Inside the Prisoner

radical television and film in the 1960s

Ian Rakoff

Contents

Printed by Butler & Tanner Ltd, Somerset

for the publishers

B.T. Batsford Ltd
583 Fulham Road
London SW6 5BY

ISBN 0 7134 8413 6

A catalogue record for this book is available from the British Library

FOREWORD

ome works, whether films, plays, or books, even people - personalities, painters, criminals - assume a mythic status completely separate from the creator's intentions or imagination. Beyond the boundaries of popularity, disgust or excellence, they become a part of the history of ourselves. They define some private part of our ego that we understand intuitively but cannot explain, even to those closest to us. They are both positive and negative icons of the general culture. The T.V. series *The Prisoner* certainly has that quality. Its very existence, in a mysterious way, captures some indefinable spirit of an era.

I only saw one or two episodes and hardly knew any of the people involved. Nevertheless, Ian Rakoff's chronicle of the struggles in the lives of the artists and technicians who made the films, written together with accounts of peripheral events and stories about other productions, held me in a way only the best biographies do, especially when they are also part diary of a period within one's living memory.

The everyday quality and scattered form gives a real sense of the hopes, disappointments and dreams of strangers, living at the same time but in parallel existence to oneself.

It made me feel nostalgic, sad and happy. It is a very clever and accurate work of film history.

Nic Roeg

PREFACE

Soort soek soort is an Afrikaans idiom similar to, but with a different shade of meaning from, the adage 'birds of a feather flock together'. Literally this Afrikaans phrase means type seeks type. It implies finding the right level, indicating how people of a similar ilk come together. It describes my involvement in film, recounted in this book, after the moral and professional turning point presented by the book's main subject. After this point, it's not merely that I no longer had to hunt for jobs. I had entered an arena in which people of a kindred spirit sought me out as I too sought them.

During the 1960s I associated with a number of filmmakers motivated by social concerns. They were rebels and they made rebellious films. Theirs was a moment in film history when shared values transcended everything else, and celluloid avarice took a back seat. For me the critical point of these associations, was *The Prisoner* television programme, first broadcast in 1967 and 1968. Among its television contemporaries, Patrick McGoohan's series was the one most driven by a sense of social responsibility. In dramatic form, it presented a picture of populist politics shaped by the manipulation of social engineering. The series' preoccupations were not themes with a ready home in the film or television industries. Most producers and film financiers, then and certainly now, would reject such a programme as not commercial. Where, they would ask, is the entertainment value? Quite rightly, the series' scripts would be read as the antithesis of Hollywood and television production values, which continue to relegate concerns of the intellect to, at the very most, a secondary place.

The Prisoner's impact on me was incalculable. As a result of McGoohan, the rest of my career was very different. Working on *The Prisoner* gave me hope that the values for which I had aimed stood a chance.

In this book, I've written about what I derived from both the programme and its creator, and I've elaborated on some of the after-effects. My net of interest has been cast widely across eclectic territory. It focuses on film, but encompasses the impact of literature, political activity, and the American comic book. For me, drawing the net in has created a homogeneity incorporating the spirit of that youthful decade, the 1960s. By consulting with contemporary sources, I have told a story of those times mostly from my point of view and drawn from my experiences of them. I do not recall with absolute accuracy but, in preparing this account, I have compared facts and the opinions of others, and I have recreated events and moments as truthfully as possible. I have omitted recollections which I can not verify.

Inside The Prisoner is my attempt at a coming to accounts with the programme, with the controversies that surrounded it and with the questions it has raised. What was it about the series that meant so much, not only to me but to so many other people as well, people across the social spectrum, people far and wide across the globe, beyond the English-speaking boundaries of mainland Britain? In this memoir of *The Prisoner* and its period that follows, I hope to add something to the answers.

A Brief Ethos Of The Prisoner

A government agent resigns. He is rendered unconscious and abducted. He awakens in an unknown village, in an unknown country. It is the Village, a community of citizens enmeshed in an all-encompassing experiment. The supreme authority behind the administration of the Village is an ongoing mystery.

The Village is totally isolated from contact with the outside world. Constant social manipulation and manoeuvring by the Village authorities exploit all mechanisms of behaviour modulation. The aim is to harness every individual and subsume each citizen's identity to the good of the state, whichever or wherever that state might be. The most advanced scientific techniques, psychological devices, psychiatric treatments, pharmacological medications and mechanical wizardry are extensively used in innumerable mind-controlling tests.

Our protagonist, and main character played by Patrick McGoohan, is the ex-agent designated Number Six. He refuses to succumb to any and every attempt at destroying his individuality. The chief antagonist, as with everyone in the Village, is a number with no name; this top bureaucrat is labelled Number Two, and is newly appointed with each episode.

In the Village, directions and commands are implemented with absolute power. The prime enforcer of the Village code of law is Rover, a six foot diameter, spherical, opaque, white, malleable balloon. It moves, breathes, apprehends or smothers to death anyone guilty of any infraction . Rover often seems to function on its own volition.

Privacy is comparatively unknown in the Village and official surveillance is all-pervasive. The single cipher of resistance is Number Six. He is the personification of every hero who has ever led a rebellion or revolution. He can not, will not, deviate from his chosen course towards freedom and humanity. He fights for not himself alone, but for all of us.

In the Village's holiday camp atmosphere, with candy-striped trimmings and a background of relentless nursery rhyme music, the entire community is lulled into compliance. It is a veritable prison with no bars.

Only Number Six seems to perceive the exact nature of his imprisonment. The rest obey and applaud, as expected by the Village authorities.

The series raises a litany of questions. There are few answers, only more questions. Is Number Six indestructible? Can he be broken ultimately, and reprogrammed to join the herd voluntarily and to march in step? Can he be discontinued from posing a threat to whomever the unseen Number One might be?

Oppression persists as rebellion pursues its inevitable quest: to be free.

1

COMING TO THE PROMISED LAND

I t was the summer of 1961 and I had just turned twenty-one. Things had not gone well for me in my South African homeland and they were poised to get worse. After the Sharpeville massacre of 1960, peaceful opposition was fast becoming a thing of the past. By the following year, the underground political group I belonged to decided that, as the only white member, I had better get out. An old school friend who'd become a detective tipped me off. The authorities were onto me. I left and found refuge in London.

For a South African politico, London represented freedom and democracy. But not every aspect of life in the British capital was better.

A coffee was impossible. It was safe only to order a cup of tea. Sliced white bread was good for cleaning windows, not for eating. Watery English beer needed much acclimatisation. Christmas lights in Regent Street were tacky.

Round the corner, Carnaby Street was plastic.

In Chelsea the signs were different. Hints of style and fashion informed a growing sense of community there, bound together by an outbreak of youth starting to abandon the past. They'd begun to come from all walks of life to the Kings Road. They saw, and they mixed sans prejudice. Traditions were challenged. Doors hitherto shut to youth, had started to open.

The contrast between closed South African society and that of London, in 1961 was immeasurable. In England I could go anywhere, talk to anybody and say anything without looking over my shoulder. The British policeman was, in contrast to his South African counterpart, a polite, friendly fellow, and unarmed.

Having resolved that England was my home, I set my course on a career in film.

The first film person whom I encountered was my landlord, the late Gordon Parry. He and his colourful Russian wife, Luisia, had an antique shop on the ground floor of a terraced house which I rented along with four others. We lived above and below the shop, at number 488 Kings Road, World's End, Chelsea.

My room on the first floor overlooked a courtyard. Half of it was a brick-walled and corrugated-iron roofed structure. I had a wash basin in my small room, and a mattress on the floor. Late night calls were a pain. The coin box telephone was just outside my door. The others occupied the top floor above.

Gordon had a sonorous deep bass voice, wore lots of blue and had a most affable manner. Large, with an ample girth, he resembled the captain of a luxury yacht as conceived by Hollywood. After directing sixteen features between 1948 and 1959, Gordon felt aggrieved that he'd been elbowed out of the film industry. I'd seen and heard about his *Tom Brown's Schooldays* and *Front Page Story*. Now he was reduced to watching over his wife's shop.

I drank endless mugs of coffee with the Parrys. Gordon's stories, of whom he'd worked with and whom he'd known, provided me with a glamorous vision of the movies. His friends included Charlie Chaplin and Dirk Bogarde, among others.

I came into the shop one day and found Gordon pink-faced with agitation.

'Where've you been?' he demanded indignantly. 'Orson Welles came to see me, and I wanted to introduce you but you weren't around.'

I was devastated.

I took menial jobs. I took clerical work. My first Christmas I packed parcels in Harrods' toy department. Deskbound, I did itineraries at Cooks. I was learning about my new country.

At a party I met a bubbly chubby girl named Alice. She had a delicious dimpled smile. She sat on the carpet next to me all evening. My pal, a Swiss chap I lived with, whispered to me.

'That is the girl of your life!'

I took no notice of his prediction but Alice kept on telephoning me. Soon we were inseparable. She moved in with me but, for appearances sake, she went on renting a room in a flat with four other girls, in nearby Pond Place in South Kensington. Alice's mother was not to know about us.

In 1962, after hundreds of letters and innumerable interviews, I got a job in the colour grading department at Humphries film processing laboratory in Whitfield Street, parallel to Tottenham Court Road. Humphries was a conglomeration of old buildings connected by tunnels whose floors battled to keep level. The lifts, simply cages, were to be avoided at all costs. The canteen was an overcrowded, cluttered room too small for the number of people who ate in it.

The colour grading room at Humphries was U-shaped and permanently in semi-darkness. There was an eerie glow from the bench lights, across which the graders wound the film, scrutinising frames through magnifying glasses. I did a fair bit of dashing round for the graders, mostly to places of deeper darkness.

The darkest place of all was the developing room. With every movement across the vast empty room, infra red lights cast changing shadows. Miniature windmills stretched over rows of long rectangular vats. Wet film rattled noisily as it raced across plastic bobbins.

The polishing room had light, but the sound was distressing and the smell of polishing fluids searing to both nostril and chest. Film was rolled round massive canvas drums with a loud whooshing noise. The palest man in the world was in charge there, and had a permanent stoop. I kept my visits as short as possible because of the chemical fumes.

Through the winter of that year, I barely saw light at all, except on weekends. I got to work early in darkness, worked the day in darkness and left late in darkness. Outside the laboratory, I wore a mask. In those days, London smog was rife. My doctor was of the opinion that my chest couldn't last long in the English winter, and advised me to return to the sunshine. Like the smog, my chest eventually cleared.

Along with a work force of four hundred, I clocked in and out daily. I wore a white coat and gloves. Most of the workers had strong East London accents. To my newcomer's ear, their speech was practically incomprehensible.

Friday evenings after work, the lads would get together for their regular weekly booze-up. One evening, I was asked along. The quantities of beer consumed were prodigious. At closing time, one of the guys called Alice to come and collect me. I was out of it.

'Sounds posh,' the chap who'd telephoned reported to me.

Alice arrived and the boys helped me into her car, a four-door Vauxhall. Reaching home, I was as sick as a dog. Alice was amused.

I knelt over the bowl and, staring at the vomit,

thought about England.

The following Monday at work, note was made of the poshness of my girlfriend. I invited the lads over to my place for a meal and to meet Alice properly.

They arrived pissed out of their skulls. One of them, Bob, slipped on the steps up to our front door, and skewered his arm on a spiked railing. I jerked it off and got him to the nearby St Stephen's Hospital.

I saw another side of England after one of the guys moved into 488. He made some decorations for a party evening. I drew the line. Most of them falsely assumed that like them, being South African, I believed in white supremacy.

'I won't have any swastikas!' I argued.

He couldn't understand my attitude. Wasn't I one of them?

Evidently it was a strange combination in this country. Rough and ready me, going out with someone like Alice. She with her curly fair hair, and her cut-glass accent from the top social stratum. She was invited to the May Ball in Cambridge. Glyndebourne couldn't be missed. Places and events I'd only heard of. She went to the continent on a skiing holiday. I wasn't included but made little of it. I was an immigrant.

The social revolution of the decade was beginning but was not yet in full swing.

Alice was illustrating a children's book on Mozart and working part-time in the City at the College of Heralds. I wore a tie to have sherry with a Pursuivant. Alice felt guilty about the money and privilege of her background. She didn't work because she had to. She felt it was the right thing to do. She'd just come down from St Andrews University.

I visited Alice's family estate near Tunbridge Wells. Her parents lived in a large, once grand, manorial house. Though not vast, the estate was dotted with cottages. Some were rented out, others occupied by staff. Alice's octogenarian father, Sir Eric, had shrunk into a wheelchair. Her mother, Lady Violet, was younger and seemingly made of steel. Sir Eric had been fundamental in building Malaya's rubber industry. During the Boer War at the turn of the century, a gun carriage had rolled across Sir Eric's skull. Severe though it was, it didn't effect him in later life. He got a medal for his war service. Later he served in Ramsay McDonald's cabinet and was instrumental in devising and implementing Green Belt policy.

During my visit, I was taken to meet Alice's mare, Cressida. Alice and I kissed in the stables. She didn't want her mother to know what was developing between us. Alice was in awe of her mother, as was, it seemed, everyone else. Was Lady Violet the power behind the wheelchair?

The cold drove us back indoors.

It was all a far cry from the film laboratory. Yet, at both ends of the social scale, there were far too many codes and rules I could not understand.

I discovered that Humphries employed whites only. At my third union meeting, I protested about the laboratory's unofficial racist policy. Nobody said a word. It was as if no one had bothered to think about it. What could I do? I went to a trade union weekend school as a delegate. It was held in a huge bleak house on the sea front at Hastings.

The deputy Secretary General of the ACTT, Alan Sapper, addressed a seminar of about twenty of us. His brief was a to present a union perspective on world politics. He maintained that anyone wanting to work in South Africa, should be hung, drawn and quartered.

'Apartheid is the most vile concept of society since the Nazis,' Sapper had declared.

I wanted to be on the same side as him.

I took my industrial problem to Sapper. He agreed to help me but the overwhelming conservative sentiment of the membership meant that the resistance to any change was strong. At the labs, the racist shop steward threatened to stop my membership ticket. However, between the deputy shop steward in the factory and representation at the ACTT head office, the ticket came through.

Humphries' race policy persisted but an opposition had been stirred.

My conflicts at the labs reminded me of the colour struggle back home. This registered more strongly when I saw a massive picture in a newspaper. On the front page of the *Daily Telegraph* appeared a huge photo of Cecil and Ilsa, old friends of mine from Cape Town. They'd escaped to get married. For them, being in South Africa meant prison for contravening apartheid's anti-miscegenation Immorality Act. This made intimacy across the colour line a crime. We met up and were soon, once again, close friends.

Cecil felt that London was no place to further his career as a jazz pianist.

'We're going to live in the States,' he told me,

and said I should come with them.

'If you stay, you must take care of Sanza.' Cecil indicated the back of fellow hunched over, watching television. We became lifelong friends.

Sanza had come to England with the smash-hit South African musical, *King Kong*. When the show's West End run ended, Sanza, along with others in the cast, was granted political asylum.

Mohajane, Sanza's friend from Soweto, was a veteran politico. He'd started early and had been arrested over a school riot, at which white-owned Rolls Royces were destroyed and fires started. He went to jail. In prison, Mohajane went into training. Out on bail, he made a run for it, much to the disapproval of his conservative parents who wanted him to stay and face the music. Mohajane hurdled the barbed wire border between South Africa and Botswana, eluding the heavily armed helicopter patrols, and ran another hundred miles into the arid southern Kalahari. Reaching a remote village, he waited almost a year before the first vehicle appeared. He got to Tanzania, where Chinese authorities issued him travel documents.

In England, Mohajane settled into studying economics, and keeping politically active. It took him many years to acquire a British Citizenship. Being white, I had acquired one a lot sooner. Nevertheless Mohajane got permission to stay.

He was a member of the Pan African Congress. I'd wanted to join but they didn't accept whites. Mohajane became a valuable moral force in my life. I admired his unprejudiced sense of right and wrong.

The Parrys were not the only film people I

met in London. Working in South Africa on a British feature film in the previous year 1960, *The Hellions,* I had got friendly with craggy-faced, Canadian method actor, Al Mulock, who played a western-style bad guy. Al's distinctive intensity, along with his reaction against South Africa's racism, brought us together as friends.

Al lived in England. After I arrived and settled in Chelsea, I arranged to meet him and our friendship continued. In London, Al launched me into the company of a much older crowd. They were grouped around Teddy and Catherine Sugden, a couple of remarkable socialites in whose flat Al lived. This was my first encounter with the London life which would later become notorious. I met people who knew about the Sugdens, but who had not met them. I never talked about the Sugdens. I remember being taken aback when I first visited them. Completely naked, Al opened the front door wide. There were other people, but Al was the only one walking around with no clothes on.

Inside, the main living room was vast, with large sofas and low coffee tables. There were thick fitted carpets. A few modern paintings hovered over vases packed with exotic flowers. Everything though casual, looked expensive.

Teddy and Catherine's flat in Malvern Court, Onslow Square, presented an assortment of people which I found fascinating. Socially they mixed young and old, past and the present, with unusual adroitness. Traditional values intertwined with the spuriously fashionable. In this way, they were emblematic of Britain in the 1960s.

At one party, I couldn't help but notice two

A youthful Ian Rakoff takes it easy in London as the Swinging Sixties begin to unfold.

very attractive girls only slightly older than me. People were whispering about them and they looked ill at ease. I wanted to keep away from them but was curious as to who they were. I later learned they were Mandy Rice Davis and Christine Keeler. Then the scandal broke. A Russian spy, Colonel Eugene Ivanov, was involved. Christine Keeler was imprisoned. Stephen Ward, another frequent visitor to the Sugden's, was arrested on a trumped up charge and died mysteriously in custody. The Secretary of State for War, John Profumo, had to resign, as did Prime Minister Macmillan.

At another party, a moustached British Ambassador cavorted about while his pretty wife told lewd anecdotes. Anyone could be anything at the Sugdens. It was a totally neutral zone.

Teddy was an elderly gynaecologist. During the Second World War, he was head of the Department of Sexually Transmitted Diseases. He won the first case for legalising abortion. Perversely, Teddy abhorred the crowds and at parties he usually retreated to a back room with a bottle of gin. There he would sit, watching his cabinets filled with live reptiles and feeding the inhabitants.

It was Catherine, Teddy's young wife, who ran the social side of things. She was slender with a husky voice, good looks and a warm generous manner. She advised me to keep my left-wing sentiment away from Teddy. Much of what went on in that flat I was too young even to begin to imagine, I was informed.

Another time, Catherine extricated me from the clutches of an attractive, predatory, older woman. I wasn't ready, Catherine told me. Drugs were involved and I wasn't ready for that either. Catherine took a motherly attitude towards me. She made sure that I didn't fall into who knows what.

There was one thing I dearly wanted from the Sugdens: an introduction to their friend Nic Roeg. They'd told me about Nic, whom Catherine felt I had to meet because he was an influential freelance lighting cameraman and because I'd get on with him. Then, it didn't happen. Much later, at the end of the 1960s, I would cut a film for Nic.

Legitimized by my union ticket, I became a trainee editor at Basic Films on the Wardour Street side of Soho Square. The cutting rooms were poky. This, I discovered, was the same everywhere; cutting rooms were dumps.

Overlooking the square, the view of grass, statues and pigeons was heartening after almost a year spent under the artificial light of the labs.

As the trainee, I made coffee and filed trims. I was cautioned against looking over the editor's shoulder. I couldn't see much training forthcoming. But at least I had got in the door.

Though Basic was primarily a documentary company, Victor, the only resident editor, cut the occasional commercial. On one such occasion, everyone was keyed up. The advertising agency was sending people round to meet Lindsay Anderson, the new director among Basic's commercial ranks. Lindsay had a reputation for being acerbic and not liking criticism. I gathered that Lindsay's presence always had a risk element. I liked the sound of him already.

As Lindsay walked in, everyone fell silent and watched him. He wore a black leather jacket with a red shirt. This, I soon realized, was his egalitarian uniform. His eyes could cut through steel and his somewhat large, patrician nose was constantly on the alert to sniff out the phoney and the false. He dumped a bunch of papers on the bench I was leaning against, and cordially introduced himself.

'You must be the new trainee,' Lindsay said, and our conversation began.

He fired questions incessantly. I criticized the Free Cinema movement of which he was the main luminary. Despite the fearsome reputation that had preceded him, he was utterly charming. Irritated by the advertising people, Lindsay used me to mock their ignorance of filmmaking.

'Isn't your uncle that famous American film director?' Lindsay asked me, having already established that it was not so. I went along with his ploy.

'Actually, he's Canadian, not American,' I replied.

After the advertising people had left, Lindsay turned to me.

'Now then,' he steered me across the room towards the editor hunched over the moviola. 'You must look over Victor's shoulder whenever you can. It's the only way that you are going to learn.'

Now, I began to learn about film.

Some months later, after I'd moved on to British Transport Films as an assistant editor, I attended the National Film Theatre in Waterloo for a preview of Lindsay's first feature, *This Sporting Life*. I went with my pal Bernard Gribble, a veteran feature film editor whom I'd met at BTF.

The auditorium was packed to capacity. I was

bowled over by the emotional intensity and all round excellence of the film. I felt it was the most realistic film I had seen from British cinema. Knowing that Lindsay would be in the foyer to find out what the audience thought, I rushed out to reach him before the crowd.

Sure enough he was there, wearing his usual black leather jacket and red shirt, standing in the foyer with a glass of red wine. I went across and kissed his hand, telling him how much I thought of his film.

'Congratulations, I've never seen anything like it,' I blabbered with unrestrained enthusiasm. I retracted what I'd said about his documentaries. I carried on despite the gathering crowd, eager to get to Lindsay.

'That's all very well,' he chuckled. 'But what are you up to that's constructive?'

I told him that I was making a film about South Africa and asked if he would look at it, when it was finished.

He said he'd like to see what I could do and I left him surrounded by well-wishers.

'I can't believe that,' Bernard said, grimacing and shaking his head. 'You actually kissed his hand!'

As soon as I had a print with sound on a magnetic stripe, I booked a basement screening room in St Ann's Court to show my film for Lindsay. I was mortified when he didn't appear. I telephoned. He'd forgotten. I made another booking. This time he turned up.

The film didn't break. The sound didn't die and the ending came through clearly. The narration, in Xhosa, concluded with the avowal: we will drive the white man into the sea.

The lights went up and Lindsay suggested a coffee at Act One Scene One in Old Compton Street.

He was unstinting in his praise for what I had done. He compared it favourably with John Krish's *Let My People Go* which had then been showing at the Academy Cinema in Oxford Street. Krish's film was documentary about South Africa based on the views of Chief Albert Luthuli, winner of the Nobel Peace Prize. Luthuli's stance was one of peace and passive resistance. Mine hinged on confrontation.

'If there's anything I can do to help you,' Lindsay said as he paid for the coffees, 'let me know.'

Now, in looking back, I see a strong connection between Patrick McGoohan and Lindsay Anderson. They had much in common. In some ways they were similar, and in others the very opposite. What they shared was a driving moral imperative, coupled with an abhorrence for the establishment and for any form of cant. They met only once. It didn't go well.

There was one South African in London whom I knew from back home and who also got into feature films. This was the flamboyant, no-nonsense, speak-her-mind Shura Cohen. In Cape Town we'd crossed paths at various clandestine jazz venues. I'd been intrigued at how freely she'd traversed the colour line. She'd always worn black with dark glasses, and had a blunt, unapproachable manner.

In 1962, I had bumped into Shura in the Kings Road on a sunny Saturday afternoon. She seemed very different to the Shura I'd met in

Cape Town. She invited me over to her place, a magnificent, light and spacious studio flat in Cheyne Walk. We became friends.

I was petrified when Shura offered me cocaine. I sniffed a line of the powdery white stuff, and wondered what all the fuss was about. On the scene around and about Chelsea, I got offered LSD. Though disinclined to the hard stuff, I dabbled with grass. It introduced me to yet more people, not heavy druggies but partial to the puffing culture. Along this route I acquired Turkish, Indian and Italian friends; all residents of Chelsea. Drugs were a common factor of Chelsea life, and eventually most of them caught up with me, one way or another.

All this had little to do with the main sway of the film industry.

Later Shura bought a terraced, double-storey house in Parsons Green Lane which she converted extensively. The interior was open-plan and the walls startlingly white. Artefacts from Morocco blended freely with imports from California and further south.

Shura asked for a trade union connection. She wanted an ACTT or a NATKE card to allow her to work in a costume department. Her house became a hotbed of film types and expatriates. As she embarked on a career in wardrobe, the people she worked with congregated at her place. In a different era it might have been called a salon. Actor Calvin Lockhart held court at Shura's. I also met Don Stroud, part Cherokee and a up and coming star for director Don Siegel. Stroud played in *Madigan* and *Coogan's Bluff* and, for a while, was involved with Shura. Peter Falk cornered himself in a high wicker

chair and sulked. Donald Sutherland gave me a lift home in a mini, a size too small for him. Mike Sarne arrived in his open-topped, mauve Rolls Royce. Figures and faces decamped from the streets of Chelsea and paraded throughout Shura's living space, as did all and sundry from London's film community. Continuity people, cameramen, sound recordists and assistant directors, all called in at Shura's. The door was always open, and hospitality always on the go. Entry to tradition-bound English society was another matter, however.

Migrating to Britain and being removed from the political conflict had certainly calmed me down. Nevertheless, the colonial savage inside of me was not very deeply hidden. I was extremely agitated and confused. The media assured me that the British class system was breaking up, but this was not so according to what I'd experienced. Alice made a botched suicide attempt because of what her snobby brother Sandy had said about us. Later, I grabbed him by the throat, and thrust him up against the wall. Alice's other brother, Neil, told me how he delayed his own marriage for a year because of his mother's attitude to his wife-to-be.

'Can't you buy her a cottage in the country?' Lady Violet had demanded. 'Surely there's no need to marry someone like that.'

Neil warned me our lives would be absolute hell if Alice and I stayed and lived in England. The disapproval of Alice's mother had already taken its toll. Alice was a shadow of her former bubbly self and had lost a tremendous amount of weight. Her thoughts, though not her conversation, were dominated with worrying about her mother's attitude towards me.

I discussed this with another South African exile, the novelist Bloke Modisane, author of *Blame Me on History*, his story of living in the poverty of Sophiatown, Trevor Huddleston's parish. My senior by some years, Bloke was critical of my relationship with Alice and drew from it a severe lesson for me.

'For all your caring, sensitivity and experience,' Bloke had told me, referring to my life in South Africa, 'you could never really feel what it's like to be a servant. But being with Alice has shown you what it's like to be seen as inferior.'

Bloke said that I should make my life in another country, anywhere but England.

'You could be happy in Lagos or Rome,' he advised me.

Within a year, Lady Violet shipped Alice abroad to get her away from me.

While working at British Transport Films, I showed my South African film to Sir Edgar Anstey the BTF boss. He praised the film generously but warned me that certain people in Hampstead might take me for a communist. Nevertheless, Sir Edgar gave me permission to leave BTF without the statutory two weeks notice in order to take up a job as a second assistant editor on *Joey Boy*, a feature film shooting at Shepperton Studios. This was a run-of-the-mill comedy by Launder and Gilliat, the team who'd written *The Lady Vanishes* for Alfred Hitchcock.

I was at work in my new job when I got a call from Alice in Switzerland, pleading with me to fly over. But I wouldn't jeopardize my first job as an assistant editor in features. This she could not understand.

Alice and I never spoke again.

Alice's absence from my life left a great void. I found some consolation in turning back to my childhood passion for American comic books. My parents had worked assiduously to wean me away from comic books. I only acquiesced to their demand when I was told that I couldn't go to university unless I gave up my comics.

I started reading comics again in London. The medium had changed radically. The 1963 advent of Stan Lee's Spider-Man, with his leap into the perils of day-to-day reality, immediately caught my attention. I revelled in stories about a superhero with ordinary problems. Not only did he battle villains, he battled to pay for his Aunt May's medical treatment and to pay his college fees. He struggled to hold onto a girlfriend, in tandem with fulfilling his social responsibilities as a fighter of crime. His hero's uniform was not indestructible; he had to sew up the tears himself. Spider-Man was not just a gimmicky costume, he was a flesh and blood person.

Between features, on weekends whenever possible, I took on small jobs, mostly in documentaries. This was only possible when located in Soho. Studio life was almost totally cut off from such activities.

By 1965 Chelsea had staked its claim as the style Mecca of the universe. Youth, filled with confidence and optimism, ran riot. Fancy dress became ordinary fare. People flocked to Chelsea to be a part of living show-time promenading up and down the Kings Road. They now swarmed in from all over, cutting across colour, race and class. It was the biggest panoply of florid, feathery, flair-filled maverick fashion imaginable. The flavour of drugs was everywhere in public and music was ever-present. An Englishman caught adrift in the Kings Road on a Saturday could easily feel he was in another country on another planet. Here I felt that, at long last, I had found a new home. Friendliness and peaceful sentiments were the order of the day. Meeting people was easy and natural as social barriers melted away.

Generally, South Africa fell out of my conversations, relegated to that place in the heart where you place things you can't bear.

The Parrys sold number 488. I moved into a ground floor flat, around the corner in Edith Grove. I shared it with a chap I'd met at an evening film class. He wanted to get out of England, far away from his public school background. He got a job in Jamaica and migrated, leaving me alone in the flat.

In 1964 after Labour won the election, the Parrys, in disgust, moved to Tunisia. Later they moved to Paris. I went over to visit them. Gordon didn't approve of my associations with left-leaning directors but it made no difference to our friendship.

We lost touch for some years until Gordon tracked me down at work. He was calling from Paris. We talked at length. I assured him that I was finishing off a job and come hell or high water, I'd get across the channel to see him.

Some days later I was at work talking to resident producer Michael Relph, an old friend of the Parrys. I was telling him about Gordon, when Relph picked up a film magazine and showed me an obituary. Gordon had died forty-eight hours after our telephone conversation. Three weeks later Luisia also passed away. She'd been in the South of France, as a guest of Dirk Bogarde.

I attended a service for the two of them, in the Russian Orthodox Church in Kensington. Simultaneous ceremonies were held for them in Tunis, Paris and London.

I took stock of my situation. Despite the freedoms erupting around me, I felt that things were winding down. I'd flopped as a politico in South Africa and got out with my white skin intact. On top of that was the painful memory of Lily Mabusela, who'd brought me up. After fifteen years of devotion, my parents had got rid of her. This had been done behind my back. I was away from home on location in the Transvaal. My parents would not discuss Lily's dismissal with me. Trying to locate her came to nothing. She'd been endorsed out of Cape Town, back to the poverty of the Transkei.

All this baggage clung to me as I tried to forge ahead in films. I needed to relocate my identity and establish some fixed points of existence. I was ripening for something meaningful to enter my life.

2

NOT OUR KIND
OF MORALS

It was 1966 and things had been going well. I'd just landed a plumb job as an assistant editor and I was about to set off on location in Ireland.

I was at my weekly judo class at the Budokwai just off the Fulham Road. I was thrown to the mat with a loud crack followed by another when my heavier opponent twisted his body. As I lay in agony on the dojo, I was instructed to get up and stand. Instead two fellow students had to pick me up and carry me across Fulham Road to Casualty at St Stephen's Hospital.

I spent a couple of weeks in a ward and then checked out with a massive plaster encasing me from my toes to the top of my thigh.

It was a week or so after I returned home from hospital that Lindsay called. I had to see him to discuss the possibility of my assisting on the imminent production of *The White Bus*.

I hobbled along Edith Grove, balancing on National Health wooden crutches, and caught a number fourteen bus up to Shaftesbury Avenue. An old lady got up to offer me a seat. Kind people helped me.

Solicitously, Lindsay escorted me to a booth at the back of Act One Scene None. Gently Lindsay escorted me onto a bench seat, stepped back and kicked me smack on my broken ankle. I screamed with pain. He sat down opposite me and refused to explain why he'd attacked me.

Two coffees later he announced that, because of my leg, I'd be too late to work on his film. Our meeting was over. I left.

Dejected and struggling up Wardour Street, I literally bumped into John S Smith. We'd never worked together, but I sort of knew him from the corridors of Shepperton Studios. On the spot, he offered me a job starting in a few day's time.

I asked what about my leg?

'Oh, don't worry about that,' John replied. 'We'll just have to work round it.'

I accepted and John began to tell me about

the project.

The film John was going to cut was for Moral Re-Armament. I felt uncomfortable about MRA but so did John. I'd already accepted the job so there was no way of backing out. It was the only time that I accepted a job sight unseen.

The film was titled *Give a Dog a Bone*.

'It's a children's musical pantomime, running at the Westminster Theatre in Victoria,' John said. 'They're doing a film version of it up at St John's Wood Studios. The good thing is that the studio hasn't space for cutting rooms, so we'll be in Soho.' John stood up straight, very tall, and lowered his voice. 'MRA, Moral Re-Armament Association, is a world wide organisation - interracial, run by stiff characters with tight, dry lips. But the film, it's nonsense, harmless stuff. It won't make the history books.'

John also filled me in about Henry Cass, the director. Cass was a bit of an old timer and this was his first feature in years. He'd been successful with two of his films. In 1948 he'd directed *The Glass Mountain* with Dulcie Gray and her husband Michael Dennison. Singer Tito Gobbi played a local mountaineer that saves a British pilot who had crashed his bomber in the Italian Alps. Cass's 1950 film, *Last Holiday*, starred Alec Guinness in one of his best screen roles.

'The films he did after those two,' John added, 'just weren't up to much.'

I commended John on knowing so much about the director's work. He told me that he'd done his homework to impress Cass, and had succeeded.

We shook hands and I was all set for

employment with a really nice guy. However, the Moral Re-Armament tag was not an inviting one. A few years previously I'd been cutting a monthly newsreel made by the Central Office of Information, a government unit, for distribution to the Commonwealth. The newsreel producer had steely blue eyes, a stiffly patrician manner and besides working for the COI, he was a big wheel in Moral Re-Armament. He'd tried to get his hooks into me to join. My wriggling out of that hadn't offended him; he was evidently conditioned for rebuttal. We'd parted amicably. Nonetheless I couldn't forget the man's proselytising zeal. I wanted absolutely no truck with it.

'They may be to the right of Ghengis Kahn but they've got plenty of money,' John observed, laughing.

It was for a cause I couldn't espouse but a kid's musical couldn't be that dangerous, I reasoned. With inane lyrics and wishy-washy music, how pernicious could it be?

The start date of the musical got put back and, by the time the filming began, I was almost out of plaster.

I went to the Westminster Theatre, to sort out and sign my contract for *Give a Dog a Bone*. The smart, recently built complex was the nerve centre of Moral Re-Armament. It was situated on a prime spot and looked shinier, and more expensive, than any of the surrounding structures. Wandering through the empty auditorium, I could almost feel its tentacles encircling the globe with insidious propaganda. I disliked the many cults now sprouting up like mushrooms in California, for seemingly instant export to Chelsea. The only difference, I felt, between them and MR was that the latter's bible-wielding operation had been going a lot longer.

The film's production manager was a high-energy chap named Chris Sutton. Of the many that I encountered in production, Chris is one of the few with whom I became pally. Production was a dirty job, often executed by shifty types. Chris was different, though, and we immediately hit it off. He was zany, enthusiastic and interested in everything. As an opera lover, he made regular pilgrimages to hear Wagner at Bayreuth in Germany. He put me on the alert about MR and said that the movement was pathologically anti-gay. He implied that he couldn't let them know about his own views on most things. I was grateful for Chris's unusual openness and frankness with me.

John and I set up our cutting room for the MR musical in a typical back street warren in Soho. I just about managed to cope with the narrow, uneven stairs which led up to a room not big enough to swing a cat. There was hardly space for the equipment, let alone us.

'I don't know how they do it,' John shook his head. 'The rooms get smaller and the equipment worse.'

'It's another dump,' I agreed, then started dusting and wiping.

John was impressed that I'd nearly worked for Lindsay Anderson.

I told him all about the film I'd made on South Africa, about screening it for Lindsay and for Edgar Anstey, and about their very different reactions.

John wanted me to know about the next job he had almost lined up.

'If you can get through this lot I may have another one you'd be more interested in. It's television but it's being done like a feature in 35mm and in colour, up at MGM. I've no idea what it's about and from what I heard, neither does anyone else. Have you seen *Danger Man?*'

I hadn't but I'd heard of it. I didn't own a television.

I reflected on the contrasts my limited encounters with television production made with my experience in features. I had the impression that in television and documentaries, accent and background counted for more than in feature filmmaking. Ability to muck in, technical expertise; these were what mattered. Who you met and whom you knew were of paramount importance. Ultimately it hinged on how your face fitted. It was all down to having a union ticket and making the connections. The mood of the 1960s facilitated the free and easy atmosphere of freelancing in features. Regardless of the feature in production, it seemed that I'd enlisted in a classless aristocracy. All my accent did was provoke the occasional joke.

In our poky cubby-hole, John and I spent a few days lolling about, getting everything shipshape with joiner tape, white cotton gloves, bobbins, charts, files, spacing and leaders.

All the potential surfaces for picking up static had to be degaussed. This was a safety precaution to forestall any likelihood of getting clicks on the sound tracks. Synchronizers and the moviola got the treatment.

I plugged in a squawk box and switched it on to test. A taxi cab came over loud and clear. I squiggled the dial until it vanished. This was a problem peculiar to Soho. The taxis were constantly creeping into the squawk boxes. They never intruded on the moviola.

Below us Dean Street teemed with life. Unlike the studios, there was always something to watch. Not only were the studios all situated on the remote outskirts of London - and I didn't have a car - but they were sterile and cut off. I loved the sleazy textures of Soho and the incredible selection of restaurants. The same went for John.

Most important now was to establish our connection with our film processing laboratory as well as the key technicians on our sound and camera crew with whom we would be working. In regard to the labs, I was pleased to learn that we were going to use Humphries.

On the first day of shooting we took a taxi up to the St John's Wood studio. John never brought his car into Soho. Parking was too much of a hassle.

In the studio, a consciously selected, multi-coloured cast of kids were swinging and singing on a sound stage under a battery of lights. A 35mm camera, blimped to make no sound, swept back and forth on a dolly shoved by a couple of grips.

During a pause between set-ups, John introduced me to the director. He glanced at my crutches but said nothing about my plaster. Cass was extremely well-spoken, with a somewhat theatrical, la-di-da lilt. He formed a solid, square shape, topped by elegant greying hair.

Shaking my hand, Cass wearily began bemoaning his fate, in a confidential tone. He had little more than passing interest in the film, he said, which wasn't helped by the awful MR types. He scrutinized my face and commented on my bookish look. If I removed my glasses, he told me, I wouldn't look that way and this might be better for my career. He looked over to the camera. John and I swapped an amused look.

'Nevertheless it's good to be directing again,' Cass added, telling us to call him Henry, and continuing in the conspiratorial tone. 'Hopefully it'll go down well in the far-flung places and no one will be converted by its insipid and inane morality. With your help we'll get through. We'll have carte blanche with the editing. They've promised not to interfere. Being moral, they'll probably stick to their word. But,' he said lowering his voice even more and giving me a most serious look, 'you'll keep running into them, prowling about like sharks hunting for juicy propaganda bits.' In a most mannerly fashion, Henry thanked us for coming to see him on the set.

'It's so good to be back in action,' he repeated and threw in a few more derisory remarks about MR. By then the camera was ready for him.

I turned round and stood face-to-face with our executive producer. It was the same man I'd worked with for the COI. His eyes were still as blue as I remembered. He shook my hand and held it. He was delighted that I was on the picture. He pronounced my name with clarity, showing me he had not forgotten. He had a strange posture, as if someone or something had whacked him hard in the small of his back. I introduced him to John and he concluded with a few well chosen words of flattery to welcome us aboard.

'Not like when you and I worked with that 16mm spaghetti,' he said with a hearty chortle before going off.

John spoke to the sound man about the click system on the musical playback and we were finished, grateful that we could return to our little home from home in Soho away from the Victoria headquarters and the studio.

I wasn't familiar with musical playback and, in the morning, John had to help get me started. That evening we screened the first day's rushes for Henry and his camera crew. To my relief, it all came up in sync. Though weary, Henry was delighted. Every time we met him, he was an uneasy combination of fatigue and delight. He prided himself on being a veteran trooper.

It was now over six weeks since I'd first got the plaster. This was longer than the usual period because I had two fractures.

When I got rid of the plaster, my leg was weird. I barely recognized the skinny fleshless thing that seemed to dangle from my thigh. It smelt nasty and looked sickly. The calf muscle and the thigh flesh had withered, and the dried up skin was itchy as hell after weeks inside the rubbing, flaking plaster cast. I went to work, limping and leaning on a cane.

Within a few days, John stopped needing to work round my leg. The limp didn't last long. Neither did the cane, though John thought I should hold onto it.

'Gives you that extra bit of style,' John grinned, adding quickly 'not that you need it, of course.'

The powers behind Moral Re-Armament, though perhaps murky, were lofty. The Dutch electronics group, Philips, were reputed to be big backers of the movement. Dwight Eishenhower's name came up a few times in conversation with the MR people; our executive producer had almost met him. An Indian Prime Minister was also mentioned. The movement wasn't short on big names.

Dutifully we plodded on. Henry covered the lengthy musical numbers with enough angles to enable it all to join together quite seamlessly. We soon had a cut of sorts, and John found it quite easy to keep abreast of the turnover of film from the floor. I struggled with the mechanical demands of playback, and the intricate numbering system.

One of the MR luminaries, Fred Perry the veteran Wimbledon tennis star, was shepherded into our cutting room for a special viewing.

At the end, he announced that he was delighted and impressed that such a fine musical pantomime might carry the word of light into the world's distant dark corners.

'It'll be nice when it's tightened up, won't it?' the benign Fred said, shaking John's hand and waving at me as he left.

'You can tell he knows something about film,' John remarked after Fred had disappeared. 'But it's already tightly cut as can be. It's a musical and there should be room for laughs.'

'So are you going to have to tighten it further? If you do much more of that we won't have enough left to be a feature, just a long short,' I said.

'None of them seem to expect you to listen,' John replied. 'They just say their say and then go away hoping you'll see the light. You know they won't insist. It's not their way. But, on the other hand, we don't want this job to drag on forever do we?'

I agreed heartily.

'They'll be queuing up in the bush to watch a 16mm print on a portable screen projected from the back of a truck,' John predicted. 'Poor people in Africa and India getting the Christian message through Moral Re-Armament.'

I groaned in sympathy.

The latter stage of post-production had been tough going, especially as we had to do all the track-laying ourselves. As *Give a Dog a Bone* was a musical, it cut down a lot on the preparation for the final mix onto one triple track. Also the re-recording of dialogue, the post sync, was minimal.

Henry Cass was satisfied with the cut. He told me to book a screening theatre and to notify the MR hierarchy.

The screening went down well all round. The tiny sandwiches laid on were excellent. Henry Cass was a genius; we were close behind. The hierarchy representatives were all pleased and they looked forward to employing us again. We appreciated the offer but we both hoped we wouldn't have to take it up. Once was enough. It had been agreeable enough as employment but the insidious tone of the movement was just too much.

John got a call from Spencer Reeve, an editor on the mooted television series. They were now desperate. Did John want the job? He said that he did and that he already had an assistant.

'I didn't take you for granted, did I?' John asked after he put down the receiver.

'Pat McGoohan is the highest paid television actor in the country, and he's pulled off his own series, along with the *Danger Man* script editor, George Markstein. It's all McGoohan's idea,' enthusiastically John began to fill me in. 'It's the show I told you about, the one being made like a feature film. And of course MGM is the closest thing we've got to a Hollywood studio.'

I looked forward to our imminent next venture, *The Prisoner*.

Secret Agent, the comic book featuring Patrick McGoohan as Danger Man. The Secret Agent before he commenced his journey into individualism.

The Gentleman Rebel

It was in the early months of 1967 and getting from Chelsea, via Kings Cross, to Borehamwood station on time was quite some feat. Then, on arrival, legging it up the High Street, racing against the clock, looking for a cab or hoping for a bus gave each day an energetic, running start. Sometimes a fellow worker on wheels would spot me and I'd get a ride up the hill into Elstree.

Behind the high wall, loomed the MGM studio stages and buildings. Their size was vast. Dull red brickwork and shapeless, rectangular structures created a look from another time. On the one hand, they resembled something ancient; on the other, a statement from the distant future. I'd already heard that, behind the guarded gates, Kubrick's epic science fiction odyssey, *2001*, was in full flood under extremely secret conditions. Also, somewhere Robert Aldrich's *The Dirty Dozen* was in post-production; an old friend of mine, Woody, was the first assistant on it.

The cutting room block seemed sectioned aside from the rest of studio life, in semi-seclusion. Our room on the first floor was, as ever, no luxury apartment but a considerable improvement on the interior conditions of our Soho location over the last six months.

We met with Bernie Williams, production manager on *The Prisoner*, with regard to our employment. Bernie was small, bespectacled and just out of his teens. He was keen, open and friendly. He warned us that we'd be up against problems we couldn't imagine. He hoped we could cope because *The Prisoner* was an unmitigated shambles. Worst of all, he said, we'd come in on the tail end of things. The best and most interesting episodes had already been snatched up by the other editing teams. We'd have to settle for the leftovers.

We were introduced in passing, to George Markstein, the script editor. He was flustered, moving fast and didn't look at all happy. But the man whom I'd later recognize as the pink-faced bald bureaucrat from the opening of the first episode was friendly and polite. He looked like a man with a jolly disposition under normal circumstances.

John and I settled in. We met up with the other cutting teams. There were four of them, grinding away simultaneously on different episodes.

The juniors, including myself, would get all keyed up and involved in what appeared to be an enigmatic, contemporary science fiction series. The senior editors generally presented a not too attractive front. Blasé about stepping down from features to television work, they conducted themselves with an assiduously maintained remoteness. John S Smith was the exception. He was ever willing to muck in with whatsoever was going on. Tea breaks would find him in the canteen with us assistants. The other editors kept to themselves.

The first episode we were given to edit had a fascinating premise. The central theme of *The General* concerned a computer able to implant extraordinary knowledge into the brain. This was achieved by imprinting on the cortex of the brain through the retina of the eye using subliminal perception. As the superimposed intellect seeped in, individual will power was sapped out. This loss of individualism and subsequent mind-control was the very opposite of the character that McGoohan portrayed in Number Six.

'It'll look better once we've put it together,' John said with determination as we viewed the plodding rushes.

If the rushes had been printed up in colour

The Prisoner crew set up for location work in The Village. Patrick McGoohan is as elegant as ever.

instead of black and white, it might have looked better from the outset. In fact the director, Peter Graham Scott, sat in with us in the theatre once or twice. He was chatty but had little to say. He was disparaging about the series and about what he'd done on it. He was totally disinterested and it showed on the screen.

We were notified to carry on with our assembly. Pat McGoohan was due to come in and sort out *The General*. We had not met him. All we'd heard so far was alarming rumour. Because of Pat's extraordinary demanding schedule as writer, producer, director and actor, he only managed to get to the cutting rooms in

John S Smith, an unusually generous editor.

the evenings, after the day's shooting was over.

John and I waited anxiously for McGoohan to appear. He was supposed to arrive at six p.m. It had gone seven. We waited and waited.

'You can see why they dropped this one on us,' John reflected with amusement. 'It's too short and too thin,' he continued, bemoaning our fate. 'There's not enough material to give much of a choice. Number Two looks a bit off all the time, as if he's just swallowed something unpleasant. *The General* has problems. This is going to be a job for the stock librarian.'

I could only agree.

The production's stock librarian was the incomparable Tony Sloman. Constantly on the whiz, loquacious Tony was a familiar face. Like me, he was an habitué of the National Film Theatre, devotedly and passionately following the different genres or directors from Hollywood's cinematic history. Tony seemed always to be there. I'd heard him in the NFT foyer and noticed him bouncing on the spot as he talked film and clutched magazines.

Tony's job at Elstree was to run the stock-shot library and handle all the back projection material. He frequently reported directly to McGoohan. Of all the cutting crew, Tony was most involved with filming. He was our link man with what was happening on set. He reported everything to everybody. There was no side to Tony, only the indiscretions of an overimaginative conversationalist. He could talk his way into, and out of, anything. Initially he'd landed the job without an iota of knowledge about the workings of back projection. He had learned mighty quickly and was, by now, a pivotal point in the mechanics of the production. The extensive use of overlapping images and numerous effects to simulate surveillance technology was a relatively new requirement in film. The material used had to be prepared specially. Sequences had to be cut and reprinted on stock with narrow negative perforations to hold the film steadier for the back projection.

As technicians, we talked about working on a film rather than on a series for television. Just as John had describe it to me, in scale and concept the production was far closer to film than television, even though it was destined for the latter. For most of us, it was cinema. The cutting room crews were freelancers from features, not television.

Seven-thirty p.m. came and went with no sign of McGoohan. We began to suspect that he might not turn up. The long wait was depressing.

There was a light rapping on our door. Framed in the door's glass porthole, was a smiling face.

'Can I come in?,' McGoohan asked with an exaggerated Irish accent as he came in clutching a gin and tonic. He seemed quite at ease in our company and said something friendly. He moved around the room sipping his drink.

John and I exchanged a glance. Where was the monster we'd been forewarned about?

John announced that we were laced up and ready to go. His sentence ended with a flourishing mock salute. John spun round on his swivel chair to face the moviola. McGoohan refused a chair. He'd stay standing. I switched on.

The tape joins clattered through the gate of the moviola and I crossed my fingers. The machine was a clumsy contraption and very unkind to a cutting print. Besides leaving scratches on the emulsion face of the celluloid, it tended to rip any imperfect joins and chew up sprockets. This meant stopping, patching and ordering reprints. It would have been more than embarrassing if the film broke. This time it went through, noisy but unbroken.

At the end of the first ten-minute reel, McGoohan said nothing and walked out.

As I battled with a faulty split spool, John

leaned over and asked if I thought Pat was coming back. I pointed out that his glass had been empty. Reassured, John remarked that he seemed to be an unexpectedly nice guy. I agreed and laced up the next reel, picture and sound.

McGoohan returned with his refilled glass and we carried on.

As I removed the last reel, McGoohan asked what we thought.

'It's probably not the best one,' John began. 'There're lots of problems but we'll get round them. Ian's ordered more library material but it hasn't come through yet.' John grinned, looked keen, and stood up. He was almost as tall as McGoohan.

There was a long pause then McGoohan lifted himself up onto the high bench that I worked on. He swung his legs back and forth as if he was winding himself up.

'It's not going to be easy, making something out of that,' he reflected.

'Oh don't worry,' John said reassuringly. 'It'll get better.'

McGoohan had certainly made an effort to put us at our ease. But, though he talked freely, he was hardly chatty. What he did very effectively was to take us on board in a personal way. The most natural thing in the world, it appeared, was to follow him and do whatever he wanted.

The division between what he was, and what he was acting, was a slender line. There was a fight going on, and it was all inside of him. I felt that I'd hate to have been around if it should ever spill out.

McGoohan gulped his glass dry and pointed

out that too many stock shots were being over used. He needed to direct more himself, he said, but finding the time was the problem. He wished us luck and said goodnight.

John and I slumped onto our swivel chairs. We were both drained. The room had become suddenly much larger with Pat's absence. His was an extraordinarily strong presence, even in the enforced passivity of the cutting room. He often lapsed into silence though, somehow, he always seemed to be implying something. Furthermore, his raw authority was accompanied by a definite softness and a genuine concern about stepping on our toes. He was not unaware of what his presence inspired. Yet he did nothing deliberately to make us uncomfortable. After some minutes had elapsed, I spoke.

'I think that went quite well.'

'I can't get over what a polite gent he is,' John started to clear up his bench.

'There was no hint of a monster,' I said as I made my way round the cutting room, switching off the equipment. 'You said you could make something out of *The General*. What did you have in mind?'

'Oh, I just told him that. I didn't want him to leave unhappy,' John said putting on his jacket. 'I'll give you a lift to the station. Everything off?'

I shut the door behind us.

We were the last to leave and someone had switched off the corridor lights. It was strange with no sounds emanating from any of the other editing rooms. The night silhouettes of the studio buildings looked even more like overgrown blocks assembled for a city of the

future. No one else was around. It was all deathly still.

As we drove out, the guard on duty in his glass hutch waved at us. We waved back and John called out a greeting.

Driving down to the station, John and I reflected that the most striking aspect of McGoohan was not just his size, though he was indisputably huge. His presence was even bigger. He appeared larger than he actually was. McGoohan took the lion's share of the space

A determined McGoohan on the move in **Checkmate**.

available, wherever he was. Most actors try to do this.

At the station, I'd just missed a train. I dug my heels in and waited. The next one was due in twenty minutes, not too long a wait. The dark, deserted platform looked as bleak as I felt, as I anticipated the journey back to Chelsea. There was no station anywhere near to where I lived. I'd catch a tube from King's Cross to Sloane Square and grab a cab down the King's Road. It was a lengthy trip.

As the inadequate *General* required more and more of Pat's attention, he seemed to mellow considerably. He was consistently polite and never even remotely unpleasant. So much for the stories put out about him, we told ourselves again. He spent longer hours with us, arriving earlier and leaving later. He offered John genuine sympathy and support. Like everyone else, John gave his all just to please McGoohan. Call it charisma, call it moral presence, call it what you will, Pat was the one to call the cards. He got the best effort out of the maximum number of people.

Pat got into the habit of sitting on my synchronising bench. Though not a very comfortable position, it provided a commanding viewpoint. John was concerned that, sooner or later, Pat would fall over because sometimes he swung his legs like crazy.

'I'm going to have a go at that,' John insisted after McGoohan had packed up for the night.

He got up onto the bench and started swinging his legs like Pat. John nearly fell off. 'You think it's some sort of religious ritual?' he wondered as put his feet back on the floor.

I said that I doubted that was the case.

'Have to try it with a drink in my hand,' John added, as we finished for the day. 'Time to go home,' he said.

At times, John would wave me away and do for himself the things I was supposed to do. He'd lace up reels on the moviola if I was occupied by talking with McGoohan.

John later explained that my job was the entertainment department. He could concentrate better, he said, knowing that I was dealing with the conversation. Other editors would more than likely have felt threatened by any assistant getting on too well with the higher-ups. This was a rigid rule of the traditional cutting-room structure but it was not for John. Like Pat, he brought to his work a strong sense of manners which, at times, ran counter to convention.

Often I'd be across the other side of the room talking with Pat while John was beavering away. McGoohan was not ready to be happy but we worked at keeping him comfortable.

'Has Ian told you where he's from?' John said across the room. 'He's a born troublemaker just like you, Pat,' he grinned.

Pat was amused at the description of troublemaker and asked where I was from.

'You have an accent. Antipodes? It's a bit light, could be New Zealand,' he said.

'I'm from South Africa,' I answered.

Pat asked if I'd escaped from anything political.

I said that I'd not been locked up, but that I'd had to leave in a hurry. I was broaching a subject that normally I seldom spoke about, I added.

The General. Patrick McGoohan with John Castle - an actor with interior.

'Not wanting to pry,' Pat sipped his gin and addressed me. 'But how involved were you?'

I replied that I'd been involved on the fringe of an anti-government group and that I couldn't really go back. I was less a politico and more a token artist member of the cell. The others were all committed Trotskyites. As I had been the only white member of the group, it was possible for me to get out of South Africa. Which I did. The colour of my skin had been a danger to everyone else as well as to myself.

This appeared to satisfy Pat. He moved behind the moviola.

'How you getting on, John?' he enquired.

'Nearly there,' John replied as he leaned over the synchronizer to check that his rubber numbers were correctly aligned.

With the stock material inserted, the opening sequences began to hang together. It was no great shakes but Pat could see that John had done well with the material he had. He was complimentary.

John beamed with satisfaction. He appreciated being appreciated.

'The subliminal crash course indoctrination could be better,' Pat muttered.

'Maybe you could do an insert,' John said excited with the possibilities. 'Some kind of spinning thing, with the light from both sides alternatively,' he went on, scribbling in the air with his finger.

Pat nodded and said that John could direct the insert.

'Get it set up and I'll have a look. I'm sure you can do better than what we have.'

John directed the insert, and while he was doing it, Pat came to have a look and added a few more ideas.

John persisted doggedly, and *The General* acquired a coherent shape. Yet, whatever he tried, it was inevitably limited. Colin Gordon was painfully stiff playing Number Two. He wasn't the right kind of bureaucrat for the part and lacked clear identity on screen. He looked as if he didn't know what was going on. Overall, *The General* seemed indifferently conceived and packaged.

Standing out, though, was actor John Castle as Number 12. His deep, throaty voice had a certain integrity. There was something going on beneath his surface. Number 12 possessed an interior. Castle's performance alone possessed a quality that functioned in tandem with McGoohan's intensity. He carried it off convincingly but his part wasn't big enough to carry the entire episode.

The General remained an irredeemably tepid piece.

We had begun referring to Pat by the name of his role in the series.

'I think you and I present a reasonable level of entertainment,' John said, trying to understand why Pat was coming to our room more frequently. 'This is a kind of sanctuary for Number Six.'

By their very nature a production's cutting rooms often present a level of calm in contrast to the frenetic activity on the floor. Also, according to rumour, things were getting progressively fraught on set. McGoohan was becoming more demanding and there was a mounting irritation among production crew as he wanted more and more, sooner and sooner. Little of this was apparent from his behaviour with John and me.

We were waiting for Pat to arrive when he called to apologize because he couldn't make it. He said he'd try the following night but, over the next few nights, we saw nothing of him. He was either with the other editors or caught up in panic meetings. On top of these, Pat was constantly rewriting what the writers had not written well enough. John and I had the time on our hands so we got round to screening some of the completed episodes. It enabled us to consider what we'd been told about the series by others on the production.

The opening episode, *Arrival*, was a stunner, we discovered. Though somewhat flatly lit, as per prevailing television requirements, the colour looked great. We could see what had so impressed the other editors and assistants. This did not mean that the editors liked or understood it; but they couldn't help but respect it. Even dry, old Geoff Foot, our senior editor who'd cut *The Sound Barrier* for David Lean, grudgingly admitted that the series was not without merit, especially for television.

Down to earth: production under way on
Arrival - the first episode.

In every conversation, among editors, any quality of creativity evident in the series had been attributed solely to McGoohan. The only good episodes were said to be the ones that McGoohan, had written, co-written or directed, or in some way left his stamp. Viewed from the cutting rooms, it seemed to be almost entirely McGoohan's show.

George Markstein the script editor of the series, was supposedly the creator of the original concept. I gathered that McGoohan was not happy with him. Markstein never ventured into the cutting rooms. Neither, for that matter, did David Tomblin, the series' chief producer. The directors seemed not to be much involved with the post-production. It appeared that McGoohan had absolute authority over everything and that his permission was essential for anything. He didn't refuse to show anything

to Lew Grade, boss of the parent company ITC, but apparently McGoohan had a slew of convincing excuses that got him delay after delay. McGoohan manoeuvred things to get independence, privacy and freedom for *The Prisoner* to be exactly and specifically what he wanted. He had established himself in a considerable position of power but he was very much out on a limb, trying to juggle too many differently spinning balls in too many separate directions. It seemed only a matter of time before the limb broke and everything came tumbling down. McGoohan couldn't sustain his isolation indefinitely. Prints had to be shown and deals had to be made, especially in regard to the all important American market.

In the middle of filming at Portmeirion, it was said, Lew Grade had asked McGoohan to come from Wales to London to meet up with Michael Dann, Senior Vice President of Programming for CBS. Dann had specially flown over to London to view some of *The Prisoner* episodes with Lew. Dann had been responsible for CBS buying *Danger Man,* and was negotiating to buy *The Prisoner.* After seeing the first few episodes, Dann was all fired up with the prospect of something so innovative and so thought-provoking that it would eclipse previous successes but he was deeply concerned about the downbeat nature of the project. Lew offered to get Patrick to allay Dann's worst fears. Lew was supremely confident that it could all be sorted out. He agreed with Dann's criticisms wholeheartedly and felt it would ease matters all round if Dann spoke to Pat, face to face. He predicted that Pat was a very sensible fellow and would definitely listen to what Dann had to say.

That evening at ten p.m. the three men met. Dann told Pat what a wonderful thing he had created. He was genuinely deeply impressed and he congratulated Pat. The location, the action, the casting, all came in for heavy American flattery. Pat listened intensely with his eyes fixed on Dann's throughout.

Lew puffed at his gargantuan cigar and said nothing.

The show could win awards, Dann continued. It could set new standards and new values, he said, but the American viewing public could not go for a loser.

McGoohan interrupted Dann a number of times, but with absolute civility. He addressed Dann as Mr repeatedly. There was no show business affectation.

'Do I understand...?'

'Did you say...?'

'Do I hear you correctly, Mr Dann?'

'I assume Mr Dann...' and finally, 'are you finished Mr Dann?'

Dann replied that he was.

'Mr Dann,' Pat started his response, 'you have outlined a perfectly wonderful show. I came here full of suspicion. I assumed you would not know what television drama was about. I want you to know that I have changed my mind completely. You make an excellent case.' Pat congratulated him. 'I encourage you, as much as possible, to make the show you're talking about. I think it would achieve exactly what you want.

'I, of course, will make this show exactly as I am writing, directing and producing it. And therefore we will both be able to do what we

want. Have I made myself clear?'

Pat went off to collect his sports car and make the long drive back to North Wales.

Lew was pleased. He felt that Dann was the only person who could've made Pat understand the message. Dann accused Lew of not listening and of not even being in the same room. Dann was convinced that Lew was wrong and that nothing would be changed.

All this had occurred before John and I joined the production. Despite it, CBS committed themselves to buying the series.

Our brief hiatus was interrupted when Pat came back to us to deal with the last sequences of *The General*. As we were working, John asked Pat what he made of the fact that our cutting room was number six.

Pat jerked the door open and examined it.

'Number six, the perfect number,' Pat muttered. 'But it's not a magic number though it's perfect according to numerology. It doesn't do any good to read more depth than there is. If you get too intellectual you could end up with something satanic like 666,' Pat looked straight at me.

Whether he was serious or joking I couldn't tell. John returned our attention to the matter at hand.

'Come on, chaps,' John clapped his hands gleefully. 'This might work.'

We went through the entire cutting copy and McGoohan said that it was ready to be shifted over to the dubbing crew. *The General* was finished; but what a finish.

In the last sequence, Number Six outwitted the mega-brilliant computer with a single word and destroyed the hitherto all-powerful machine. The ramp leading up to the banks of machines wobbled underfoot. It seemed it had been made of cardboard, or very thin painted wood. Every footstep seemed to shake something, everything was so flimsy. For the finale, there were a few flashing lights and, with the dramatic weight of an electrified Christmas tree collapsing, the overgrown computer got smoked out.

There was little of excellence in the episode. It offered an interesting premise but it had not been interestingly executed. It was ludicrous, but it was over.

'Are you going to tackle another episode?' Pat asked us.

If Pat didn't know then who did, we wondered.

The next morning we were allocated *It's Your Funeral*.

After viewing all the material, we weren't sure it was any better than *The General*. It might even have been worse.

John told me to cheer up. We were still employed, he said, even if we were about to start sweating again over another undeniably duff episode.

As before, John told McGoohan that it wasn't that bad and that he was confident he could do something with it. This time, even John's great generosity couldn't rise convincingly to the occasion. Again, so little material was shot that it seemed likely to be the episode with the largest amount of library material. The director had disappeared in ignominy during the shoot after a flare-up with Pat. McGoohan took over the directing but, apparently, not soon enough.

The genesis of *It's Your Funeral* was one of the oddest of the series. The commissioned writer, Michael Cramoy, was given a limiting brief. He was to write a story around existing stock material. This was the least original script in the series, a fabricated, uninspired storyline implanted in material already shot, like the cut-out games for children where heads can be switched to different bodies. This primary weakness was compounded by further carelessness in the production.

The skeleton of the plot was the double-double-cross. The Village authorities planned some housecleaning to get rid of the outgoing Number Two. The blame would be placed on a non-existent underground, thereby providing a convenient excuse for reprisals. The only serious fly in the ointment was Number Six. Could he be prevented from interfering and exposing the assassination plot? To protect innocent people, Number Six had to protect the departing Number Two. The Seal of Office, worn round the neck by the retiring Number Two, was secretly a bomb. It was to be detonated before being transferred to the new Number Two.

An elderly East European watchmaker, naïvely committed to freedom, had been duped into believing that he was part of an underground resistance movement which, in fact, did not exist. His blonde daughter realized that her father was being manipulated. She tried to convince Number Six of the false plot and enlist his help to thwart it, thus saving her father from otherwise inevitable punishment. The frail old watchmaker had to perfect his detonation device in time for the handing-over ceremony. His faith in the veracity of the plot was unshakeable. He was determined to strike a blow for freedom.

Perhaps the script could be viewed as plausible. However the production lacked pace and was afflicted with particularly weak casting.

Derren Nesbitt, playing the episode's incoming Number Two and arch-plotter, claimed that he didn't know what the episode was about, let alone the series. No one gave him any direction during shooting, he complained, so he played to the gods and himself. Unsurprisingly his performance appeared misplaced. His sense of drama veered too close to pantomime. His cumbersome heavy-rimmed glasses were a prop beyond his abilities to carry. The chubby, beach-boy image he projected was out of kilter with any serious intent behind his No 2. Unfortunately, the episode's direction was unable to compensate for such deficiencies. On screen everything was turgid and unconvincing. The elderly watchmaker appeared disproportionately neurotic. His daughter played by Annette Andre, usually a fluent and compelling performer, was stiff with fear. Off-screen, we were told, the actor playing the father had been reduced to tears by McGoohan. Andre, it was said, had been painfully intimidated by McGoohan's rude and dismissive attitude to her.

Whatever the reason, everyone involved seemed committed to burying *It's Your Funeral*. If John S Smith could make something out of the material we had, he would emerge an indisputable genius.

Closing up for the night, John asked me how Lindsay matched up to Pat. John had heard much about Lindsay, but had never met him.

'John, I'm still just getting to know Lindsay, so what I have to say is from a limited point of view.'

Although comparing Lindsay Anderson and Patrick McGoohan was inevitable, such judgements are best made retrospectively. Both men went against the grain. Both were anti-establishment. However Lindsay was dominated by a fierce intelligence and Pat by a raw intuitive passion. Both had monstrous egos. Yet Lindsay functioned from the head. Pat functioned from the heart and shot from the hip. Neither was capable of recognising their common ground. Lindsay was suspicious of success and Pat was suspicious of the intellect.

Lindsay was a polymath with considerable savvy and know-how. Physically he was a strongly built barrel with a solid right hook. Whereas McGoohan towered in physical height, he didn't have much to say. When he eventually squeezed out a few words, they were measured, laconic or ironic. There was little difference between McGoohan's off-screen persona and his performance. In person, he was only spasmodically loquacious. In the series, his tight-mouthed control was an irritably attractive feature. His stance projected angry defiance as he busted icons and fomented rebellion. I didn't say all of this to John at the time. Instead I found a way of summarising what the two men shared.

'Both of them are gentleman rebels,' I said.

4

BETWEEN KAFKA AND BRECHT

Even though I did not go to work on Lindsay's *The White Bus*, our friendship continued. We'd kept in touch. We'd talked on the phone, and met up when possible. He'd encouraged me to write a script. Now Lindsay had invited me over for a meal at his home in Greencroft Gardens, West Hampstead. I decided that it would be inadvisable to talk about *The Prisoner*.

Lindsay welcomed me warmly and put on a record to which, he said, I had to hear. It was Alan Price's single, 'Simon Smith and his Amazing Dancing Bear'. Lindsay was planning to meet up with Alan Price. He felt that it might be possible to get Alan to produce socially relevant material. The stridency of Alan's style had certain Brechtian overtones, he maintained. He was also concerned that I wasn't 'with it' vis-à-vis the world of popular music.

There was nothing palatial about Lindsay's living conditions. His somewhat gloomy basement garden flat was how I imagined Brecht might have lived. The rooms were dimly lit and poorly heated by calor gas and fan heaters. The place was sprawling and spacious, but cluttered. There were stacks of books everywhere. The kitchen was tiny and the ancient gas stove appeared to be leaking. He didn't care much for material things, though he had specific tastes and opinions on everything. In his polymath manner, he embraced everything with unbridled curiosity and inescapable criticism; everything, that is, except for my interest in American comic books. This he dismissed as idiosyncrasy. He did not accept that comics were yet another medium in which popular values were examined and questioned.

We chatted about Brecht. When I first arrived in Britain, the East German Berlin Ensemble was in London. I got to see *Coriolanus* and *The Threepenny Opera*. They were performed in German. I could not understand the words but the impact of both plays seemed to transcend the language barrier. Both had been exhilarating experiences.

Lindsay told me about Poland, from where he had recently returned after directing *The Singing Lesson*, a 35mm black and white short about a blind and elderly singing master. Lindsay loved working in Eastern Europe. He felt more appreciated there than he did in Britain.

As Lindsay opened a few cans of minced meat, he instructed me to go into a back room and introduce myself to his mother.

A plumpish, grey-haired lady was seated on the edge of a bed watching the door. She had a somewhat haunted look. She blurted nervously, in a Scottish accent, that her son frightened her. He was too rigid for her liking, she complained. He was too demanding and uncompromising. I could not begin to guess why she was telling me all these things about her son.

I was summoned to stir a pot in the kitchen while Lindsay made a phone call.

Over a meal of mince fried with onions, served with pieces of limp lettuce, and bread that had seen better days, Lindsay asked what progress I'd made on the script.

While I washed up the dishes, Lindsay read my latest draft of *The Application Form*. I could hear him groaning vociferously in the next room. He'd given me masses of instructions, all of which I had implemented. Finally he summoned me out of the kitchen. He'd made very few changes, except that he'd deleted what I took to be the main scene.

'Of course it is,' he explained, ' but there's no need to overstate your case. Get rid of the scene

and the whole thing becomes more mysterious and effective. It's not bad now,' he continued, 'It's probably as good as it's going to get. You'd better stop any further rewriting and submit it somewhere.'

I said I'd send it to the BFI head of production, the mad Aussie, Bruce Beresford. Lindsay said they'd go for it. It caught the mood of the time and was more a homage to Kafka than a rip-off. Despite my decision not to mention the programme, I pointed out that it was also a product of my working on *The Prisoner*.

Lindsay made a dismissive remark about my working in television and that I had better get busy at some serious filmmaking. He couldn't envisage me being led astray by the appeal of money and mediocrity but I'd better be on the lookout, he cautioned me, because I left myself wide open and people couldn't resist taking advantage of that. He cited the incident of the young Belgian director he'd sent to me.

'I only sent him to you to get help with the idea for his next film,' Lindsay gave one of his over the top sighs. 'But no, you had to feed him and put him up for a fortnight.'

'You thought his film about the bomb was very good,' I countered, 'and so did I.'

'That is not the point.' Lindsay raised his eyes up at the ceiling.

The Application Form was a dark piece about a poetic innocent caught up in a bureaucratic nightmare. A loyal citizen falls foul of the authorities. The accusations are never defined, a sentence is never quite passed and guilt or innocence never established. In the end, however, the innocent is killed.

Lindsay was convinced that it would make a good vehicle for my directorial debut. I said that I wasn't interested in becoming a director. As he had done so much work on the script and practically written it, I wanted him to direct it.

'You wrote it,' he said. 'So you must direct it, if you get the chance.'

Lindsay recommended more books which he felt I should read. These were to help my education, which he felt was limited. I was given D H Lawrence's *Sons and Lovers*. On his suggestion I had already got through *Out of Africa* by Karen Blixen.

What would McGoohan have considered for recommended reading, I wondered.

I made the scene deletion as Lindsay had recommended and took the manuscript up to Scripts on Gerrard Street in Soho. This cluttered tiny office in Chinatown had cornered the market for quality presentation of feature film scripts. At the least my project would look professional.

At work, John encouraged me to tell Pat about my project. I said we'd better wait and see if anything comes of it.

John didn't wait. During a lull in the evening's work he started to inform Pat about the quality of my writing. Pat responded politely, but didn't seem overly interested.

Afterwards John said we'd have to work on getting McGoohan to really see me as a writer. He felt I deserved every chance and, though I knew a quality director like Lindsay, John considered that I didn't have family or the right connections in the business. If Lindsay was more

commercial and churned out more features, I'd probably be okay, John suggested.

Meanwhile we plodded on, snipping away at *It's Your Funeral*.

I got a call from Bruce Beresford at the BFI. He wanted to see me. Without any qualms, John gave me the time off.

I spent a morning listening to Beresford flapping about in his congested BFI production office in Dean Street. I could not see how Bruce had landed such a prestigious and powerful position. Then, I could not see beyond his brash manner. 'Well the board approved, and you got a grant,' Bruce informed me. 'But first, you'll have to produce a test sequence.' Bruce swung his feet up onto his crowded desk, with his hands folded behind his head. 'I can recommend what scenes you might tackle but it's up to you. Lindsay was involved with this, you said, but there was nothing in any of your correspondence about him.'

'I had a fantasy that he would direct it,' I admitted. 'Especially after all the work he put into it.'

'Be bloody good if you got him to direct it,' Bruce changed his posture, and leaned forward eagerly. 'Ask him till he says yes.'

'Are you mad!' Lindsay seethed when again I broached the subject of him directing my script. 'I'm not going to direct your film. You've got to do it. Don't you want to become a director?'

'Not really,' I replied feebly.

'For God's sakes! Just do it.'

Meanwhile, back on *The Prisoner*, John Smith made another unbridled pitch on my behalf to McGoohan.

'Pat,' John said, leaning away from the movieola, 'do you know about Ian and his writing?'

Pat replied that he did not.

'You should,' John continued. 'What he writes fits right into *The Prisoner*. And he is definitely talented.'

I kept silent. I had no inkling that John had intended making such a strong pitch on my behalf.

The discussion about my writing concluded with Pat agreeing to read *The Application Form* and a script I wanted to submit for the series. I was mulling over an idea that might be appropriate, I told him, but it would be different, hopefully very different.

'I'll have a read,' Pat assured me. 'Drop it in my office when it's ready.'

Lindsay Anderson. The thinker, thinking.

MY FAVOURITE GENRE

The MGM canteen had a high ceiling and a strong echo. The incessant clatter of utensils was continually present. Tony Sloman led our little group of assistants to an empty table. Tony slumped down and began eating without interrupting his verbal flow. The back projection requirements were never ending and Tony's work there kept him in the heat of things. We editors all saw him when we made the odd visit to the set for some reason or other but, in the main, the strict off-limits rule was maintained.

The Prisoner was almost as secretive as the nearby Kubrick unit. Between our own tight schedule and Kubrick's, little was ever seen or heard by us of *2001 A Space Odyssey*. The production occupied plenty of studio space in a big block, at the far side of the studio, that butted onto the vast back lot. We rarely saw anything, however. At one stage, I glimpsed a couple of actors in monkey suits but that was all. Occasionally female art students could be seen slumped on the steps of C stage, out in the sunlight, resting their eyes after the task of painting Kubrick's night skies. Tony and Mark Davies, another assistant, were often trying to chat up the girls. Tony had taken great delight in asking Kubrick if we could have some of his stars for *The Prisoner*. As a result *The Prisoner* night skies would sparkle with the *Space Odyssey*'s hand-painted stars.

Sitting down next to me in the canteen Eric Mival, newly elevated from assistant to music editor, asked me if I'd heard about the looming crisis on the series. Though cheery, Eric was easily the most serious of our lot. He was the closest thing on the unit to a clean-cut Christian. He was far from narrow or intolerant but I would never hear him swear.

'Yeah, man,' Mark joined in as he sat on the other side of me, 'they're desperate for ideas.'

'That's right,' Tony bounced in his seat. 'We can all give it a try and maybe get our names up on the credits.'

'Ian,' Eric addressed me. 'You've done some

writing haven't you? Have you thought of doing a script?'

Before I could reply, Tony chirped in.

'Course he has. He's writing a western.'

'Tony, it's early days.' I interrupted. 'I've hardly begun and, besides, you've read nothing.'

'How can I read it before you've written it?' he demanded. 'You better get it done so that I can read it.'

I had told Tony in confidence about the script. I was taken aback by the way in which he blurted it out. I remembered our western encounter, prior to *The Prisoner*, in the NFT foyer. We'd got chatting at a season of films by Budd Boetticher, one of the great masters of Hollywood B-feature westerns. Our meeting was brief and we'd only met properly at MGM.

'A western,' Eric adjusted his glasses and grinned at me. 'How could you fit a western into the format?'

I had no reply.

'Be great if one of us pulled it off,' Mark nudged me and unwrapped the macrobiotic lunch which his wife had prepared.

Tony began to hum discordantly. It was the theme tune from Fred Zinneman's *High Noon*.

'Ian's already started his script. *Do Not Forsake Me Oh My Darling*, That's the title,' Tony announced across the table.

I told Tony to belt up. He dashed off to get something more to eat.

Mark repeated my title and mused over it while adroitly clicking a pair of wooden chopsticks. He gave me a narrow-eyed, mischievous look.

'Bloody *High Noon*. You'll chuck in some sex and violence though, won't you?'

'That's out then,' Eric chuckled. 'Pat would never go for anything salacious.'

'I'm sure Pat could stretch his boundaries if something good enough came his way,' I maintained, 'as long as it's not exploitative.'

Bearing a large pudding, Tony returned and sat down.

'Just write what you like,' Tony said emphatically, spreading his custard across something spongy. 'You've got nothing to lose, have you?'

David Naughton, the youngest of our bunch, came over and tried to join us. Everyone was furious at him. He'd managed to cause masses of unnecessary work for all of us that day because he'd messed up the morning's rubber numbering, the system for printing matching numbers on picture and sound reels for synchronisation.

It wasn't the first time Naughton had messed up something. Although smaller and younger than the rest of us, he was by far the most showy. He was always boasting about how he could get things done by the shortest possible way, with the least amount of effort.

We all started to have a go at him for not pulling his weight.

'Have a heart, you guys,' Naughton protested. 'Last night was incredible. How could I say no? I can't help it if I'm irresistible.' He flashed a gold crown as he drew a chair from the next table to sit with us. 'I can't help it if I had a hangover and was late.'

'Get lost, squirt,' Mark said threateningly, 'and have those numbers redone before we get back from lunch.'

Naughton laughed, and Mark stood up.

'Pull your weight or I'll personally see you trashed back into the Pinewood post box you crawled out of,' he growled.

'Calm down, I'm going,' Naughton said, backing away from Mark. 'You take this nonsense too seriously, mate. You're all nuts. It's just a job.'

Mark made a move and Naughton dashed out.

'Cretin,' Mark said, sitting back down.

I never thought that Mark was really going to whack Naughton, or that Naughton thought that Mark would do it. Mark exuded brotherly love and peace. He made no bones about being right up to date, doing drugs and being hooked on macrobiotics. His dress, his walk and his talk were all quintessentially of the period, of the moment. On sunny days Mark would take his lunch break out on the back lot, ploughing his way through the *Glass Bead Game* by Herman Hesse, or rereading his favourite science fiction author, Alfred Bester, accompanied by rice balls with tofu.

'What's up chaps?' John S. Smith joined us with his tray of canteen lunch. 'What are you lot plotting? I saw Naughton going off. Have you all been getting at him?' He grabbed at a seat. 'He hasn't messed up the rubber numbering again?'

No one answered John as he sat down.

'What is this?' John moaned as he stabbed something flabby floating in his greased plate. 'It doesn't look very good.'

A date had been pencilled in on for shooting my test sequence on *The Application Form*. All the elements of the project seemed slowly to be coming together but, in the meantime, I had a

western to develop. It may have been only a remote possibility but it was definitely something worth aiming for, I felt. In fact, I had rather more confidence in my capacity to write a western than I had in my skills as a potential film director. With the former, I had special help.

That evening, at home in my flat, I got out some of my favourite late 1940s and early 1950s Dell western comic books. Roy Rogers gave me little to sink my teeth into; he kept on blaming half-breeds for every possible villainy. This was no use. Not only did they smack of racism, *Roy Rogers'* pages were more crudely drawn than the more liberally oriented *Gene Autry* comics. The latter had an atmosphere that began to suggest ideas. I turned to some more recent Two Gun Kid stories. Images seemed to ride straight off the page.

Ghost towns, way off the beaten track, and false façades seeped into my thoughts. There was also a good-natured saloon hostess, a corrupt judge, and a young maverick psychopath, slick with a gun and quick to use it. These would all be stirred up by the arrival of a nameless hero, very much off course. I felt I had the beginnings of a story but how could the whole thing be incorporated into the Village?

Besides being an avid collector of 1949-55 period Dell westerns, the first feature film I had worked on had been a western of sorts. *The Hellions* was a British film made on location in South Africa.

For me, the direct similarity between South Africa and the Village had been obvious. The country's apartheid system was the Village legislation writ large. Under the draconian laws of apartheid, the entire population was rigidly controlled. The religious white government claimed biblical motivation as its excuse for their own experiment in social engineering.

The Hellions' production unit was composed of a mixed South African and British crew. British technicians I worked alongside provided my first big encounter with anyone from overseas. It was tricky for those technicians in South Africa, a world away from the studios at Pinewood where a number of them had learned their craft. However they learned quickly not to speak their thoughts. They all realized the dangers of the police state.

It was then 1960 and a time of great change in South African history. Endless laws were being passed to categorize people into separate cubby-holes in order to facilitate the control of black by white. At the same time, a long history of passive protest was rapidly giving way to armed resistance.

The Hellions was a not very successful remaking of *Gunfight at the OK Corral*, the Hollywood classic directed by John Sturgess. The story was set in the Transvaal in the 1860s. A family of outlaws starts a reign of terror in a small village until, finally, the locals rise up against them.

After *The Hellions*, I returned home to Cape Town. The political group I belonged to was on the cusp of committing itself to an armed struggle, but the time had not yet arrived. I had carried a gun, and the leader of the group had ordered me to give it up. Most of the group had opposed open violence. But political events were overtaking pacifist views.

Personal memories of the resistance in South Africa were infiltrating my western. Vietnam and the burning of draft cards were big in the news.

The call to arms was being resisted across America. Public opinion was far from as patriotic as it had once been. Too many deaths and too many burning bodies had appeared on television. I deliberately did not try to separate my ideas from these events. If it was good enough, I reasoned, McGoohan would swallow it.

I got underway, expanding my initial concept and incorporating the necessary elements. It had to have a current relevance and resonance, more than just a story, more than just an entertainment. The Village and its accompanying psychology wouldn't be difficult to tap into; my South African background provided it all.

Gene Autry #63. One of the all-time great cowboys, and Ian Rakoff's source of inspiration. **Gene Autry** #39 (back cover).

6

RUMBLINGS OF DISCONTENT

McGoohan told John to stop. I flicked off the moviola switch and moved aside. 'It's the directing,' Pat said, 'but that's what you're stuck with.'

'Give me five minutes, Pat,' John said, pulling the cutting copy from the machine then slapping the picture reel and the striped magnetic sound reel into the synchronizer. 'I've got an idea.' He glanced at me. 'Tell Pat some more about your life in the Village and your goings on out there. How you, too, were a rebel.'

Pat took a sip, and looked at me.

As I went on double-joining another reel of cutting copy, and patching some torn bits, I told Pat how back in Cape Town, I'd started a school magazine for a charity. It had been closed down after three issues. Nothing was made clear but the reason was probably the serial I wrote in the magazine about Jack Johnson the Galveston Giant, the first black world heavyweight boxing champion in 1915. Having a black hero in every

issue had not gone down well at my school, SACS, the oldest white school in Africa.

While John laboured on, I talked to Pat more about my troubled school history.

'I ran the Civic Society for a while. I gave a talk on race and about forty boys turned on me. I got in a scrap, got caned and kicked out of the Society.'

'Did they keep you censored after that?' Pat enquired.

'Over here chaps!' John broke into our conversation and summoned us to the moviola.

The reel didn't look a whole lot better but John had certainly improved it; and quickly.

Pat announced he was off.

From our first floor window I watched Pat's slender figure flitting between the lights and the shadows across the cement surrounding the windowless stage monoliths. The high corner lighting created a wartime Stalag look. Pat disappeared and a moment later he reappeared on his bicycle. He was on his way to the Red

Free For All. The Village marching for democracy.

Lion Pub at the bottom of the road to meet David Tomblin.

John and I mused over the present hierarchy of the series. Ultimately all paths of power led to McGoohan, but the levels of subordinate power formed the contours of a variable and uncertain terrain. Though the shadow of David Tomblin appeared to be dutifully close by Pat, even Tomblin's shadowy role seemed to change. As the production had progressed, doubt among the ranks had grown. A contract was no guarantee with McGoohan in charge. No one was secure. Stories of conflict with an increasingly demonic McGoohan were rife.

Directors and actors had ugly confrontations with Pat. Things changed with phenomenal rapidity and lines were being rewritten while the camera was turning.

John had a good nose for finding out. He had discovered that a major rift had opened between McGoohan and his script editor. There was a threatening shortage of money, a possible close down at any moment, and worst of all, an increasing dearth of ideas. Everything seemed fluid and up in the air, getting more so as time pressed on. No wonder McGoohan often appeared chronically distressed. It was a heavy, heavy weight and it finally rested on his shoulders alone.

'You better get on with your western, hadn't you?' John urged me. 'Before it's all too late.'

John was still going at the cutting with undiminished determination. The limits of *It's Your Funeral* were not going to get the better of him. At the end of an afternoon, he suggested I take off. He had it all under control, he said. He had everything he needed and I could catch up in the morning. John wanted me to go home and carry on writing. I took off.

In the corridor I met Mark. He was also leaving.

'That old fart has fired me again,' Mark scowled, referring to his editor Geoff Foot. 'Geoff hasn't got a laugh in him,' Mark complained, as he offered me a lift home. 'He calls McGoohan that out-of-control maniac.'

Mark, tall, good looking and catlike was in constant conflict with his immediate boss. Nonetheless, Foot was by far and away the best editor at work on the series. He was, without question, a consummate professional.

Geoff Foot was a small man with a large chip on his shoulder. He resembled a dried-up yachting captain with a dash of the RAF flown in. He eyes were either blankly disinterested, or looking somewhere else. Working in television was an obvious step down for such a high flying feature film editor and it was irredeemably bad chemistry between him and Mark. To Geoff, Mark was a complete anathema. Mark was chronically unreliable and insisted on doing the most menial jobs in his own time, at his own pace. Mark's laid back attitude drove Geoff to despair. Mark was incorrigibly defiant and

Geoff was unbending. Mark was repeatedly fired and hired by Geoff who, underneath his military façade, was a genuinely decent type.

Mark was motivated by absolute faith in all that McGoohan was trying to do. He idolized McGoohan and was proud of his association with the series. McGoohan could do no wrong. Mark's personal identification with Number Six, also convinced him that McGoohan was an avid drug taker.

A lot of people talked a lot about drugs. They were thick in the air at the time, literally and figuratively. I picked up no hint that Pat ever had anything to do with drugs, beyond any legitimate medications he might have been prescribed to keep that incredible stamina going. His boundless energy and drive clearly came from within, sans stimulants. What was without doubt, though, is that the social reality of drugs entered a substantial aspect of the world which *The Prisoner* inhabited; and Mark, more than any other young members of the crew, was the resident barometer of what was going on outside *The Prisoner*.

Mark was in touch with the very latest, most way out music. He was near monkish in his adherence to the basic tenets of eating and living the macrobiotic way. Visiting Mark at home was a religious culinary experience.

The macrobiotic thing was big. The new style of eating, from Japan via Belgium, was gathering ground. Ceres, a specialist store, had opened in Portobello Road and was soon followed by a macrobiotic restaurant in nearby All Saints Road. Mark was in on all the healthy food developments and was in cahoots with the two brothers who'd launched Ceres, spreading the word of George Oshawa's teachings on the principles of yin and yang. I bought the Oshawa books and read them assiduously. I learned to be cautious in any culinary relationship with the dark toxic forces inherent in the extreme yang. I moved away from aubergines and mushrooms, and later learned the joys and virtues of organic brown rice, miso and tahini. For that moment in time, I was fascinated.

What also attracted me to Mark was his circle

Checkmate. The chess game. Unlike chess, with its clear-cut rules, not everyone on the series could make the right moves.

of friends. His flat was a centre for a group of Biafrans. One by one, they shipped themselves off to Africa to fight for their independence in the Nigerian civil war. I felt comfortable in seeing Africans mixing so freely with a white Englishman. The patriotic Biafrans were a mixed bunch. Some were in music; others were film technicians. All of them were chomping at the bit, eager to get back and fight for freedom and for Biafra to keep control of the vast oil fields.

Mark's dream was to have a camera of his own and become a free, floating filmmaker, drawn by whatsoever visuals he fancied. His thinking, and the little films he created, suggested that Mark could be the one to go the furthest of us all.

Driving back from the studio, Mark invited me to his place for a macrobiotic meal. I said I couldn't. I had to work on the western.

At home, I had to disregard the doom and gloom forecasts of the series in order to carry on the writing. I couldn't very well both press on and accept that it was all likely to come to an absolute halt. Rumour had gone as far as predicting that the expensive series was condemned to be one man's folly, shoved on a vault shelf, collecting dust and nothing else, never to be seen or heard.

7

ANOTHER VILLAGE, ANOTHER COUNTRY

Though supportive of my writing, John was sceptical about my writing a western. 'It's such an American thing,' he said tentatively. 'I can't see us lot over here ever making a western. It's not British. It's never been done.'

'That's not so,' I corrected him. 'There was a British western, and I worked on it.'

'I know what films you've worked on,' John shook his head, not believing me. 'You've never mentioned any cowboy film.'

'On location, a British South African co-production,' I explained. 'The Ken Annikin film of ...'

'*The Hellions*,' John swung his hand and snapped his fingers. 'Of course! It came and went. Richard Todd!'

'My first film experience, thanks to a pushy friend of mine.'

We recharged our sugarless coffees and settled down. I filled John in about my introduction to

cinema, and to the South African cowboy film.

He smiled when I asked if he wanted the works.

'Absolutely, give me the gory details of when you became a celluloid cowboy.'

It all began when Randal, an old pal of mine, came back from London after being kicked out of RADA and Central drama schools. It was 1960, the year before I left South Africa and we were both about twenty years old. Randal had landed the juvenile lead in a play for the Leonard Schach touring company. My old pal was appalled by my situation. I'd dropped out of university, left home, and was living in the impoverished Malay quarter of Cape Town, Skotches Kloof. My place didn't have a bath, a shower or a phone. Randal nearly jumped out of his skin when he saw the size of my cockroaches.

Skotches Kloof was an area designated under The Group Areas Act as non-white. Technically, I was living there illegally but, by keeping a relatively low profile, I had not yet been spotted by the police. The character of the apartheid regime was going through a major change. In Sharpeville, a township near to Johannesburg, a peaceful demonstration against the Pass Laws had ended in bloodshed. Sixty-nine unarmed people had been massacred and many more were wounded. Almost all the victims were shot in the back as they tried to get away. It was indefensible and the horrors of South Africa hit the headlines of the world press in a big way.

Since the massive post-Sharpeville demonstration in Cape Town, I'd been dragging my heels, not involved in much of anything. So, when Randal came up with a suggestion, I said I'd go along with it. Randal had made a connection with a film on location near Pretoria. He reckoned that he could get me a job. I pointed out, that, though I'd done plenty in the theatre, I had no experience with film. Randal assured me it didn't matter. He was going to set me up and I was going to pull it off. For once I would have to behave like him, he stated emphatically. We went out and he made a telephone call.

I was met at Pretoria station by Willie Hertz, the Afrikaans production supervisor. He was a huge, fat fellow who had trouble with his breathing and kept on taking off his thick rimmed glasses to wipe away the sweat. It was as hot as hell in Pretoria and when we got to the location village, Britz, it was even worse. Everything looked hazy in an endless expanse of nothingness. The earth was being fried. I could feel the heat searing my lungs; I could taste the hot dryness. The light, though, was incredibly

brilliant.

To get me the job, Randal had dished out a few lies. I did exactly what Randal had warned me not to do. I told Willie everything. I was not from England, as Randal had told him; and I had no experience in film, only in theatre. His friend and my friend, Randal, had deliberately misinformed him. I apologized. None of it seemed to worry Willie in the slightest.

'You're one of those people I can read like an open book,' he told me. 'There's a job as assistant director I can give you. At least I can know where I stand with you.'

Willie mentioned a weekly wage and we shook hands.

Everything was chaotic and disorganized. Willie was sure that I'd pick things up quickly. My being bilingual was an added asset; but he was curious about my peculiar Afrikaans accent. I explained that my family was from Namaqualand. Namaqualand was a vast remote area along the west coast just below South West Africa, the ex-German colony where my mother was born. Willie had evidently never met anyone from Namaqualand. It was huge but it was mostly arid, lifeless and thinly populated. Everyone had heard of Namaqualand; few people had actually been there.

I was booked into a Pretoria hotel, and teamed up with Dawie van Heerden. He'd been a location manager and assistant director all over the place. He claimed he had found locations for John Houston on Lake Tanganyika. As Dawie was only a few years older than me this seemed extraordinary. Nevertheless, it seemed that Dawie had been on every major film across East Africa.

Dawie and I got on like a house on fire and soon we became inseparable. Out at Britz under the hottest sun imaginable, we worked together with manic intensity and a small army of labourers. We moved trees, we levelled hills and we handled some of the firearms. Dawie was the big Mr Fix-it on the unit.

Out on location, I rocketed around the rugged terrain in a four-wheel drive jeep. Going to and from Pretoria, Dawie drove his Alfa Romeo at breakneck speed. We were both continually stripped to the waist and burnt to a crisp. It was all hard, physical work and I loved it.

The English technicians were an alien breed. But loose and effortless as they may have been, they were inescapably aware of the country's laws. They didn't like the atmosphere which seeped in everywhere, especially in a small Afrikaner backwater such as Britz. You could smell dust and Dutch Reform Church everywhere.

One evening after a heavy drinking session, Dawie wanted me to meet his girlfriend. The idea of dropping in unexpected at such a late hour did not bode well but Dawie was adamant.

The girlfriend refused to let Dawie in. She yelled through the locked door that he was drunk.

'She's cheating on me,' Dawie slurred angrily.

Before I could stop him, Dawie climbed onto a railing and, with his arms folded over his head, took a flying leap and plunged right through a window. As the glass shattered, a half-undressed man ran out the front door.

I went in. The girl was sobbing hysterically and blood was pouring from Dawie's forearms.

I drove Dawie, in his Alfa, to Pretoria hospital. Shards of glass were extracted from his arms and no serious damage was found. He had a few stitches but the wounds were superficial.

By the time all that was over, dawn was breaking. The bandaged Dawie was back at the wheel and we were racing off to work, clocking up well over a hundred miles per hour. He thanked me profusely for backing his play. It was now guaranteed that I was his friend for life.

There was some kind of unspoken animosity between Dawie and Jamie Uys, the Afrikaans co-star and producer. I only noticed that Dawie avoided him.

Jamie Uys was a sensitive, cultured man, from a distinguished Afrikaner family. I'd met his cousin Uys Krige on Clifton Beach in Cape Town. Uys was one of the foremost poets in the country. His work had been on our school curriculum. Despite the impeccable Afrikaans lineage, the Uys family were all reputed to be vehemently anti-apartheid.

'Why have you read so many books, Ian?' Jamie wanted to know. 'Do you read purely for education, or for entertainment?'

I said the two were inseparable and he asked what I had read. Many of the books I mentioned were banned and therefore hard to come by. He'd read the same books but he was not familiar with the American comics.

'When he came to power, Malan banned *Superman* and *Captain Marvel*,' I told Jamie and he smiled.

In the film, he played an avuncular, pipe-smoking storekeeper. Off-screen he was exactly

Ian Rakoff with veteran Spaghetti Western actor Al Mulock during work on **The Hellions**.

the same. There was something extremely benign about Jamie.

'Were you around at the Clarenden Square incident, after Sharpeville?'

I hesitated before deciding to answer.

'I was in the heart of it. I was almost in touching distance to a Saracen tank, not that far from Philip Kgosana.'

'There were no white demonstrators,' Jamie sucked at his pipe and lowered his voice.

'There was another white,' I shrugged. 'A girl named Sagov in a Mercedes driving Kgosana through the mass to negotiate with the police. She was from one of the wealthiest families in the Cape Town.'

'You were there in that mob, just a stone's throw from Parliament, amongst thirty thousand natives?' He muttered incredulously. 'It could've ended apartheid there and then, ' he whispered. 'You must have been terrified,

though.'

'No, that was the extraordinary thing. It was the safest I ever felt. It didn't matter that I was white.'

Jamie thanked me for being so open with him, for trusting him. Punctuating the air with his unlit pipe, he declared that we must speak again. We had things to talk about, he said.

A call from make-up interrupted us and Jamie disappeared behind one of the western façades lining the dirt track road through Britz. Only a couple of the buildings had usable insides. One was the saloon and the other was the store run by Jamie.

The lead, Richard Todd, personified my every fantasy of the British stiff upper lip. He looked okay on horseback but I imagined him looking far more at ease as a World War II flying ace: more of a dam buster than a veldt sheriff. Opposite him was Ann Blythe, a refined English rose who, despite her milky white complexion, seemed to bloom out under the hot sun. I gathered that she was the girlfriend of Irving Allen, the boss of Warwick Films, under whose aegis we functioned as Eon Productions. Irving never made it to Britz. He was in London, racing to finish one of two films being made on Oscar Wilde.

The most villainous looking actor was without question the Canadian, Al Mulock. His teeth were permanently clenched tight, as if he was holding something bilious deep inside. His face looked as if it'd been worked over by an Indian hatchet. Al, the introvert graduate of Lee Strasberg, was method all the way. At times his mouth was so drawn in that it appeared to be forcibly stitched up. His sallow sunken cheeks and lined face gave him a haggard and haunted look, albeit encased in sunburn.

In the script, he was the first outlaw to bite the dust. When it came to his catching it, Dawie and I got involved. Jamie had to shoot Al by mistake. As Al got it in the gut, Dawie and I were crouched behind a wooden counter. When the shot fired, we jerked the wire attached to the back of Al's belt, lifting him off his feet. The tomato sauce blood spewed out from his guts as he writhed on the floor.

Dawie had plans for when the film was over. We would go from *The Hellions* to Windhoek, in South West Africa where he owned a diamond mine. We'd do some prospecting and then go

onto a feature due to shoot in Kenya. He wasn't the only one with plans for my future.

Randal had been in touch. He was performing in Johannesburg, thirty-six miles from Pretoria. He was convinced that I could get into the Schach company, as a stage manager and small-part actor.

Would I have to choose between acting and Dawie's diamonds? I was more concerned about politics than I was about job prospects. However, I was interested in keeping in contact with Jamie. Across the country things were getting no better; they were getting worse.

The laager mentality was digging in more and more. South Africa was on its way to becoming the acknowledged polecat of the world. This

The Hellions - a British film shot in racist South Africa.

Village which encompassed the whole of South Africa was rapidly passing more onerous and restrictive laws, arresting more people and denying everything. The bible and the gun were firmly in the saddle. It had become almost impossible to make any conversation across the colour line, let alone share a coffee. The Cape had lost its liberal independence. Segregation signs appeared in every public place. Buses, lavatories and park benches were all unequally divided between white and non-white in English and in Afrikaans. The control of people's movements was absolute and fear was everywhere. The paranoia that would engulf Number Six was already alive and well under the apartheid regime.

I found Dawie in a fracas with one of the labourers. I knew the chap to be sluggish and I'd had some words with him. It hadn't done much good; but the way Dawie was treating him was wrong. I'd asked Dawie not to try any strong-arm tactics. So far Dawie had brought none of the racial stuff into play. I saw the chap trying to back away from Dawie. It looked very unpleasant.

'*Nee baas, ek doenie daardie ding,*' the chap was shaking his head.

I hurried towards them. Dawie started screaming and looked as if he was about to hit the guy.

I rushed between them and warned Dawie that, no matter what the guy had done, he'd only get to him over my dead body.

Dawie blurted out some racist expletive and pulled out a massive knife. I'd already reached for my hatchet. For a moment it was a stand-off.

About a dozen labourers gathered around. My heart was pumping a mile a minute but I wasn't going to back down.

Dawie muttered something, lowered his knife and walked away. Later Dawie offered to forget the incident, and that we could go on as before. I accepted his offered hand and said that, if the same situation came up again, I wouldn't hold back.

Dawie laughed and said I was crazy but there weren't any more such incidents.

As the production drew to a close I decided that, ideally, I would like to stay on with Jamie's company. He'd convinced me that I could find my political expression in film.

I got an opportunity to see some documentaries that Jamie had directed. One of the films showed how the government was replacing the terrible township shacks with proper houses. It was unmitigated propaganda.

Later, at the end of picture party, Dawie repeated his partnership offer. I refused and we drank enough to sink a battleship.

While we were getting boozed, Jamie came over to me. I let loose in a loud, intoxicated voice. I told him that I'd seen his documentaries. My opinion of him had changed. If he could work for the government, I couldn't work for him. I accused him of betraying every decent value I thought he stood for and, unsteadily, I walked out.

The next morning I had a well-deserved hangover. I was packing my things when Jamie came to see me.

'The English executive producer, Rudkin, had some advice for me,' Jamie sat down, crossed his legs, and filled his pipe. 'He said I could do away with all the others working for me, but that I should keep you,' he lit his pipe. 'Within a year, I promise, you'll get your chance to be a director. I'm willing to forget what you said to me last night. You were drunk.'

'Jamie, I remember every word I said, and I was drunk,' I said continuing with my packing. 'But, I can't forget those films you made. They were propaganda films for the government, which I know you don't believe in.'

'But they lied to me. I believed those facts were true,' he said uncrossing his legs and leaning forward. 'I will not tackle anything like that again. I can promise you that,' he assured me and got up.

We shook hands and that was the end of that.

'So your western experience isn't just from comic books,' John chuckled, back inside the MGM cutting room. 'Did you ever see Jamie Uys again?'

'No, but I nearly did,' I told John how a couple of years later Jamie telephoned me at Shepperton studios.

' I was really pleased to talk with him and made an arrangement to meet. Later, I had second thoughts. I couldn't go and see him. I liked him far too much. I was frightened that, if he made me another offer, I'd accept. At the time I'd just put an end to the romance of my life. I felt useless and homesick,' I explained. 'I got his call in the cutting room while I was an assistant on *Joey Boy*.'

'I was at Shepperton then,' John exclaimed. 'I was dubbing for Kubrick, on *Doctor Strangelove*. It was like working for royalty. Do you remember David de Wilde? He was the only one that knew how to make Stanley's Nescafé. He stayed with Kubrick for years, and ended up not cutting for him, but doing household chores in Stanley's house, before he took the hint to get out,' John shook his head. 'I suppose I should have stuck with Kubrick,' John said sorrowfully. 'But I had a wife and kids, and I got a chance to dub *The System* for Winner, for an extra five pounds a week.' John laughed ironically at his choice.

'Didn't Nic Roeg light *The System*?' I asked and, as John nodded, I told him that some friends of mine knew Nic, and said that I should meet him. We carried on swapping reminiscences and our experiences in film, as we awaited word from McGoohan.

By now it was very late, and though Pat had not called us, it was unlikely that he'd turn up. We closed up shop and went home.

8

FALLING DOWN

John had to drop a list of credits into Markstein's office. He told me to take them instead. It might be good for me as a beginning writer, he said, to take the chance to meet George properly. I picked up the credits list and stepped out, glad to get a breather from the long hours confined in the cutting room.

I knocked on George's door and went in. He stood up from behind his desk and welcomed me. By this time, we'd already had a few brief chats. Whenever I'd seen him, outside a stage or in a corridor, he'd been exceptionally convivial.

Markstein looked like a quintessential apparachik, the bureaucrat behind the secret agent, the one who had the authority to press the button but who couldn't find it. He was bald, stout, bespectacled and usually ebullient. He was not a man of action. He was a thinker. But, at the time I came to meet him, his façade was crumbling and power was slipping away.

George told me to help myself to coffee as he went through the list I'd handed him.

It was proper coffee.

Having made a few minor changes, George gave the list back to me, and fetched himself a drink.

As I sat sipping, George paced about the room and talked unhappily about his shrinking role on *The Prisoner*. Some of his remarks were disjointed and his sentences not very clear. He was aggravated about the way he had been treated. He didn't name the cause but waves of discontent kept on coming out. A few more sentences and it was apparent that everything referred to Pat McGoohan.

'If you don't want your ideas hijacked, left out and shoved to the margin,' George complained, 'then television's not for you.'

I said that I didn't think it was. I'd set my sights on features and told him about my BFI grant. I told him about Lindsay's involvement.

'You can't go wrong there,' George said positively.

I asked if *The Prisoner* was originally

conceived by him. He was emphatic that it was his.

George told me that he'd been cultivating the idea since he'd worked for Britain's Intelligence Service during the Second World War. One of the most intriguing government secrets had never really been made public. His idea was to expose it and to reveal a dark period in British history.

'My idea would have been closer to fact than fiction,' George said, 'brainwashing and social control in the post-war era. Troops would be receptive to new thinking and might have to be manipulated before returning to civilian rule. That could be dangerous for the governments of many countries.

'After the war, the British Intelligence Service was formulating methods on how to implement change according to their way of thinking. For this there was a special military camp, in the north...'

What George told me was fascinating.

'I didn't get a chance to discuss my western,' I reported back to John. 'But he told me how *The Prisoner* got started.'

'Whose idea was it?' John asked me. 'Markstein's or McGoohan's?'

'George said it was his,' I shrugged. 'I suspect Pat would say the same.'

At home that evening, I put aside my western to have a go at constructing the type of story that George had in mind:

Towards the end of the Second World War a high-ranking British officer, recently engaged in espionage behind the enemy lines, regains consciousness in a barely furnished room with iron bars. He has been drugged by his colleagues.

A white-coated psychologist with an East European accent, accompanied by two guards, informs the officer that he has been selected to participate in a top secret experiment. The officer refuses to go along with anything until he knows more.

It is the officer's duty to obey orders and not ask questions, the psychologist warns. If the officer persists with his uncooperative attitude, he will be punished. On the other hand, he could benefit tremendously. If he wants to regain his civilian identity in post-war Britain, he'd better not make a fuss. A man of his type can't just be released back into the community, knowing what he knows. In the meantime, the war is not yet over, he is informed, and all he needs to know is that his being here is with the approval of his own government.

Looking out of the window, the incarcerated officer recognizes the bleak terrain of the Scottish Highlands. Armed soldiers in unrecognisable uniforms patrol the grounds with dogs on short leashes. Loudspeakers issue commands in a variety of languages.

The officer explodes in a rage. The psychologist orders the guards to restrain him. Once the officer is subdued, the psychologist produces a syringe. As he injects the struggling officer, the psychologist reiterates that all is being done for the officer's own good, and for the good of the country which he has served loyally for so many years.

I'd been writing for writing's sake, with no

goal in mind and no destination. I didn't show it to anybody, including George. It wasn't long after this that George acrimoniously left the series.

Up at the studio there was an even heavier mood of imminent doom in the air. Grade was losing his enthusiasm. The experiment he had financed was going in the same direction as McGoohan: off the rails. Everyone was trying to step carefully. No one knew anything for sure.

Another day began with conversation. John and I talked about anything but the torturous slog on *It's Your Funeral*. I gave John my latest update, fielding the story problems I needed to get through on my western.

While John went to sort out some coffee, I worked through a mound of trims spilling out of the bin onto the floor. It was a mindless chore which was good for relaxing.

I was far away, traipsing through an imagined Wild West, when John handed me a coffee. He returned to what seemed to him the basic difficulty with my story.

'How can you get the western into the Village?' John asked me. 'It's just not in the format.'

'That's no problem,' I tried to articulate my line of thinking. 'Firstly, almost any human conflict could easily be incorporated into the format of the western which is so all embracing. In comic books different genres used the western format. Science fiction and romance got the

It's Your Funeral. Derren Nesbitt - a new Number Two - tries to pass judgement. An ineffectual Number 100 watches.

western treatment, as did stories about the Nazis. So why not the Village?'

'But how will you actually move from the Village into the West?' John asked.

'I'd just jump in, West first,' I answered. 'The tricky bit will be getting out of the West and back into the Village. But with the right drugs and medication,' I pointed out, 'one can be manoeuvred into believing anything.' Then I launched into a lengthy explanation.

'I'm assembling the main characters as western archetypes,' I told him. 'The mentality of the cowboys must match the characters you'd come across in the Village. First comes McGoohan, an ex-sheriff, now a horseless drifter, walking with his saddle across his shoulder. That idea I took from an early 1950s *Gene Autry* comic. The drifter is captured on the outskirts of a western town which exists on no map and is proudly named Harmony. Gun law prevails. It's an open town. Sheriffs get gunned down routinely.

'So, who runs the town in the way that a Number Two would? The powerful corrupt, smart local Judge. He has no name. He's just the Judge. He thinks he knows everything about everyone who comes into his town, and that includes the drifter. The Judge is always in the saloon, playing patience. He knows how to prod, stir and manipulate. Literally, he has the patience.

'The Judge wants a new sheriff whom he can trust. When the drifter is not interested, the Judge's cronies get to work. They devise and stage events designed to get the drifter to settle in and adjust to life in the isolated, cut-off

western town. The locals all claim to like living in Harmony. But the cowboy drifter refuses to adjust and stay. The ex-sheriff's a virtual prisoner in a town that's anything but harmonious.'

John was all ears.

'I read a *Two Gun Kid,* or *Kid Colt Outlaw,* comic in which the unfriendly town was named Harmony. It was a Marvel comic from a few years ago, about 1963.

'In my story, the locals resent the intruder because he doesn't like the place they're all proud of. They roughhouse him and the Judge has him locked up for his own good, for his protection. To them, the outsider has behaved in an anti-social way and it's dangerous for him to go around free. People don't like that kind of thing. They don't like somebody who's different. Especially as he doesn't carry a gun, and because he was once a man of the law.

'The main premise has a South African origin. I was at a party when a white guy took exception to my black companions, who were members of a group of political activists. I reached for my shoulder holster. I was ready to shoot the racist but one of my group stopped me. "You shoot and we pay," he told me. Later, I was warned. If I'd wanted to go from associate to full member of the group, I'd have to be more disciplined and give up the gun. It was irresponsible in that world, at that time.'

'You carried a gun?' John interrupted me.

'I gave it up for politics,' I told him.

I tried to explain and then went back to the western. 'So who's the Judge got to back his play? There's the usual bunch of heavies. They're wild and looking for action or fun. But they're not up to much. The Judge needs a sheriff in his pocket and the drifter fits the bill.

'The Judge has a young sidekick, the best gunslinger in town. He can't talk. He's manic, he's crazy and only the Judge has control over him. He'd be fighting in Vietnam if he wasn't playing in a western.

'The pivotal point,' I continued, 'is a saloon girl singer named Cathy. She has to be good looking and has to fancy the beleaguered stranger, or need his help. He does something which impresses Cathy, and then stands up to the Judge. He gets into trouble and she takes the risk of trying to help him. That's when cowboy Pat's problems really begin. Of course McGoohan won't co-operate. The girl appears to hate the Judge and everything he stands for. But is she genuine or is she in some convoluted way working for the Judge?'

'Sounds interesting,' John said thoughtfully. 'But this romance thing, you know Pat will never go for that. And how many fights does Pat have? I hope no horses get shot.'

'Well it's America, it's the West.', I replied. 'There's shooting and killing. You can't have a western without action or one that's only psychological. Right now they're going crazy in Vietnam, in the war that everybody says they won't win. But the stranger is not a pacifist or a conscientious objector. His position comes from strength, not weakness.

'Anyway, the body count grows and all because of Cathy. She is a sensual woman who can turn men's minds. The crazy Kid, the mute gunslinger, can't keep his eyes off her.

'Manipulating Cathy is the Judge's best weapon in his fight to control the outsider. There's drinking. There's card playing. I don't know about dancing, some in the background. That's what goes on in frontier saloons. It's a sadistic time in a sadistic place. If Pat wants a western, he'll have to buy the whole ethos, the whole myth. If I start to water it down, it'll run away into nothing. It's got to be real,' I said emphatically. 'Not only will I take the Village into the West, I'll bring the West into the Village.'

'You've lost me,' John frowned. 'Is it going to end with a shoot out in the Village?'

'There aren't any guns in the Village,' I told

Living In Harmony: the stranger and the judge - prior to reverting to Number Six and Number Two.

him. 'But the power behind the Village believes in guns. It'll all happen in the mind but, in the end, reality will force an entry,' I moved a few paces as if I was bow-legged, and spoke with a drawl. 'I reckon Pat could handle a cayuse an' look real dandy on one o' them four-legged wind-eaters.'

'But can he wear a hat?' John shook his head. 'That's defeated the best of them.'

I pointed out that I had no intention of writing caricature. My West was no jokey affair. It was a serious place.

'What if he doesn't like your western?' John asked. 'He's always been nice and sweet with us, but,' he tapped his temple, 'no one really knows what's going on in that head of his.'

'Look, I don't know anything,' I said. 'I'm working on it and I may not even get it finished in time, let alone get Pat actually to read it.'

I completed a draft of my western, titling it *Do Not Forsake Me Oh My Darling* just as Sloman had forecast, after the song that played through Fred Zinnemann's *High Noon*. This was the epic western in which one man is pitted against a whole town and wins through. The film has been said to have been an allegory of Senator Joseph McCarthy's witch hunt tearing into Hollywood at the time when the film was made. When most were running scared of McCarthy, Zinnemann stood his ground, and successfully slugged it out in a weight above his own. He moved to London before McCarthy succeeded in getting him. There were, in fact, aspects of *High Noon* which I had born in mind when writing the script. However, it was material I found in American comic book

westerns that provided the most significant source of inspiration.

I showed my first draft to Tony Sloman. He was encouraging and saw none of the pitfalls that worried John. Tony declared that I had incorporated all the basic hallmarks of the western, and that it fitted into *The Prisoner* format. He predicted that McGoohan would love it.

'And even if he doesn't, he'll take it. Because they haven't got a fresh idea between them. They're all played out and desperate. Markstein's off the boat so who's at the rudder?' Tony demanded. 'Who can think, out of who's left?'

I was surprised when John stopped me from going home, especially as I had an appointment.

'We won't be going late,' John explained, 'but Pat's due soon so you'd better hang around. You'll still make your meeting. Is it your producer?'

'Yes, but he's hardly a producer, he's just willing to help. A bit of a modest character.'

'You mean not like us?' John joked.

Pat arrived. Immediately John told him that I was about to direct my BFI grant film and that I was writing an episode for *The Prisoner*. He felt that Pat should look at what I had written, both because it was progressing well and because it was in tune with *The Prisoner*.

'If it's going to go on,' John added, 'you'll be needing fresh talent, won't you?'

Pat nodded and asked about what I had written.

'It's a very novel idea for a western,' John answered for me.

'That's interesting,' Pat looked at me. 'How far have you got with it?'

'*Do Not Forsake Me Oh My Darling* is the title,' John got in. 'Ian, you don't have that much left to do, do you?'

'I'll have something finished in a few week's time,' I replied gingerly. 'Will that be too late?'

'No, you've got time. For the moment, all decisions are up in the air,' Pat said. 'Things are changing around a bit.'

John patted the moviola which was laced up and ready to go. Pat moved over behind him.

'It's okay, Pat and I can manage without you,' John said and Pat nodded.

I grabbed my things and sped out, elated beyond belief. McGoohan had agreed to read my script. John was a magician.

I'd found Alan Patillo through a trusted old friend, a dubbing editor. Though mostly employed in the cutting rooms, Patillo had also directed animated and puppet productions. Among others, he worked on *Thunderbirds* for the Andersons. He directed for television but he cut for features. He straddled both camps, both media. By a strange coincidence, he had also dubbed *The Hellions*. Patillo was a sensitive, pleasant enough chap and we settled easily on terms for his help on *The Application Form*. No money was involved. We observed the restrictions of a BFI budget.

I was getting actors, seeing technicians and going ahead on the test sequence. Patillo offered to do what he could, but balked when I said that he would be the producer.

'Oh no, Ian,' he objected. 'I'm not a producer. I'll just do what I can to help. I've got a car so I can fetch people and things. I can watch over the props, but I'm not a producer.'

On the telephone Lindsay snapped at me for whining on about having to direct. I was lucky that I'd got money to start my film, he told me. I had to do it, especially as he didn't think I was equipped for any kind of straightforward career. Oddities like me can sometimes thrive in the directorial role, he argued. He cited McGoohan as an example and laughed.

'You've got the chance to do something, so do it, and don't quibble. Miriam's been helping you with the actors, hasn't she?'

I said that Miriam was being generous with her time and effort.

'What more could you ask for? Miriam Brickman is the best casting director in the country.' Lindsay said and asked. 'Got the camera crew?'

I said that I had.

'Actors?'

'Got Wallace Eaton,' I replied.

'Ah, that's a good one. Must use him in something one day,' Lindsay said and began singing into the telephone. '*Take it from here...*' He paused. 'Coming from the colonies I don't suppose you even know what that is.'

I told him that I did.

'And you say your producer drives a Porsche,' Lindsay commented. 'I like that, shows some sense of money. You don't know much about money, do you?'

Patillo, though not remembered by Lindsay, had been in the Aldermaston CND march in 1959 against the nuclear bomb, along with the concerned thousands following Bertrand Russell

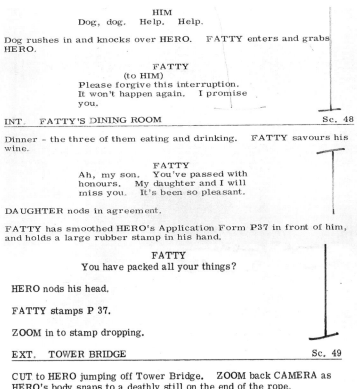

```
                                HIM
              Dog, dog.   Help.   Help.

     Dog rushes in and knocks over HERO.    FATTY enters and grabs
     HERO.

                               FATTY
                              (to HIM)
              Please forgive this interruption.
              It won't happen again.    I promise
              you.
     INT.  FATTY'S DINING ROOM                              Sc. 48

     Dinner – the three of them eating and drinking.    FATTY savours his
     wine.

                               FATTY
              Ah, my son.    You've passed with
              honours.    My daughter and I will
              miss you.    It's been so pleasant.

     DAUGHTER nods in agreement.

     FATTY has smoothed HERO's Application Form P37 in front of him,
     and holds a large rubber stamp in his hand.

                               FATTY
              You have packed all your things?

     HERO nods his head.

     FATTY stamps P 37.

     ZOOM in to stamp dropping.

     EXT.  TOWER BRIDGE                                     Sc. 49

     CUT to HERO jumping off Tower Bridge.    ZOOM back CAMERA as
     HERO's body snaps to a deathly still on the end of the rope.

     VERY LONG ZOOM BACK to show bleak London.


                         END  OF  FILM
```

The Application Form - pages 26-27 of the screenplay. The defeat of an individual without Number Six's resources.

and Cannon Collins. I mentioned this.

'Trust you to find a lefty for a producer,' Lindsay muttered. Wishing me luck, he ended the conversation.

For a weekend, my flat became a studio. Lights, cables and camera boxes crowded my tiny, one-room flat. I warned everyone to watch out for my comic books.

For filming, I had selected from the story a three-minute section that involved a dirty old man being caught in the act of molesting a young blonde. The old man is tried, found guilty, chained and beaten. This is witnessed by the hero, played by Wallace, who was transferred from one half of my flat to the other and given a ludicrous lesson on how to commit suicide with the minimum of mess. We got through the lot in one weekend. Everyone was most encouraging.

My continual misgivings over the value of my

Wallace Eaton - a British comedian in a serious role.

Alan Patillo - Ian's reluctant producer.

directing a test section of *The Application Form* were accurately confirmed in the rushes. Everything was painfully laboured. The acting was almost uniformly wooden and devoid of any spark.

I couldn't do the cut up at the studio as the only 16mm equipment there was in the projection facilities. I got access to a cutting room at Dateline, in seedy Flaxman Court, just off Wardour Street. Dateline was managed by Marlene and John Fletcher. Understanding that it was a BFI production, they gave me their facilities free of charge. They seldom turned away anybody in need. Dateline was then a well known underground route for helping people

break into the restrictive film industry.

The following weekend, I showed an unfinished cut to Patillo. He told me that I should have selected scenes from an earlier, rather than a latter, part of the script. I finished the cut and submitted it to Bruce Beresford at the BFI. I did not feel confident about the submission.

I carried on chiselling away at the western, and waited for the reaction from the BFI. I'd given in my notice to John. However, unlike my former stint at BTF, I was working out the statutory two weeks.

9

LICKING MY WOUNDS

Pat's time on *It's Your Funeral* was up and he had stopped coming to see us. The final details had been left in John's hands.

I asked John if he'd been given his notice. He said he had not. I asked him what he had lined up.

'Nothing,' he said. 'But maybe I can wangle something here, get another episode.'

I pointed out that everything seemed pretty uncertain and no further productions were in the pipe-line.

'Well,' John held up a finger. 'I had a nose round the vaults. There's an episode that none of the other editors want to touch with a barge pole. Apparently, it's Pat's least favourite. I had a look at it. I thought it's really good, much better than the two we had. I'm going to ask Geoff if I can have it.'

'They've already got my notice, so you'll need to drag someone else in,' I said trying to make casual conversation.

'You'll be all right,' John nodded and beamed. 'You'll direct your film and then Pat will commission you for a western screenplay, won't he?'

I told John that he was being overoptimistic. Bracing myself for disappointment, I rang the BFI.

Bruce said I could come in and see him if I wanted. I didn't want. I asked him if my worst fears had been realized.

'Well there's yes and no,' Bruce hummed and hawed for a bit. 'Everyone still likes the script but well...'

I interrupted Bruce and told him that I'd seen already that it was lousy.

'Putting it that way, I can't but agree with you,' he paused, 'but what about having another go at getting Lindsay to do it? Without a test sequence of course. I think I could pull that off.'

I doubted if Lindsay would do it in a million years, I said. This concluded my association with the BFI film production board.

Listening intently, John gawped at me.

'Do you want to stay on if I get another episode?' he asked.

I shook my head. My notice only had a few more days to go.

My old pal Woody knocked on the door and came in from down the corridor, where he'd been working on *The Dirty Dozen*. We'd always popped out for teas and drinks. Now we had a date to have lunch. We'd never been on the same film together, but we used to keep in touch and, when in the same studio, we'd have lunch together. Today was our day to catch up.

I got into Woody's Lotus Elite and we zipped out of the studio. Woody always knew where to find the best pub lunches in the vicinity of whichever studio he was at. Neither of us would drink at lunch times but the best nosh was definitely in the pubs.

My friendship with Woody Woodward started at Shepperton when he was employed on the Richard Brooks's version of Conrad's *Lord Jim* in 1964. I was impressed by Brooks. He'd made *Elmer Gantry*, with Burt Lancaster, one of my favourite films. Woody and I had instantly hit it off. Back then Woody was tooling around on a 750 cc Norton. Typically we would zoom off into the greenery around Shepperton looking for a pub in which we could eat.

Currently, Woody was assisting Teddy Darvis. Teddy was an overweening, puffed-up editing veteran. He'd studied in England and stayed on to work for his fellow countryman, Alexander Korda, back in the heyday of British cinema when it had the Hungarian director at its helm.

He and Woody had just spent fifteen months at MGM cutting *The Dirty Dozen*. An American editor had been brought in and had rapidly ousted poor Teddy. The film was now in Hollywood with the dubbing crew, and Teddy was sitting out his last moments of employment.

At lunch with Woody in a Borehamwood pub, I enthused about the overall qualities of *The Prisoner*, excluding the two episodes John and I had tackled. As ever we ate well and gossiped. Woody had an enthusiastic appetite for a man whose stature was just broader than a beanpole's. I listened to his stories from all the time he'd spent on the present movie, meeting the Hollywood stars.

'I think Lee Marvin was about the nicest,' Woody told me. 'He sure liked his drink. though.'

'What other vices did any of them have?' I asked.

'Telly Savalas had his poker school in a corner of the set. After filming, he'd head for the gambling casinos in the West End. There was some kind of deal by which all the actors got given a Jag. One story was that Savalas had to sell his Jaguar to get home, he'd lost so much gambling.'

We both laughed.

' I don't know if the story's true but it's a good one, isn't it?' Woody smiled. 'The only actor that came in to watch any cutting was John Cassavetes. He was a very nice man and seriously interested in the editing process.'

On the way back to the studio, Woody asked me if something was wrong. I told him about my BFI disappointment.

'But honestly, I had no illusions about becoming a director,' I tried to sound nonchalant. 'Now I've proved myself right.'

'Oh, I am sorry,' Woody said, swinging through the studio gates with a squeal of tires.

We got out of the car.

'I'm also finishing on Friday,' Woody said, 'and I'm flying off to visit my parents. They've got a flat in Malta by the sea. Why don't you come with me? My parents are terrific and I'm sure they'll like you. Take a break from it all.'

Before leaving the studio, I went to Pat's office to deliver my two scripts. The reception room was poky and nondescript. There was a desk and a few chairs. I saw nothing personal anywhere.

Roger, the one-eyed secretary, was unfriendly. People didn't just leave things for Pat to read, he told me. I told him that Pat was expecting me to deliver something, and went.

It was almost summer when I flew off with Woody to spend a fortnight in Malta at the family flat in Buggibba, overlooking St Paul's bay.

The days and nights in Malta were well lubricated with generous lashings of gin and tonic. Everything was pretty loose and there always seemed something to laugh about. The sun was brilliant and the Mediterranean was calm.

Every morning, I'd be out early on the veranda tap-tapping away on a portable Olivetti. I was writing a fictional history of Shaka the Zulu. I'd been on the project on and off for ages.

'What is that?' Mrs Woodward squealed as I took out my Asprey note pad and scribbled

David Woodward - Woody escapes from MGM to Buggibba, Malta.

down something she'd said.

'Don't worry, mum,' Woody chuckled. 'He does that kind of thing all the time. He's becoming a writer. He jots down lots of thing, such as the nonsense you sometimes come out with.'

Father and son hooted with laughter.

'I really don't see what can be interesting about what I say.'

'Time for another,' Woody's father, the Wing Commander, announced and set about refilling our drinks.

'Don't worry, mum,' Woody put his arm round his mother's shoulder. 'You'll get used to Ian. We all do.'

One day, while out swimming, I thought I was really in for it. I was exhausted; I could barely stay afloat and I doubted that I could swim back to the shore. Panic was setting in as I trod water and gasped for air. The rocks weren't that far from me but I didn't think that I'd make it.

'Ian! Ian!'

I saw Woody beckoning me, looking fraught, keenly aware of my desperate situation, about to plunge in and swim to my rescue.

His presence reinvigorated me. Summoning my last reserves of energy, I lashed out.

Woody helped me up the slippery rock.

'I should've warned you about the backwash at this time of day,' he said. 'When I couldn't hear the typewriter, I came to look for you.'

I sat hunched over, clinging to my knees, shivering with fright.

'You better have a drink after that,' Woody patted me on my back, and we headed for the flat.

As the days fled by, the gins got bigger and went down faster. They were the perfect medicine.

10

DO NOT
FORSAKE ME

Back in London, I wasn't sure what my next move would be. I faffed round a bit and telephoned Lindsay. He asked if I'd recuperated from my director's strain and insisted on seeing my rejected BFI test sequence.

We went into Dateline to view it on a Steenbeck, a 16mm flatbed single screen machine. Looking at my final cut, Lindsay agreed that I was not destined to become a film director.

Lindsay asked if I had any cutting work lined up. I told him I hadn't. I wasn't eager to leap back into the rat race. I wanted to stay at home and carry on writing my African epic.

I called John S Smith at MGM to see how things had worked out for him.

'It's still going on,' he said jubilantly. He'd successfully talked his way into cutting *Dance of the Dead*, the episode which he'd found consigned to the shelf. 'Everyone still thinks it

must be rubbish, and I definitely think it's terrific. You'd like it too,' he enthused. 'It's got atmosphere, and a really good Number Two. It's got mystery, surrealism and adventure.'

He'd got another assistant.

'Have you heard anything from McGoohan?'

I said I hadn't.

'I'm sure he'll be in touch,' John assured me. 'Things have quietened down, so he'll have some time. He said he'd read your stuff. Pat isn't the type to say something like that unless he meant it.'

A few days later, I got a call from Roger, Pat's secretary. I was given an appointment to see McGoohan. I wondered if John had prompted Pat.

I had got to MGM at ten-thirty a.m., a good half an hour before my appointment. In the alcove room outside Pat's office, Roger told me that he didn't know where Pat was, or if he was coming in. Roger flitted in his pinched gait

Checkmate: Setting up the mind for when chess enters life.

about the small reception room. I struggled not to stare at his glass eye.

I settled into reading Scott Fitzgerald's *The Pat Hobby Stories*, about disasters facing the writer in Hollywood. It was not a good choice of reading matter. As time dragged on, the tribulations of Fitzgerald's abused writer in Hollywood started to get to me.

Eleven o'clock, my appointed time, came and went. So did eleven-thirty.

'I've no idea where Pat could be,' Roger reminded me.

'That's all right,' I said. 'I can wait.'

Twelve o'clock. Twelve-thirty. I was starting to doubt that Pat would show. When he was late for the cutting room, he used to telephone at least. I read another unhappy Hollywood story.

It was past one o'clock when the door behind me swept open, and Pat lurched in. He didn't notice me. Or so it seemed. He had a brief garbled conversation with Roger, strode past, and closed his office door behind him.

I looked at Roger; he turned his good eye away from me. I waited another eternity. As a punctilious character, it was never easy for me to have to wait for anyone. I had finished reading the Scott Fitzgerald.

The door to Pat's office opened a fraction. His head peered round the edge, and glowered at me. He looked flustered and his features were tinged with annoyance, as if he didn't expect me, as if he didn't want me to be there. It was already awful, and it hadn't even begun.

'You'd better come in,' Pat said with a face far

different to the one I'd met in the cutting room, the face I was familiar with, the face I'd watched on the screen, the face for which I had written a western.

There was nothing civil about the way in which Pat beckoned me.

For the first time, I entered McGoohan's office. It was an unusually massive room, even by studio standards.

Pat pointed at an easy chair to the side of his desk.

'You can sit there,' he said with unfamiliar gruffness.

I eased myself onto the chair. The worn cushion sank under my weight. I felt a spring as I went down further. My knees were high up and my bum nearly scraped the floor.

Pat paced round the room. Thus far, there seemed to be nothing at all good about his demeanour. He was pacing about as fast as when he was the thoughtful Number Six on camera, alone in his room and agitated.

I glanced up at the clock on the wall. I'd been in the room over five minutes, and I was still waiting for him to start. I did not dare open my mouth.

Pat looked as if he was growing before my very eyes, bigger and bigger. At last he stopped behind his desk and stood, tapping his fingers on the top of the desk. He stared straight at me.

'I have just had a meeting with Lew Grade,' Pat said coldly, as if it was my fault. 'It's all neat and easy on the surface. But the accountant still comes to pry. I've seen him hovering around.'

'Excuse me,' I cleared my throat and asked what he was talking about.

Pause. I don't think he heard me. Or he chose to ignore me. He was in full flood, oblivious to my being there. Or so I thought. I could follow no strand of logic as he went on about problems, persecutions, not being allowed to be left alone. Then, as if he'd burned something out of his system, he became relatively calm and stood leaning with his fists on his desk.

The mood was only momentary and it soon changed. Sitting down, he lurched into a full-scale attack. He had read my scripts and he was not happy.

I tried to lean attentively forward but my decrepit seat wasn't built for it. I slid straight back. Was this the inescapable torture chair? The usually cryptic McGoohan was deluging me with words but it was impossible to grasp what he was saying. Angry words were pouring out. This was not any McGoohan I had imagined.

This had nothing to do with my writing, he told me, but it was important for him to tell me things. Again I tried to sit up forward, and again I slumped back. I wanted to move to the inviting-looking sofa but I couldn't budge and, now, I didn't dare. McGoohan was sweeping round the room, prowling near and past me, like some predatory shark. Why was he pointing at me? Why was he now behind his desk, slamming a leather briefcase on it. Why?

The problem was that Lew Grade was letting him down, and not behaving as he should, McGoohan said. Lew Grade didn't understand. Of everyone he felt that Lew should be the understanding one. He was no different from all the others. George Markstein was briefly referred to. The context eluded me.

Gene Autry no. 70, page 1. Gene learns about the new no-gun theory.

'That's what you should be doing,' McGoohan raised his voice and smacked the briefcase. 'This case could belong to Lew Grade, and that's the sort of thing you should be writing about. The power, the politics, the money behind it all. He's the one that's in control. He's the one that says stop and go. We've thirteen episodes near completion, and four more to go. After that, who knows? It could all end with the twenty-six episode run. It could all end tomorrow, even today. You should be writing about Lew Grade,' he repeated emphatically and swung the case off his desk.

I had no idea what was going on. I certainly had no idea of what was to follow.

'This is what you should be writing about,' Pat slammed a bottle of Malvern mineral water

on the desk.

I wanted a drink, but didn't ask. He was banging the bottle up and down, up and down. Where in God's name was it all going? I was slipping into the role of punch bag and his verbal swings were getting harder and drifting closer. What was he acting out?

My heart was beating so fast and my head was pounding so much, I was worried that I might pass out. My mouth felt dry. I assessed the distance between me and the door to determine whether I could make a dash for it. If things continued as they were, there was no telling how it would end; or what would happen to me.

Why didn't the phone ring? Why didn't Roger appear with some urgent message? Why were we so alone?

'...because otherwise you will become a writer of despair,' his words pierced through my wall of mounting paranoia. 'That's why I say write about Malvern mineral water. Wash your thoughts and clean your mind. That stuff you wrote was completely on the wrong track. Get rid of those dark thoughts you brought from wherever it is you come. You've got to begin writing on a different level, just forget about your script. Put it behind you, you have to change direction. You've got...'

I did not know which of my two scripts he was talking about. He'd mentioned no titles. His criticism appeared to apply to both. Did he mean that a bottle of Malvern water should appear in *Do Not Forsake Me Oh My Darling*? Was he suggesting that the briefcase should be in *The Application Form*?

'Well, what did you make of the western?' I

asked fearfully.

He looked at me blankly and shook his head.

Had he not read the western?

'*Do Not Forsake Me Oh My Darling,* that's what I called it,' I added.

I waited but he said nothing and promptly returned to the Malvern water and the briefcase, which he started moving across the top of his desk, side by side.

'You could be a writer of value but you'd have to get the despair out of your system,' he said and repeated the word despair like some mantra. Despair was my crime; despair was my sin; despair was my problem. I had to be cured. It was imperative.

Pat moved away from his desk and over towards me. He towered over me, squeezing his fists. His face got more flushed with increased anger. I thought he was going to reach out and grab me. It was frightening and, with each passing moment, it was getting more so. I had never heard him so voluble or so enraged. Never in the cutting room and certainly not on film, not even in the opening sequence when he banged the desk in front of Markstein; when the cup and saucer jumped in the air; when his anger was lost under a wave of thunder and lightning.

Obviously I had no chance of a scriptwriting job. He didn't even mention my attempt at a western, and I wasn't even sure that he had read it.

I glanced at the clock. He'd been at it for well over an hour, and still he was going on, indefatigable, without letting up one jot.

I could only think of escape as Pat expanded

and the room shrank. My head was spinning and my heart palpitating to bursting point. His voice reverberated and battered up against my eardrums.

As he stepped away from me, I wondered again if I could I make it to the door and flee before he got out of hand and threw me from the window, or something worse. I tried to lean forward in readiness to make a dash for it. My thoughts were jumbled. I shouldn't have read the Scott Fitzgerald while waiting. I shouldn't have bothered to come in the first place. Why did I have to subject myself to such an ordeal, such an inquisition devoid of questions? Who was I fooling in thinking that I was in the running for screenwriter?

There still had been no reference to *Do Not Forsake Me Oh My Darling.*

I didn't dare look at the clock again. I didn't dare to look away from Pat. It was horrendous, but it was also magnificent. If I survived the performance, I'd certainly have something to remember. But I could not clarify in my thoughts, why now, and why me? What had I done to deserve this? What did I have to do with Lew Grade? I'd never even met the man.

Simple. I had written rubbish. Not according to the BFI and Lindsay, but according to McGoohan. I could only conclude that he was so appalled by my western that he couldn't even mention it. My mind was packed with questions and no answers were in sight. I was frightened witless. This was like nothing I had ever experienced. I could not delude myself that it was some act for my benefit. It was all too real.

McGoohan paused. He looked as if Number

Six had taken over. Inwardly I prayed. I, the agnostic, was calling out to the Lord above.

How long had I been there? Was the clock telling the truth, was it really going on towards two hours? I could hear myself breathing more heavily. Had I passed my limit of endurance? Even if I'd wanted to I could not have moved. I was immobilized with fear. This man had absolute control over me. I was helpless jelly and there seemed to be no end in sight.

I felt destined to be a prisoner of *The Prisoner* in that one room forever and ever. This was my doom, my punishment. And for what? For being an inadequate writer?

I prayed again for some interruption, for the phone to ring, for Roger's glass eye to appear. For any distraction. How long was it going to go on? Why hadn't he just kicked me out? Was it a test? I blinked and quickly squeezed my eyes, not daring to rub a hand across the accumulating moisture.

Pat returned continually to the despairing nature of my writing. But to which screenplay was he actually referring? From out of a drawer he produced my scripts. Was he going to tear the damn things up in front of me?

'These are yours,' he said handing me *The Application Form* and *Do Not Forsake Me Oh My Darling*. 'You can go now.'

Defeated and depleted, I scrambled up out of the chair, and hoped that I could walk in a straight line. I did not feel at all safe walking out with my back exposed towards him. I wanted to walk out backwards, but that would have been ridiculous. Until I reached the door, I didn't believe I'd make it without collapsing. Besides

any tilt in the balance designed by him, might trigger off something even more uncontrollable.

With great relief my hand gripped the door handle.

'Ian,' Pat snapped as I drew the door open.

From the far side of the room his voice sounded a million miles away. I stopped and cautiously turned. It was all too much. Hadn't he already done me in? Now what did he want?

'Yes, Pat?' I asked without releasing my grip on the handle. I needed to hold on to keep myself steady. 'Yes, Pat?' I repeated, thinking how idiotic my voice sounded. 'Yes, Pat?' I said yet again and cleared my throat.

'Want to write a western with me?'

'Yes, Pat!' I blurted.

I tried to say something else but could not manage anything. I had been emotionally pulverized and could hardly believe my ears. No matter what he'd say or ask, 'Yes, Pat' was the full extent of the entire vocabulary I could muster.

I was going to be a writer on the series.

'You'll get the standard union minimum. Under the contract, you'll get the protection you need.' Pat stood up behind his desk. 'Is that all right?'

'Yes, Pat,' I replied once more.

'You can write. You're a writer. You know that, don't you?'

I couldn't just dollop out yet another 'Yes, Pat.'

'I know that now, don't I?' I said laughing nervously.

Pat did not laugh. He didn't smile either. No new feature appeared on his stony face.

He moved out from behind the desk and advanced over towards me.

'You've already got most of it down there. It's a proper western,' he nodded. 'It's different but it fits into the Village effectively.'

I left with what I interpreted as high praise ringing in my ears. I floated past Roger. I noticed something on his desk. It was a memo about *Do Not Forsake Me Oh My Darling*. It had all been decided in advance and Roger must've known. I supposed he could've told me and put me out of my misery from the start. No, I decided. Given the set-up, Roger would have been fired.

The probability was that Pat had already

thought of tackling a western, though apparently nothing quite as bleak, dark and foreboding as I had written. It seemed to have just happened that I was on the right wavelength and had come along with an idea which had already been bandied about. Yet there had been no acknowledgement of this. Instead, I was on the brunt of an inquisition without questions, the full treatment of emotional and verbal torture. Did he have to bring me so to my knees before lifting me up? Or should I blame it all on Lew Grade? If yes, Grade must have been quite something to have got Pat going like that; something more than just a bag of gold and all the power money entailed.

Gene Autry no. 70, page 15. The no-gun theory triumphant.

11

Buying a Soul

Within a week I was back at the studio. With great pleasure, I signed my writing contract. Now there was hope that, as a writer, I'd get my name attached to the series. In those days assistants didn't get credits.

I settled in with Pat in his office. Roger brought us coffee. Pat was as only Pat could be: indestructible and friendly. He implied that his other collaborations with writers on the series had frequently been inadequate. I had the right mentality to make a go of it with him, he told me. He would be demanding but he knew this wouldn't worry me. He said that I'd managed to incorporate almost all the essential elements; all it needed was a bit more work.

Production dates were being scheduled for the last four of the first seventeen episodes. Everyone was keen to do a western, Pat told me. Despite his friendliness, he began to seem more distant, more remote. He was a remote character but now he was even further away. His voice was lower, his eyes glazed, and his posture less animated.

Roger came in and said to Pat that Jack Shampan the art director, had the sketches and a model to show him. Pat apologized for having to go off. He told me to carry on with the dialogue back in the Village and left me to my own devices until he was next available.

'I've made some notes,' he said. 'I'll give them to you at our next session.'

I felt okay with Pat, but hardly relaxed.

Pat went off to the art department and I headed for the cutting rooms. It was the one place I knew there'd be a semblance of calm.

Mark was sorting his way through a bin spilling over with trims. He asked me to stick around as he was nearly done. I settled on the synchronizer bench, waiting and swinging my legs, imitating McGoohan's behaviour in John's cutting room.

The session with Pat rankled. I kept on feeling that we were both trying to reach each other, but

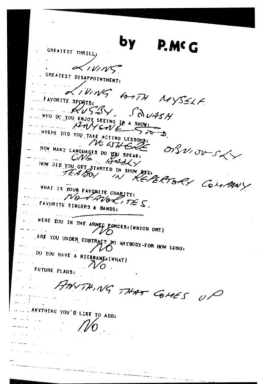

by P. McG

GREATEST THRILL:
Living.

GREATEST DISAPPOINTMENT:
Living with myself

FAVORITE SPORTS:
Rugby, Squash

WHO DO YOU ENJOY SEEING IN A SHOW:
Anyone good.

WHERE DID YOU TAKE ACTING LESSONS:
Nowhere obviously

HOW MANY LANGUAGES DO YOU SPEAK:
One Badly

HOW DID YOU GET STARTED IN SHOW BIZ:
Teaboy in Repertory Company

WHAT IS YOUR FAVORITE CHARITY:
No favorites.

FAVORITE SINGERS & BANDS:

WERE YOU IN THE ARMED FORCES:(WHICH ONE)
No

ARE YOU UNDER CONTRACT TO ANYBODY-FOR HOW LONG:
No

DO YOU HAVE A NICKNAME:(WHAT)
No.

FUTURE PLANS:
Anything that comes up

ANYTHING YOU'D LIKE TO ADD:
No.

An extract from McGoohan's cryptic response to an ambitious questionaire.

had yet to grasp a common language. I had no qualms about the way the script could develop but I felt that, somehow or other, I was standing on precariously shifting sand.

I felt that Markstein's departure was not a good thing. Markstein was the intellect, a thinker. There seemed to be no one else around with George's breadth of mind. No matter how much Markstein might have irritated and disappointed Pat, he was solidly grounded in the brains department. It appeared that something new had been gathering force inside Pat, simmering away, heading for implosion or worse. I was lost in this train of thought when

Mark's voice broke in.

'I was well pleased to get the news that you landed the writing commission. I thought for sure Sloman would get it,' he bent over to pick up some dropped trims. 'Still, old Sloman claimed that he knew all along you'd be the one to get it,' Mark said, smiling. 'Just hang on, I'm nearly there. Don't mind the wait, do you?'

I wasn't going anywhere and I didn't mind. Mark was working in his usual relaxed way. It excluded all frenetic activity. He managed to keep above it all. This might have been the effect of drugs. Whatever, his company was consistently sympathetic.

Mark told me that the esteemed Geoff Foot had moved on to a feature. Having survived four firings from Geoff, Mark had got himself allocated to the replacement editor, who had yet to start. Seemingly, the ructions between Geoff and Mark had got so tense it was a miracle that Mark had kept his job.

'Funny old geezer, Wing Commander Foot,' Mark reflected. 'After all that trouble I gave him, I know for a fact that he was considering asking me to come on the big one with him.'

I had once seen Pat outside the sound stage, chatting, or should I say listening to Mark. I noticed Pat eyeing Mark intently and wondered what had sunk in. Later, on seeing the final episode, *Fall Out*, I suspected that quite a lot about Mark's character had registered on McGoohan, albeit not very deeply. The part played by Alexis Kanner in the last episode I felt, in the writing, to be influenced by Mark. However, in the production, Kanner's supposed embodiment of the spirit of the moment seemed

an uncomfortable contrivance. It was all yeah, man, with hair cropped unfashionably short. The part was frilly and superficial.

By contrast, there was something sensitive and inescapably real about Mark. He may have embodied much fashionable sentiment, but he also exuded considerable thoughtfulness.

Pulling on his shaggy sheepskin coat, Mark suggested:

'Let's go to the studio bar and quaff a few,' he said checking that all the equipment was switched off.

'Look, mate,' Mark said to me as we entered the studio bar, known to us then as Stage Nine. 'Get an eyeful of that...makes you want to puke, doesn't it?' With a conspiratorial chuckle, he eased me over to the edge of an attentive crowd encircling Alastair McIntyre.

Alastair was the high-falutin, fast-talking editor that cut for the Polish film director, Roman Polanski.

I was no Polanski fan. I had admired his first film, *Three Men and a Wardrobe*. However, I found his first feature *Knife in the Water* distasteful, irrespective of the quality of filmmaking. I abhorred its undercurrent of sadism. His later British-made film *Repulsion* I found equally repugnant. The clincher for me had been in Wardour Street, a couple of years previously, at the old Hammer Theatre in the basement of the building. I went there to hear Polanski speak. Film technicians had packed in

Alexis Kanner in **Fall Out**. An electric Kanner impersonates the spirit of the age.

to listen to him. On stage that evening Polanski looked small and pale. His English, though faltering, was perfectly understandable. He strutted onto the stage radiating an aggressively arrogant manner and his words followed suit. He started his address to an audience of British technicians by attacking them.

'Most English film technicians should be selling washing machines and not working in film...' he declared, and carried on in this vein.

I wondered if anyone would shout him down, or maybe sling a tomato. Not a murmur. The lot of us just sat there and took it on both cheeks.

Leaning against the MGM bar with his arms on the counter, Polanski's editor was holding court and pronouncing on all and sundry in a manner which appeared to have been learned at the master's elbow. I gathered that Alastair was just visiting friends at the studio. He wasn't working there. No more big features were slated to come into MGM. From our position on the edge of the crowd, we could hear Alastair loud and clear.

'...Polanski doesn't think much of British technicians. He told me I was the exception. I can't honestly say that's not true...'

'Now look, mate,' Mark said in my ear. 'You can't let the fucker get away with what he's saying.'

'...soul, what's in a soul?' McIntyre demanded scornfully. 'I'd sell my soul for a pint of bitter, I would...'

'I'm still just an assistant, but you're the fucking goods, mate. You're the writer now,' Mark nudged me. 'You got moral and social responsibility to take care of, haven't you?' Mark bent over narrowing his eyes at me. He was a lot taller than I was. 'You can take the smartarse down a peg or two, can't you, mate?'

'Alastair,' I said, and he swung round to face me.

'What can I do for you, whoever you may be?'

His drinking cronies laughed.

Mark edged supportively closer.

'Was that a genuine offer,' I asked, 'about selling your soul?'

'Of course it was,' he replied with a derisory laugh. 'You want to buy me a drink in exchange for my soul?'

'No, I don't want to buy you a drink,' I answered. 'But I do want to buy your soul.'

'Really?' Alastair laughed. 'Tell me more. I'm open to all offers.'

'I can't buy you a drink, but I can pay you the equivalent price if you'll sell me your soul,' I explained and pulled out a note pad and wallet. I took the top off my pen and started to write.

Alastair eased himself upright. There was silence as I drafted an agreement for the purchase of his soul.

'I, Alastair McIntyre,' I read aloud as I wrote, 'agree to accept the sum of one and sixpence in exchange for the exclusive ownership of my soul.'

I held out my pen to him.

'If you sign that, I'll give you the cash. What you do with it is your business. I'm presuming

that you haven't done this sort of thing before, and that no one else has any claim on your soul. Is that correct?'

For a millisecond, Alastair hesitated.

'Of course not,' Alastair said with slightly forced bravado as, shrugging and laughing dismissively, he put pen to paper. 'Of course I'd prefer the drink rather than the cash, but I'll take what I can get.'

I turned to Mark and handed him the pen.

'Will you please sign as a witness?'

'Sure thing, mate!' Mark snatched the pen from my hand and signed. 'It's a pleasure,' he said and the broadest smile I had ever seen crossed Mark's face.

I placed the money for a pint of beer on the counter in front of Alastair. He emptied his jug and plonking it down slid the cash across to the barman.

'Another pint, if you please.'

A fresh pint appeared in front of Alastair.

'That was great, that was bloody marvellous,' Mark told me with absolute delight as we left.

Later, after taping the one and only testimony to Alastair McIntyre's soul on the inside door of the metal cabinet in John S. Smith's cutting room, I forgot all about it. Probably it disappeared along with the rest of the rubble when the studio was demolished.

BATTERED AGAIN

At my next session with Pat, he handed me Ibsen's *Brand*. McGoohan had come to public prominence playing Brand at the Lyric theatre in Hammersmith in 1959. This part brought him to the notice of television and launched him on the *Danger Man* series. I gathered, from sources other than Pat, that the critical acclaim for his performance had been unstinting. It put him on the path which was to make him the highest paid actor in television. It was from this position of power that he was able to set up *The Prisoner*.

Things seemed to be going well with the western. Pat appeared to be satisfied with what I was doing. I carried on scratching away.

After a couple more sessions equally notable for their brevity, Pat said he regretted that our meetings had become so cursory. He wished he had more time to give me. All between us was sweetness and manners, albeit hardly palsy-walsy. There were certain barriers that could not be overcome. Remote he began and unreachable

he stayed. Happily, though, I saw no repeat appearance of the character who had terrorized me during my horrendous first interview.

Again something seemed to have changed about Pat. He was going out of his way to be more polite. What was afoot? Was I being groomed for the chop? Despite this, Pat made future collaboration sound no less a possibility, and more a fact. Consistently, I was getting mixed signals.

I didn't like the idea of being summoned to meet Pat in the Red Lion pub with David Tomblin, the producer, who had survived as Pat's right hand man and general factotum. The production company of *The Prisoner* was set up by McGoohan and Tomblin. Markstein had spoken unflatteringly about Tomblin, and the few chance encounters I'd had with Tomblin had not gone anywhere.

The pub was a huge, high-ceilinged, dull place. It felt, smelt, and looked dead. I was informally introduced to Tomblin at the bar and

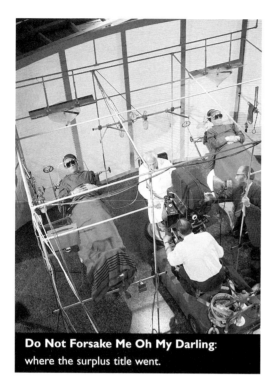

Do Not Forsake Me Oh My Darling:
where the surplus title went.

given a drink. Neither of them suggested sitting down. Talking about the script, Pat and I discussed a saloon scene to establish the Kid's bad character. I suggested stubbing a cigar out on somebody's neck, though I thought it probably too sadistic. Pat agreed and Tomblin made no comment.

Standing between them I felt like a dwarf with a couple of giant redwoods. Tomblin wasn't as impressively big as Pat, nor did he have the same presence, but he was almost equally huge in physical stature and bulk. He never looked me in the eye. When occasionally he spoke, it was somewhere between a mutter and a mumble. I found Tomblin's company disturbing.

As usual the pub was almost deserted. Other members of the unit were not in the habit of

frequenting the Red Lion. It was McGoohan's private office in public.

Tomblin was going to produce the western. Was that why I was invited? It was about the only explanation I could find.

I regretted that Markstein was no longer around, and I was grateful that Tomblin was not involved with the script.

'Can you come up with another title?' Tomblin handed me another beer. 'I mean it doesn't have to be that title does it? You could use another title, couldn't you?'

'I suppose we could,' I agreed. 'A more relevant title might be better.'

'So what you want to call it?' Tomblin said, taking a sip.

'There's a line in the draft about living in Harmony,' I said addressing Tomblin but watching McGoohan in the giant wall mirror behind the bar. The place was empty and shadowy. It had almost a western feel to it. 'The town's named Harmony, or it was in today's session wasn't it?' I glanced at Pat.

'Yes,' he replied taking a deep swallow.

'So we could discard *Do Not Forsake Me Oh My Darling* and go for *Living in Harmony*,' I said.

'It sounds better,' Tomblin finished his drink and offered me another. I declined. I had a train to catch and it was already late.

'Can you come in earlier tomorrow morning,' Pat asked as I did up my jacket. 'About nine-thirty?'

I said that I'd be there. We all shook hands and I went, happy to be leaving.

The next morning Pat was already in his office

waiting for me. Something was up. He looked more concerned than was usual, decidedly perturbed. He told me to sit down because he had something to tell me.

Obediently I sat, avoiding the low chair I'd felt locked into during my inquisitorial interview. I had no desire ever to be that low down again.

'I'm sorry but I'm going to have to let you down.'

My heart sank. I'd thought everything was progressing well with the writing, so what had happened? Why did he look so agitated? Had he decided that now my writing just wasn't good enough. Was another writer taking over? I'd heard plenty about that sort of thing, but it wasn't what I expected from Pat. He'd seemed pleased with what I was doing. I waited in silent apprehension as he walked about, delaying the final blow. He looked as deeply serious as only McGoohan could. Was he going to flip? Was I going to get a repeat performance of my initial interview? Was I in for it? I glanced at the door, and again went through the terror of calculating the distance of my escape. My worst fears raced through my imagination at breakneck speed.

'Pat, what is going on?' I asked.

'The series is in big money trouble,' he replied.

Was I going to have to work for no money? This was hardly a tragedy. Contractually I'd been put on the absolute minimum writing fee which was a rate considerably less than what I'd been earning in the cutting rooms. As long as he was satisfied with my writing, I'd work for free if I had to. I seriously wanted my name on *The Prisoner*.

'Don't worry about your writing, ' he said as if he could read my mind.

Then what?

'Your writing's fine, but I won't be available to finish it off with you,' he began to explain to me. 'I'm leaving for Hollywood. When I come back, there won't be time to do more work on the western. It'll have to go straight into production. The script has to be completed while I'm away.'

Pat paced round the room.

'Everything is up in the air. I've accepted a part in a Hollywood film for the sake of *The Prisoner*. It'll mean that we can do another four episodes. Then, we'll see how much further we can take it. We intend going up to twenty-six episodes. You'll do four of them.'

He looked out of the window, away from me.

'But for now, this will have to be the last of our collaboration. I'll leave you in competent hands,' Pat assured me. 'The best hands I know. Nothing to worry about.'

I *was* worried.

'David Tomblin will take care of you,' Pat sat down with his copy of the script, and I finished my coffee. 'He's read it and he likes it. He's very keen on it.'

'Pat, can you just up and leave in the middle of it all?' I asked without disguising my astonishment. 'Is it that critical?'

'It's a matter of financing the last four episodes to get them made the way I want them to be. Otherwise, I could have it taken out of my hands. I can't get out of going if I want to save the series. You see that, don't you?'

I couldn't see anything. Worst of all, I

couldn't envisage a fruitful collaboration with Tomblin. To me he was a mystery, with an indefinable role and a well-hidden agenda.

I asked Pat the title of the film in which he was acting.

'It's by John Sturgess, *Ice Station Zebra.*'

'That is great,' I exploded enthusiastically. 'One of my favourite westerns is his *Bad Day at Black Rock*, with the one-armed karate expert, Spencer Tracy.'

'It's not a western,' Pat informed me. 'It's in the North Pole with spies. Interesting other actors. Rock Hudson, and Ernest Borgnine.'

'So how much time do we have left?'

'I'm leaving tomorrow,' he answered. 'This is our last session.'

'Well then, I better get the most out of you here and now,' I said whacking my copy of the script.

'I'm sorry about all this, but there's no alternative. There's not a lot to do on the script,' he told me. 'I'm leaving you in good hands,' he repeated, as if that made everything okay.

Of course everything was far from okay. I remembered a remark Markstein had made about Pat during one of our brief conversations in the corridor to the production office. George had intimated that Pat had great intuition, but was capable of going notably wrong. Pat, he'd suggested, had one blind spot: no one could advise him. This I had felt rarely while collaborating with Pat. Generally with the script development, I found him to be receptive and responsive.

I attempted to put aside my growing apprehension about the production. We switched back to the work at hand.

Beginning at the beginning, Pat said that he accepted my approach of foregoing the standard introduction to each episode, and plunge right into the action.

'David can sort that out, but in principle that's it,' Pat said.

I asked what David Tomblin had to do with the western, besides producing and now on the script. Pat said nothing. I went on.

'You are going to direct it, aren't you?' I asked apprehensively.

He ignored my question, or didn't hear it. He was too busy flipping through the script intently.

So for the start the Sheriff, McGoohan, would go into the Marshall's office and resign, handing in his badge and his gun.

I was still concerned that it would be too confusing to start like that, even though I'd written it that way. Now I thought starting in the Village might be better. I voiced my doubts.

'You had a good idea. You should stick by it.' Pat reprimanded me. 'Get your audience having to think right from the beginning,' he insisted.

Pat seemed to be allocating some sort of power to me, but in fact it was only words. With him out of the way and left alone with Tomblin, what power would I really have? I doubted that I would have anything. It would be like being back assisting in the cutting rooms. As part of the creative process, I thought I was entitled to more of a say; or so I inferred from Pat's intermittent flattery. Now it was as if my indispensable contribution was going out the window fast. I tried to rid myself of paranoid reflections and carry on with the job for which

I'd been contracted; but my heart was no longer in it from the moment Pat informed me that he was going off to Hollywood.

I was only half-listening as he continued talking about the opening.

'Let them think they've tuned into the wrong channel. Keep them mentally off-balance until the last bit where Number Six wakes up on the sawdust-covered wooden floor of the saloon, out of his cowboy clothes and wearing his piped Village jacket. At least until the bicycle placard in the commercial break.'

'Fine,' I responded resignedly. 'It would give us more screen time for the western story.'

'No it won't,' Pat said. 'It'll give more screen time to the plot back in the Village. That's what you need to work on.'

We skimmed through some alterations Pat had proposed and I had implemented. But his attention was off-kilter. He had too many things on his mind and too much to get done. My time was up.

We said goodbye. He wished me luck; and I wished him luck. I can't remember shaking hands.

Despondently, I headed for the cutting rooms.

I popped in to see Tony. He greeted me effusively and reminded me that he knew from the start that McGoohan would go for my western. Eric joined us and said that it was lunch time.

Walking along the corridor, I noticed new faces on the editing crew. They didn't look happy.

'Good to see you,' John jumped up from behind the moviola and shook my hand vigorously. 'I'm ready for lunch, if that's what you're here for, mister screenwriter.'

We left John's replacement assistant hanging up trims.

'What's this about Pat going off to *Ice Station Zebra*?' John asked me.

Before I could reply. Tony was answering.

'He's getting three quarters of a million and the chance to work with proper stars and a name director. That should give him a different perspective. Film and not television.'

Tony held the canteen door open as we all filed in.

While queuing with our trays, a dubbing editor who'd joined the series just before I'd left the cutting rooms made a snide remark to me.

'I remember you,' he said unpleasantly. 'What you doing back here, sniffing round for a job? Desperate, are you?'

'You'd better be careful what you say,' John said leaning past me.

'What you mean?' The dubbing editor looked up at John.

'You're scheduled to lay tracks on the western, aren't you?'

'What of it?' The dubbing editor asked defensively. 'What are you getting at?'

'Well, this is the writer,' John spoke slowly, and clearly. 'That means that he's your boss. You'd better watch what you're saying.'

The dubbing editor shut up. We collected our food and settled at the table.

'John, I've just had the wind knocked out of my sails,' I told him. 'Pat's going off and leaving me to finish the script with David Tomblin.'

next morning at Webber Douglas, the drama school she attended. I could not turn her away.

In the morning, Tanya made no moves to go to her audition. She was slurring her speech and her eyes were practically closed. She'd emptied a bottle of sleeping pills. Then in a welter of tears she stumbled out.

Later I got a call from a hospital. I was told that she nearly died. They'd pumped her stomach just in time. The nurse had my name as the next of kin, not her parents in Dulwich.

A few days later Tanya came back for her teddy. She promised not to subject me to more trials if I'd let her stay. It went okay and then, after a few days, she went back to her parents.

I was woken in the middle of the night by Tanya calling from a coin-box. She'd been locked in a home, but had escaped. She wanted to see me. She gave a startled cry.

'They're from the clinic. They're after me...' another cry and the phone was cut off.

The next day I called Tanya's parents. I was told coldly that their only child was in safe hands and getting the best possible treatment.

I got a call from Tomblin and trudged off to Borehamwood. The session with Tomblin was no better or worse than I had expected. It was plodding, it was gloomy, it was inescapable. I came at Tomblin from every angle trying to find common ground and found none. I took the blame upon myself. I was failing as a professional in not being able to strike the right chords.

After a few more meetings, I had to face facts. I was slipping away, or about to be eased aside. Tomblin's short sentences were getting even

shorter, and he was clutching a pencil all the time. Previously he'd put it down and leaned back in his chair. A few times he said that he saw the western as potentially one of the most interesting in the series. He was talking aloud, but not to me. He was testing his thoughts. He could have been sitting alone or talking to a tape recorder.

At our last collaborative meeting, Tomblin sat behind Pat's desk and I waited opposite. His hands were laid out on top of some script pages and his head sloped forwards as if his gaze was diving between the papers and the desk right down towards his feet. He told me that we weren't making progress. He thought I'd contributed as much as I could to the script. There was no longer any reference to it being my script. By the end of the conversation, it was his script.

As he was going to direct *Living in Harmony*, he knew exactly what needed to be done, he said. There was nothing more I could give to the project.

I asked what made Pat change his mind about directing it himself.

'There won't be time for him to prepare between getting back from Hollywood and start of shooting,' Tomblin muttered, avoiding my eye.

He finally sat back in his chair and looked at me.

'You don't have to stick around. If you got something else to do, you can get on and do it. I can do the rest by myself. You must have other things you'd rather be doing,' he said ushering me to the door. 'You got things going on, haven't

'That's not good news,' John commiserated.

The next day, I reported for my first session with Tomblin. We sat in Pat's office and I waited while, slowly, he read through the script. He asked a few questions, but nothing of significance emerged. I don't know how Tomblin managed it, but he was even less talkative than Pat. I asked if we should meet the next day.

'Yes, I suppose so,' he said unenthusiastically.

The following day, I found Tomblin settled in and scribbling away, waiting for me.

'I got a few ideas I thought I'd like to put in,' Tomblin notified me. 'I don't think your script has been going the right way. I'm sure you'll see what I mean, and agree.' He pointed out various sequences. This was inadequate, it seemed, and that wasn't good enough.

'Pat's left me in charge because I know what he wants,' Tomblin said without looking at me.

Tomblin was making me feel more and more uncomfortable.

'I'm going to direct *Living in Harmony*,' Tomblin announced.

'There was talk of Pat directing it,' I told him, struggling to sound casual.

'I don't know about that. I'm looking forward to do the western,' he said folding his arms.

He carried on reading the script as if I wasn't in the room.

Trying to communicate with him was like banging my head on a brick wall. Nothing I said or suggested seemed able to provoke a response. Keeping my worst fears at bay was futile. I had no ill-feelings towards him, but I was deeply shaken up. There was an ugly twisted little knot growing in the pit of my stomach. I was being stifled by the prolonged silences that emanated from Tomblin like a suffocating shroud. I asked if I could open a window.

'Yeah, if you want to,' he mumbled indifferently without lifting his head from the page he was rereading for the umpteenth time.

I opened the window and went back to my seat. He was still on the same page. Mindlessly I sat there watching the dream that McGoohan had stirred, disappearing up the chimney. Given how close Tomblin was to McGoohan, I'd expected him to make some effort in my direction and meet me halfway. In this I was totally wrong. Everything was going to go at his pace, and his alone. Fast or slow, I couldn't match his step. We walked and we talked in diametrically opposite ways.

I felt terrible. I felt utterly and completely played out.

'I think that's enough for today,' Tomblin declared, getting up.

I accepted his decision with relief, and left.

Stupefied, I stumbled out across open space between the building which housed Pat's office and the cutting room block. I didn't know what I could do. Without Pat around, I was powerless to do anything. I hoped that John wasn't too busy. I needed to cry on his shoulder and tell him that it was all falling to pieces.

I didn't feel at all up to it when I got home and found my friend Tanya on my doorstep, hugging a teddy bear and singing 'Daddy wouldn't buy me a bow wow.' Her large, light-blue eyes were moist. She'd been crying. She was terrified of something she couldn't explain and frightened of an audition for a part she had the

'Count yourself lucky to be out of this mess.' Number Six resigns.

you?' he paused, holding the door ajar for me.

'A friend of mine wants to go to East Europe, and I was thinking of going with him,' I said. 'I told him it would have to wait until I'd completed the western, and collected my final payment.'

'I tell you what,' Tomblin said with a quite unexpected air of magnanimity. 'I'll do you a favour. I'll give you the money that you're owed out of my own pocket. Otherwise, you only get your last payment when we start production,' he paused. 'You can give me your residuals.'

'What are residuals?' I asked.

'Residuals? That's the money the series won't be making,' he mumbled. 'Be a miracle if the series even gets shown. We got to throw all we can in to the pot, to keep it going. Pat's throwing his Hollywood earnings in to complete the production.'

'He is?'

Tomblin nodded, went back to his desk and wrote out a cheque. I folded it and slid it into my Asprey wallet. Tomblin moved ahead of me, and held the door open again. 'Count yourself lucky that you'll be out of this mess,' he said and shut the door behind me.

ANOTHER JOURNEY, ANOTHER LOSS

My close friend Peter Tribe, a journalist, saw that I was in a state. 'Has Tanya been round?' he asked.

Very briefly I told Peter about the goings-on. I also told him that my stint on *The Prisoner* was at an end.

'Good!' he commented decisively. 'That means that we can take that trip to Bulgaria and Greece we talked about. I don't start my job on the medical paper till September. Give us plenty of time to forget about things back here. We both deserve a good break, and you look run down.'

I'd met Peter some years before at a film lecture in Kensington library. That was in 1964 when my cinema interest had been intensifying. I'd chase after lectures on the subject, haunt the National Film Theatre and read film history voraciously. Over the previous years I had assiduously attended the BFI history and film appreciation courses. This was where I'd learned about the Free Cinema movement, and Lindsay

Anderson's seminal influence. I'd seen films such as *Every Day Except Christmas, O Dreamland, We are the Lambeth Boys,* and *Together.* It was films like these, with their driving social concerns, which led me to my first job in the cutting rooms at Basic Films. The gruff Leon Clore was boss. He had been a financial angel of the Free Cinema movement during the 1950s.

When I met him, Peter had just come down from Cambridge. He was surviving by gambling in casinos and betting on horses. Though taken with neither activity, I was impressed by Peter's keen ability. He was a serious fellow and I liked that. He was also a devout Catholic, which intrigued me. Peter seemed to have more of a moral concern for things than most people I met. We became firm friends.

My Tomblin débâcle still plagued the hell out of me. Though I trusted Peter wholeheartedly, I didn't want to talk about it. I felt the same about Tanya. I kept both incidents squeezed up inside me, and tried to concentrate on what lay ahead,

Polyjanna, Yugoslavia: 'a medieval village with elderly inhabitants and old houses built of wood.'

Peter Tribe is third from right in the second row, Ian Rakoff on the left sitting down.

not behind. I looked forward to going to places I'd never been and Peter was one of the most companionable friends I had. He was also going to be doing the driving. I'd failed my driving test in Britain and my international licence had expired. Luckily, I didn't like driving and Peter did.

Peter's car, a battered Triumph TR6, was a shaking, rattling, and rolling contraption that spluttered and coughed, had a nervous disposition, and frequently needed coaxing back to life with bits of string and odd pieces of wire. Peter could do amazing things with oddments.

We plotted the route so that we'd get some visits to cathedrals. Every Sunday would find us hunting out a church. I liked going to cathedrals and I liked the fact that Peter had no inclination towards proselytising. He was not a religious fanatic; just an effortless, habitual believer.

We got a cross-channel ferry from Dover to Calais and belted across France. Peter drove fast. We kept the top down all the way.

'Peter!' I gasped as we veered across the open road.

'Sorry,' he said slowing down and keeping in a straight line.

'You remember the time my dad found you lying asleep on the ground at our bungalow?' Peter asked. 'He said you looked as if you'd never had a bad dream in your life.'

'That was the weekend we saw *The Cherry Orchard* at Chichester, directed by Lindsay,' I recalled. 'Celia Johnson and that incredible roar in the middle of her performance. Shook the whole place up.'

'Last year, when England won the World Cup,' Peter remembered and asked if I knew where we were.

I said no, and we sped on, leaving things in England further behind. We cut across the top of Italy and entered Yugoslavia

We drove off the beaten track and ended up in Poljana, a medieval village with elderly inhabitants and old houses built of wood. There were no young people except for a few who'd come to visit grandparents. The young visitors had bulging muscles like factory workers from an Eisenstein silent epic. A few spoke some English.

The hospitality and generosity of the local people was unstinting. We began each morning swilling slivovitch under the early morning shade of the apple trees. It was peaceful and calm. It was a relic of an ancient past. It had nothing to do with any outside world. I could not help but compare Poljana's remoteness with that of the Village in *The Prisoner*.

The McGoohan débâcle had followed and still haunted me. At every hint of these feelings, Peter would suggest moving on. He drove and I tried to forget.

'You did write to your friend Donna in Sofia?' Peter asked. 'Will she be there?'

'Yes, she's expecting us.'

'Good, that's where we'll go,' he laughed and stepped on the accelerator. 'Better get out the map.'

The only map we had was in the back of my pocket diary. Neither of us had got round to buying what might be called a proper map. And we never stopped to buy one. What for? We had the time and the curiosity to make mistakes. We had no schedule or destination. The aim was only to get out of England and feel that we were somewhere different.

From Yugoslavia we made for Bulgaria. We stayed in Sofia with my friend Donna, and her family. Peter and I shared a bed in part of a room curtained off for us. Living conditions were pretty crowded, even amongst the better off. Donna was home on holiday. She still lived in London where she was trying to get her film producer cousin to find her an opening in movies. We'd met at a do in Shura's house. Donna had not been taken with Shura.

'She's the type that reads only the dust covers,' Donna commented, 'not what's inside them.' Donna had assisted me on a documentary I had cut a few years previously. Our friendship had blossomed.

In Sofia, Donna took us to a restaurant frequented by the literary élite. We sat in a splendid garden under a floral canopy. Waiters shambled indifferently amongst the tables wearing white, ankle-length aprons. The patrons were elderly caricatures of the East European intelligentsia. The food was rather plain. Bulgaria was Bulgaria and nothing was lavish. It was a stringently modest society compared to how we existed in London. I was beginning to get an inkling of why Lindsay was so taken with East Europe.

We were advised us to steer clear of Greece. The Colonels had just taken over. We pressed on down towards the Greek border.

We crossed the border safely enough. On

seeing personnel carriers with armed soldiers as we left Thesolonika, we kept off the beaten track. We veered along the winding coastline in search of a place to settle down for a while.

It didn't look promising. The Junta Colonels had made the atmosphere pretty steamy. People were suspicious, especially of an almost broken down sports car carrying two oddballs, neither of whom spoke a word of Greek.

While eating at an isolated café overlooking the Aegean, we got into conversation with the owner. He had a smattering of English.

'Where are we?' Peter asked. 'What is this place called?'

'Kadir Raga,' the owner told us.

We were joined by a family of Italians with a holiday villa nearby. They were rabid anglophiles and wealthy enough to indulge their tastes, right down to the young man's brogues.

'See, I only wear English shoes,' he said, wiggling his foot proudly.

Their villa was open and easy, and Peter and I were generously welcomed. But the atmosphere was inescapably fearful. The father was back in Italy and, since the Junta overthrow, he'd become *persona non grata*. The newspaper he owned in Milan had openly attacked the Junta.

The wife and children said it was dangerous for us to stay with them, but they persuaded the Greek café owner to put a couple of beds on the roof. There was a reed covering overhead.

I took one of the café tables and a chair, and set up my typewriter. Each day I beavered away writing my epic on Shaka the Zulu.

'Aren't you writing another television script?' Peter asked me. 'I mean, you're on your way.

Shouldn't you take advantage of that?'

'Peter, for all I know, my name won't even be up on the screen.'

Occasionally an army vehicle came snooping along the coastal road. We kept well out of sight and Peter hid the car in the Italian's garage. No one seemed to stop in Kadir Raga.

We had an idyllic three weeks basking in the Mediterranean sunshine and soaking in the Aegean. I did masses of writing and felt I was getting somewhere. My sad memories of MGM seeped away. But soon enough, it was time to get back. We'd been away from home for over five weeks, and Peter had his new job to start. If he was late for that, his mother would never forgive him. She'd always disapproved of his cavalier lifestyle.

'Is that what you went to Cambridge for,' she had complained, 'to learn to gamble and bring home long-haired friends?'

On one visit, Mrs Tribe had tried to cut my hair but I got away.

Driving back through Yugoslavia, we met a chap who invited us to stay at his home. It turned out to be on a housing estate on the edge of Zagreb. No one spoke any English, but somehow we got incorporated into the family and slept a night in their crowded flat.

Peter slept like a log but I was awakened by a continual chorus of sexual sounds from our hosts.

With the first light Peter and I were woken by our insistent host. He took us down to the ground floor and urged us across a vast, bleak courtyard to another high-rise building which, on its ground level, housed a glass-fronted store.

The Greek coast near Thesalonika. The rooftop where the writer lived.

We joined the short queue of impatient men and sleepy women.

At seven o'clock, the store opened. Our host bought bottles of slivovitch and we were away back upstairs again for a meal whose delicious abundance and meaty contents exceed any notion of the term breakfast. The booze flowed. Then it was time to depart. With much hugging and words of affection, we went down to the car. My case which had been strapped onto the back of the boot, was gone. The case had contained my lengthy manuscript on Shaka the Zulu. I had no copy of anything. I was devastated.

For me, the journey back to England was travelled in a haze. Was there some lesson I should have absorbed? All that writing and nothing to show for it. On top of *The Prisoner* writing débâcle, I found the loss of the African manuscript almost too hard to believe. If there was some moral to be learned, however, it escaped me.

I struggled to think positively. I'd enjoyed sea and sunshine, and got a good tan. The trip had cleared some blocked tubes in my psyche, but I couldn't shake the demoralising cloud of *The Prisoner* that hung over me.

I bolstered my depleted ego by considering my connection with Lindsay Anderson. My association with McGoohan might have become a thing of the past; but my bond to the values of Lindsay marked my future.

MEN OF CONSCIENCE

Back in London, I was acutely aware that *Living in Harmony* was in production. I kept well away from MGM. I still didn't have a television and I deliberately avoided keeping in touch with what was happening on *The Prisoner*. I couldn't face it. I was smothered with my sense of letting McGoohan down. As far as I was concerned, I'd hit the high point of possible standards on television and I wanted little more to do with that branch of the media.

Nevertheless, I couldn't go back to where I'd been working prior to the series. I no longer wanted to be a top-earning assistant on second-rate British comedies or mediocre thrillers. To break into feature filmmaking as a young editor was near impossible. The top ranks were overcrowded for the amount of films being made. The same went for assistants getting into the closed club of features. I thought I might have to settle for documentaries but, for the time being, writing was going to be my goal; despite

the loss of my manuscript in Yugoslavia.

The association with McGoohan had changed my direction. He was the role model for me to be myself in the all-absorbing world of film. McGoohan was a thinking, caring, egalitarian. I believed in him as a valid moral force. McGoohan refused to permit the dictates of commercialism to dilute the ideas he had in mind. Steadfastly he pursued a provocative course to engage his perception of the truth. In effect the realisation of the series was, first and foremost, a political act. Had McGoohan been a politico in my home country, I would readily have thrown my lot in with him. Indeed, in South Africa, there was a figure to whom I could compare McGoohan's *Prisoner*.

In Cape Town, when I was about fourteen, in the mid 1950s, I read *Naught for Your Comfort* by Bishop Trevor Huddleston. His was the very spirit of the oppressed of Sophiatown, a township on the periphery of Johannesburg. Too close to white areas, the township was later bulldozed flat by the authorities. What Huddleston stood for, so articulately and so spiritedly, in Sophiatown captured all that I could respect. He uncompromisingly opposed every form of white supremacy, no matter what the law stipulated. In his book, Huddleston set out the reasons why apartheid was absolutely and totally wrong. He never threw bombs - his credo would not permit that - but his words resonated across the country with explosive impact. Huddleston was unique and he was a devoted man of the cloth. He would not be silenced in his almost solitary war against apartheid. Even within the ranks of his own church, he was a man alone. Why couldn't other white people share Huddleston's values and total commitment? This was a painful ache that was my constant companion in my years of living under apartheid.

In the mid-1950s, my older brother had been an untalented jazz pianist. Jazz and boxing represented two ways in which it was possible for a black person in South Africa to acquire some degree of personal freedom.

On Sundays, my brother threw open the doors to our father's house for the musicians to come and jam, ignoring the laws that made such mixing illegal.

The music was heady, serious improvisational modern jazz. No one danced or dared even speak.

Jazz men and women of all colours attended. These included Shura, dressed in black with dark glasses. A trend-setter, she was in with all the musicians and barely greeted my brother; or me, for that matter. I was just a bit younger than her but, then, the difference in age seemed measured more in aeons than in years.

My father, at his best, was a benign liberal who tolerated the mixed gatherings despite the obvious risks involved. Ours was a charming and verdant, white neighbourhood nestling on the lower slopes of Table Mountain. When our house reverberated on Sundays, the oppressive world of white South Africa disappeared. The music echoed up the mountain, a sonic eulogy to humanity. It was, literally, the sound of freedom.

A genteel youth of fifteen once appeared and played a trumpet like a dream. It was Hughie Masekela. I recall that, once, a lengthy riff of Hughie's fell into competitive harmony with the Moullie Point foghorn. Like a slowed-down metronome, the foghorn blared out rhythmic bass throbs, calling on all life to pause and wait and drawing a veil across all that was ugly.

Hughie carried on playing until the mist lifted.

Hughie's trumpet had a history. Louis Armstrong had presented the instrument to Trevor Huddleston when they met in Louisiana. Armstrong told him it was for the most talented youth playing in the poverty of Sophiatown. Huddleston had given the trumpet to Hughie Masekela.

Years later I was at the Africa Centre in King Street, Covent Garden, with a fellow filmmaker, Lionel Ngkane, also living in London. He introduced me to Hughie, then a grown man and a world-famous musician. 'Grazing in the Grass' had rocketed to the top of the American charts. Hughie and I found we'd had friends in common back in Cape Town. After we'd had a bellyful of each other's stories, he thanked me for the trip down memory lane. I forgot to ask him about the trumpet.

At that same gathering Lionel, also from Sophiatown, introduced me to Bishop Trevor Huddleston. He was tall and stately in his crimson robe. Shaking his hand, I said what a pleasure it was to meet him.

'In childhood,' I told him, 'you made me believe that not all white people were evil.'

He roared with laughter.

Still later, in the early 1990s, about the time that apartheid collapsed, when Trevor Huddleston was approaching the age of eighty years and living in the St James's Refectory in Piccadilly, I saw him strolling by in flowing crimson. After greeting him, I asked him if he'd be prepared to read something I'd written.

'By all means,' he replied and waved his hand to indicate the fine Georgian building across the paved courtyard behind us. 'I live upstairs. You can drop it in with my secretary downstairs.'

I duly delivered 'The Incident'. It was a treatment for a film about a court case in post-apartheid South Africa. A farm labourer killed a litter of puppy dogs by accident and was mercilessly tortured to death. The film was to be an account of the lack of change in changed times, and the need for truth to facilitate reconciliation between the races. It was from a true incident which an old pal had brought to my notice.

I heard nothing from Huddleston.

Months passed. I sent the Bishop a polite note asking if he'd had time to read 'The Incident'.

By return post, I received an apologetic letter and a brief but studied response to what I had written. It also said that he wanted to meet me. I arranged to take him to lunch at BAFTA, the British Academy of Film and Television Arts, almost adjacent to St James's Church.

BAFTA is a society that offers membership and a meeting place for television and film technicians. Its annual awards are the British equivalent to the Oscars. At lunch times, BAFTA's rooms are usually pleasantly uncrowded. I strolled into BAFTA arm in arm with the robed Huddleston.

Tony Sloman walked past us as we sat down. He stared but didn't come over. A member I didn't know, apologized for intruding, and asked if he might shake the Bishop's hand.

For the next few hours we were left alone. I have known few people who have been so effortlessly open. Our conversation ranged from the politics of his friend Nelson Mandela to the Bishop's personal sexual drive.

Huddleston told me that what I had written was needed to be said about South Africa's onerous past and questionable present. He saw no chance of my finding anyone who'd back such a film.

Looking back I see similarities between what Huddleston achieved and to what McGoohan aspired. Religion and ethics were close companions for both men. This was evident in the manner in which they conducted themselves; in what they said and in what they didn't say. Both were distinctively morally aware characters. Both were strong positive identities who did not compromise. Both carried religion in their stride, but never pushed or inflicted it. They

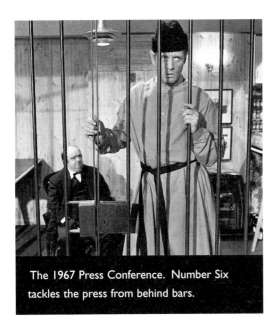

The 1967 Press Conference. Number Six tackles the press from behind bars.

would be initially shown on the ITV network, in black and white. Much of the programme's impact was diminished as a result; the flat lighting, prevailing throughout most episodes, would suffer even more with its transfer to black and white transmission.

After the screening, the journalists were escorted to a reception on a curtained off section of one of the sound stages. Stationed at one end of the cordoned-off area was the iron-barred cage. This was the set which featured in the penultimate episode, *Once Upon A Time*. Wearing the ankle-length crimson robe with a black Russian fur hat, McGoohan conducted the interview from behind bars. Beside him Angelo Muscat, the mute butler of the series, served beers through the bars in total silence. He was

injected their respective and markedly differing vocations, pastoral religion and television drama, with moral and political drive. McGoohan was Roman Catholic; his church, despite its chequered history elsewhere, had resisted apartheid when other faiths and branches of Christianity just knuckled under.

On Wednesday, 20 September 1967, half-way through the filming of *Living in Harmony*, Pat McGoohan held a press conference. He too wore crimson, albeit a Kosho costume from the martial arts contest in the episode *It's Your Funeral*.

The press were shown the first and second episodes, *Arrival*, and *Chimes of Big Ben* projected onto the big screen at an MGM preview theatre, in colour. 1967 was the year that BBC2 introduced colour television. As it then stood, none of the other channels were equipped for colour broadcast. *The Prisoner*

Alexis Kanner (on pennyfarthing) under surveillance by an out-of-character Patrick McGoohan.

helped by a couple of extras wearing piped blazers, the distinctive Village uniform. Surrounding the cage were pieces of decor from the series' props department including the inevitable penny farthing bicycle. Ever resourceful, Jack Shampan, the art director, had created an amalgam of sets from leftovers, rather in the way that Clough Williams-Ellis went about creating Portmeirion, governed by what was available.

Cryptically, McGoohan answered questions with questions. He wanted to know what were the journalists' reactions to the first two episodes. What did they think was the significance of Rover, McGoohan asked. What was their interpretation of the meaning behind the symbols decoratively incorporated into the dressing of the series?

Questioned about the medical experimentation witnessed on screen, Pat threw back the reality of Christian Barnard whose first heart transplant patients dropped like flies. Was that sick, he demanded, was that sadistic?

McGoohan took his stand, played it straight, gave nothing away and strove for provocation. He massaged his media attackers; he manoeuvred past his detractors. His skill was masterly in turning the tables. Close up, his personal magic was awesome and seductive. But he lacked the something which could endear him to people. It was not dissimilar to Lindsay Anderson's own uncompromising temperament.

Patrick McGoohan on location. As ever, in control.

Pat continued asking the press more questions. In attack mode he was relentless. His attitude to the media was no less bullish than his stance in the programme as Number Six.

A journalist criticized McGoohan because the series conveyed no sense of development. There was no continuity of story from episode to episode. There was no progress in his captors' attempts to break him. Where was the logic? A journalist asked.

'Let me ask you two questions,' McGoohan snapped back. 'You're living in this world? You must answer "yes" to that,' he went on without pausing. 'Do you find it always logical? No? That's your answer to that.'

McGoohan emerged from the cage and posed for a photo call. Alexis Kanner had a go on a penny farthing and hit the deck unceremoniously.

To the rear of the cage, a curtained backdrop was drawn aside to reveal food and drink. Behind the buffet tables was the egg-shaped global chair. Decked out like Village citizens, waitresses served refreshments to the assembled press throng.

McGoohan left the interview, and returned shortly wearing his costume for the western, which he was scheduled to shoot in the afternoon. Later, members of the press were invited onto the set during the filming of *Living in Harmony*.

The shooting of the seventeenth and last episode was a matter of mere weeks away.

15

FACING THE SCREEN

I got a call from the studio inviting me to a screening of *Living in Harmony*. I invited Shura to come with me. She was more than willing to zap up to North London in her Triumph Herald.

'What's wrong?' Shura snapped at me as we approached Borehamwood.

'Everything,' I replied and told her about my last meeting with Tomblin.

'There's no sense in brooding on it,' Shura grumbled. 'You'll discover how it turned out soon enough.'

The guard on gate duty was a new face to me. I had to explain who we were and where we were going. He told us where to park.

As we entered the main preview theatre, I saw Tomblin. He was too busy to greet me. The theatre was half-packed with crew and people I didn't recognize. All of them seemed to know Tomblin.

Shura wanted seats towards the back. We sat where she wanted. I would usually sit near the front in a viewing theatre, preferably the first row. For once, I wanted back seat anonymity.

Living in Harmony burst into life on the large MGM screen. When the credits came up, I found my name had survived. Tomblin had taken producer, director, and screenplay credit. The original story credit Tomblin shared with me. I was relieved that my name had not been totally dumped.

Watching the episode was like having my insides torn out. For a moment I couldn't believe I'd written any of what I was seeing. It seemed familiar but from somewhere far away and long ago. Dialogues struck chords.

Playing the saloon hostess Cathy, Valerie French looked every inch the veteran of innumerable Hollywood westerns that she was. She almost carried the episode and her presence gave *Living in Harmony* a genre verity. I felt uncomfortable about the Mexican small-part character, which bore some distinctly racist overtones. To my absolute delight, the film was

Living in Harmony: roughhouse in the town square.

not as flatly lit as most of the episodes. There were shadows, and it conveyed a mood. I was impressed. The western setting looked suitably authentic. Unlike some of the sets in other episodes it didn't look like cardboard and papier mâché. Nothing wobbled. I thought the transition from the West to the Village was made incredibly well. I was impressed by the horse wrangling, the fight scenes and the general atmosphere. McGoohan looked like a regular inhabitant of the Wild West. He wasn't bad on a horse but I wasn't sure about the hat.

I had trouble believing that, creatively, it was all Tomblin's doing. I just didn't expect it to be technically as good as it was. There was another

strong influence there, I felt. I may have been mistaken but, like my former colleagues, I felt the real credit had to belong to Pat.

And who wrote what, finally? Doubt assailed me, despite most of the dialogue having a familiar ring to it. I told myself that I should just be grateful that my name was on the screen. I wondered what Tomblin had said about my contribution to Pat, or if he'd explained my absence. Had he mentioned the handing over of my residuals to the cause completing the series? How was the money that I might have got eventually used? These were not questions I thought I could ask aloud.

I shrivelled in my seat at the tasteless

denouement, the prolonged strangling of Cathy. It struck me as excessively, unhealthily sadistic, not at all what I'd visualized emerging from what I'd written. For this, I wasn't happy that my name was on the credits.

After the screening, I congratulated Tomblin and asked where Pat was, as I'd like to see him. Tomblin told me that Pat was too preoccupied to see me. He wasn't available, he said. I was painfully disappointed.

I got into Shura's Triumph and we headed back to the relative reality of Chelsea.

I never did get to speak to McGoohan again.

I did not delude myself into thinking that Pat might ring me up and commission me for another script. I'd heard nothing about the series going on after the seventeenth episode.

On the Sunday night after *Living in Harmony* had been transmitted, a fourteen year old boy

Living in Harmony: in the saloon. The nonchalant stranger seems to be in a standoff with director David Tomblin (far right).

had killed himself. The father attributed his son's suicide to the lynching in *Living in Harmony* and an American western episode also transmitted the same evening. Was the boy's suicide the reason why the gratuitous death scenes in *Living in Harmony* were re-cut?

Reading about it in the newspaper, I was stunned. Could I be implicated in the horror, I asked myself. Or would my objection to the death sequence exonerate me? Was there anything I could have done?

This resulting incident heightened my desire to disassociate myself even further from what had once been my episode. Yet the experience of having made a personal and professional commitment to the programme could not be gainsaid; and it compelled me to take stock.

Despite my difficulties with the production, working on *The Prisoner* had set me a new standard. Ultimately I'd got my name on something I believed was worthwhile. I was determined not to slide back into working on tepid comedies and mediocre features as I'd done prior to McGoohan's series. This was all changed by being on *The Prisoner*. It showed me that somehow or other I could carry on and make a career for myself, getting involved on serious projects with serious people. I realized that I did not have to suspend politics in order to have a working life.

I resolved that come hell or high water I'd, somehow or other, have to get on to Lindsay Anderson's next film, whatever it was.

16

REBELLION IN SOUTH AFRICA

Lindsay recommended me for an editing job on a short feature; black and white, on 35mm. *The Burning* was the first film by Stephen Frears, who Lindsay knew from the Royal Court Theatre. The film was a co-production between the BFI and Albert Finney's Memorial Films, with additional backing from Karel Reisz. But it was to Lindsay that Stephen had turned in his hour of need.

The film was about a day of revolution in South Africa. Stephen, with first-time editor Mary Brown, had spent months cutting it every which way. After they'd screened it to me in a Soho basement preview theatre, Stephen paced back and forth in front of the empty screen and listened to what I had to say. He was a swarthy, solidly built fellow who wore sneakers and moved like he had all the world's problems on his shoulders. My advice was to discard the cut they had, join everything back together and start all over again.

Stephen was appalled at the amount of work I was suggesting had to be done. I saw no alternative. I didn't think that snipping here and there would make much of a difference.

I didn't feel ready to take it on. I was settling into becoming a writer and, besides, Stephen already had an editor. I offered to help out part-time.

Lindsay called me. He'd talked with Stephen and he was amused by the way in which Stephen had spoken about me.

I told Lindsay that I'd offered to help out part-time as a supervising editor.

'That half-baked attitude won't get you anywhere,' he fumed. 'It'll be a proper job and a full-time commitment. You can carry on with your writing after you've cut the film.'

I waited before Stephen phoned.

'We've put it all back together,' he told me. 'I've booked a theatre to screen the rushes, and I've extended our booking for the cutting room. Can you be at Dateline, tomorrow morning at nine?'

Mary Brown, the editor, bristled in my company and I wasn't relaxed with her. Being a woman in film editing was a rarity at that time. The cutting rooms were, in the main, a white male English enclave. Mary had a healthy energy, a thoughtful presence and a keen mind; but she was hardly experienced enough to edit. She disliked my high-handed manner. It was a tricky predicament for both of us. We were not getting on.

Lindsay came into the cutting room almost daily to keep an eye on Stephen and me. I remember my first editing shock with him. One of the longest scenes took place in a kitchen where a servant had a long dialogue with the elderly cook. Stephen had cut the sequence, I don't know how many times, and had never got it even to begin working. I took the restored footage, mainly inadequately shot, and recut it to produce a dramatic order. Stephen was delighted.

Viewing the completed sequence, Lindsay complimented me on how I had cut it. I felt a great sense of achievement.

'But if you remove it,' Lindsay pointed out. 'It will make the whole film work much better.'

'But it's now the best scene in the entire film,' Stephen objected.

One of the best qualities that Stephen possessed was being open and responsive to criticism. We took another look at the sequence on the moviola and then deleted the scene.

From this point on, the cutting proceeded from strength to strength. We worked with considerable ferocity and intensity, and the material at last found a life of its own.

I visited the Memorial production offices, off Piccadilly in Sackville Street, as I had done on several occasions.

Being there was unlike any previous experiences I'd had in the industry. There was an extraordinary civility about the Memorial set-up. It was different; and better. There was nothing rigid about Memorial. Informality was the order of every day. Everyone employed there seemed to be treated equally. No ill-feelings simmered. Nobody wanted what somebody else had. Equally, nobody seemed to be at Memorial just for the job or just for the money. It was the film industry, but also it wasn't.

Of the directors supported by the company, I briefly met Mike Leigh who, like Stephen, was directing his first film under the Memorial umbrella. Mike's beard was trimmed neatly and his demeanour was somewhat austere.

My main points of contact at Memorial, however, were three people: Daph, the secretary; David Barber, Memorial's resident accountant-cum-production man; and Finney himself

Daph would talk in hushed, conspiratorial tones.

'...do you really think so? I don't believe that,' she said. She'd want to know who was doing what and why. Later, she'd debate aloud the morality of her actions, and everybody else's. Daph was a case of orderly and trustworthy chaos. We became confidential pals. She disliked the secrecy and the cant endemic in the film industry. When occasionally things got frenzied, Daph was the resident tonic.

David Barber had started in the film business working for Leslie Grade, younger brother of

Lew Grade and Bernard Delfont. At Memorial, Barber did all the budgets and made it his business to know exactly what was going on. In person, he was so restrained that being laid back would seem like aggression by comparison. He was also amenable, but sometimes thought he was smarter than he was. He nearly got his head bitten off trying to cross swords with Lindsay. Barber used to bitch a bit, but not maliciously. He had reservations about his accountancy label and leaned more towards the creative side of the business. One way or another, he got pretty involved with whatever was happening.

Albert Finney carried the responsibilities of his burgeoning, creative empire quite unselfconciously. Off-stage and off-screen, he was more the person and less the actor: gentle, serious and friendly by turns. He'd made his directorial debut, and swan song, with *Charlie Bubbles*. Although written by Shelagh Delaney, it appeared to be a personal, poetic statement of Albert's own on his life, his success and his relationship with his modest roots in the industrial north of England. It was a work of substance, though quite the opposite to the rebellious subjects to which I was drawn.

Out of all of them it was Albert whose curiosity would prompt him to take my interest in comic books seriously.

I can also make a comparison between him and Pat McGoohan. Like McGoohan, Finney was a large, solidly built man. Both had strong screen presence, though in different directions. Both were stars of stage and of screen.

Stephen sauntered into the Memorial office. Daph pointed out that his sneakers were

Albert Finney: the man who gave the British film industry a sense of the ensemble.

undone. He took no notice, plonked his rump on her desk and reached for her phone.

'It wouldn't hurt to ask,' Daph said irately. 'Why must you use my phone, and why must you sit on my desk, and why don't you do up your laces?'

'Daph, stop going on so,' Stephen mumbled, putting the phone down, sliding off the desk and tying up his laces. Then he picked up the phone again.

Daph smiled.

'Hello chaps!' Michael Medwin, Finney's friend and partner, strolled in smiling and waving at everybody. He asked Daph something. She told him he'd left it too late, but promised to give it a try if Stephen would let her have her phone.

'Just do what you can,' Medwin looked round.

Michael Medwin: the ever-supportive and unusually civilized film producer.

Albert Finney: The actor as detective in **Gumshoe**.

'Has anybody seen my dry cleaning? It should have been delivered. I have to put another shirt on.'

'It's in there with Albert,' Daph pointed at Finney's office, and picked up the phone as Stephen put it down.

Albert, putting on a jacket, came out of his office as his chauffeur walked in the front door.

'Got your clubs downstairs,' Finney asked Medwin, and nodded to Daph as he walked past.

'Oh, Albert?' Daph called breathlessly after Albert.

'Later, Daph,' Finney waved a no-no and glanced at Medwin now walking out beside him.

'Clubs in the car, all set to go. Lovely day. Sean meeting us at Sunningdale?'

'Not sure, depends on some audition,' Finney shrugged slightly.

'Oh, really?' Medwin said with interest. 'Is that the Columbia offer?'

They stopped just beyond the open glass door and waited for the lift. I watched them and listened to what they were saying.

'But Albert, you must take a lunch with Lindsay,' Medwin pleaded and Finney grunted.

'Is that a yes or no?' Medwin asked.

They got into the lift still discussing the matter. Stephen came over to me and asked what was going on. I told him about the proposed lunch with Lindsay and we left together.

Outside the building I stopped to see if I could remember where it was that I'd come to see director Michael Winner.

Stephen had not known that I'd worked for Winner, but he knew where his office was located. He pointed it out and, as we strolled back to Soho, I told Stephen about one of my more memorable encounters with Winner. It was in 1964, on his film *You Must Be Joking*. I was first assistant to editor Bernard Gribble. Winner had wanted to check a particular frame. I rushed the relevant cut reel, end out where the frame was easily accessible.

'I asked for a clip, not the whole fucking reel,' Winner barked. He jerked the centre bobbin out of the reel, strew the film across his office and stormed out.

I spent ages on the floor fiddling to get the film back into the reel.

Less mediocre rewards awaited me now.

When we got back, Lindsay was in the cutting room waiting for us, surrounded by an attentive audience. As we walked in, he was verbally tearing some new film to pieces, to the obvious agreement of his listeners. They swiftly dispersed, leaving Mary to set up the reel we were about to tackle.

Lindsay asked how dear Albert was, and I told him that he'd gone off with Michael Medwin to play golf. Lindsay asked me what I made of Albert. I responded favourably, using the word nice. Lindsay complained that nice was an empty word with no real meaning. I shouldn't describe anybody or anything as nice. I mentioned that I had spoken to Albert about comic books. Lindsay turned to Mary and announced that both Albert and I were retarded. This was proved by our having conversed on comic books.

'Poor Ian,' Lindsay said sympathetically and patted me on the back. 'What can we do about

your illiteracy?'

I said I should listen more intensely to Lindsay Anderson and that would probably cure me.

'Don't be facetious,' Lindsay scolded. Then he folded his arms and leaned back.

I pressed my foot on the peddle and we were off.

Lindsay disappeared for a pee. By the time he came back, Mary was packing her things and was on her way out.

Lindsay said it was a pity she had to go. I'd already arranged another assistant. Later that afternoon Gerry arrived. He was trying to get work as an assistant director in features but he'd agreed to help us out. He wasn't keen on the cutting rooms, he said. He wanted to be where the action was, close to the camera; but while he was with us he was willing, dependable and pleasant enough company.

Lindsay came round to my place for a meal. The first thing he did was to open his battered leather briefcase and take out a pair of well-worn slippers.

I grilled two chicken breasts and made a salad dressing in my somewhat decrepit kitchen. Lindsay sat on the board covering my bath and sipped from a glass of red wine. He asked me if I planned to move. I said that if I ever did that it would still have to be in Chelsea. I didn't think I could live anywhere else.

'What a trendy attitude,' Lindsay laughed.

Over our meal, Lindsay interrogated me about my background. I said I felt uncomfortable talking about it. It was bad enough being a white South African. He told me that he had some cousins in Cape Town but he had no

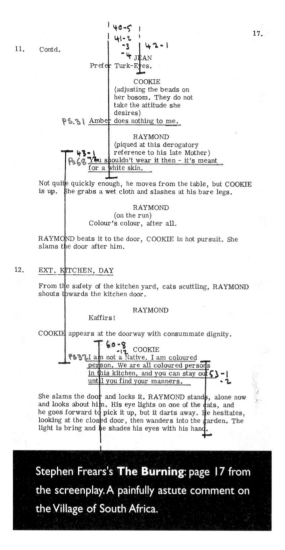

Stephen Frears's **The Burning**: page 17 from the screenplay. A painfully astute comment on the Village of South Africa.

intention of going there.

Puttering round my flat, Lindsay was appalled to learn that I had no television.

'How can you work in films? How can you be so out of touch?' he demanded and then changed subject as he scrutinized my shelves. 'Are these,' he asked, incredulous, 'all comic books?'

I replied that there were more in cardboard boxes under my bed. He shook his head

disparagingly and complimented me on the fresh coffee I'd made. I told Lindsay that it was Blue Mountain from Jamaica. I bought it at the old coffee shop in Rathbone Place. He knew it, but thought that far too much fuss was made over coffee. At home he made instant, he told me. I said I'd noticed that.

I strolled with Lindsay to the number thirty-one bus stop. There was no tube station near my place, as Lindsay would have preferred. Lindsay thanked me for a good evening and said he'd be in the cutting room a bit late the next morning.

'Poor Stephen,' Lindsay said as a bus swung towards us. 'He's had a rough time editing his masterpiece, so we can't let him down.' Lindsay hopped on the bus.

As it drew away he paused on the platform and waved.

Roland Starke, Stephen's screenwriter popped into the cutting room. He was open, chatty and deliciously bitchy but, as soon as Lindsay walked in, he went silent. I announced to Stephen and Lindsay that I was going out for a coffee with this writer and fellow Capetonian. I wanted to tell him what I thought of his script.

We went to Act One Scene None. Over coffee I told Roland how good I thought the script was. I was keen to meet him because most writing about South Africa was worthless. I felt comfortable with the moral premise which I felt was behind *The Burning*.

'You probably see more than I wrote. I'm a bloody white South African with no political involvements.'

I asked if Roland was from Starke, the famous florist family in Cape Town. He was, and that's why he couldn't stand flowers.

'But is the film any good?' Roland whined. 'I don't want something that's just fucking worthy.'

'Of course it's good,' I reassured him and told him that it couldn't do better than have Lindsay involved.

'I know,' Roland flung his head back. 'That's what worries me.'

We shook hands in Old Compton Street and parted, intending to meet up again. A fortnight later I got a call. Roland was in the running for a feature commission. He was in a panic. We spent a weekend drinking whisky, rewriting dialogue and intensely enjoying scribbling together. Between the whisky and my input, Roland's sense of dialogue took off. He got the commission.

I was crossing Wardour Street with Lindsay when Tony Sloman came over. With a broad smile, he told me about an interview he'd had with Michael Winner. He was told not to cross Winner's path or he'd end up like the one other young man who did so. That was Ian Rakoff, who, as a result, Winner had claimed, had never again worked in the British Film industry.

Tony asked what I'd done to Winner on *You Must Be Joking*. I told him about contractual exploitation and how I'd come up against the production manager. After some dirty tricks, I brought the union in. It had cost the production a packet. Winner had wanted me fired, but it would've cost too much to replace me. I stayed to the end. Winner, it would seem, had not forgotten.

Tony said that I should come over to his place on Sunday evening, then rushed off.

Lindsay smiled. He was the one who'd sent me to the trade union to help me with the Winner production in the first place.

'What'll you get up to at his place on Sunday evening?'

I told Lindsay that Tony didn't have a television but did have a 16mm projector with a collection of Elvis Presley films. We'd also been discussing my writing a medieval screenplay. Then I raised the subject of comics.

'But most important is that I take him an IW reprint with a sexy advert on the inside cover with Quinn O'Hara, a Hollywood starlet of B-features.' I told Lindsay. 'Quinn will be there on Sunday. IW comics were bootlegs from the 1940s and 1950s reprinted in 1963 and..'

'That's enough,' Lindsay held his hand up. 'Enough!'

I informed him that Albert had been round to my place to look at comics. I'd shown him Russ Manning's *Tarzan*. Albert had compared the angles and shadows with what he'd been trying to achieve with *Charlie Bubbles*.

Lindsay told me that I was wasting time with Finney.

17

Close to the Heart

I was on my way to Dateline when I bumped into Roy Benson. I'd met him in the freelance cutting rooms at Shepperton, working for Kubrick. Roy was flashily dressed, straight off a Carnaby Street rack, right down to his winkle pickers. Highly agitated, he asked if I had time for a coffee. He'd been on the lookout for me, he gabbled. I said if he calmed down and told me what was going on, then I had the time for a coffee.

'I'm editing a film, *Magical Mystery Tour,* for the Beatles,' he blurted 'and I want you to assist me.'

I told him that I was fully committed and, much as I'd like to, I couldn't pull out of what I was cutting. I said I'd think of someone suitable to assist him.

'A lot of people would give their eye-teeth to work with the Beatles,' I said encouragingly.

Roy gave me a run-down on what it was like working with the group.

'Paul seems to be the one behind it all,' Roy began, still very much on edge.

I pinned back my ears ready for a barrage of words.

'I collected all these cans of film from Ringo's hotel room. The stuff was shot on all different kinds of stock. So the first thing is sorting it all out. That's a nightmare in itself, as you can well imagine. The continuity girl gave me piles of paper and asked if I was the editor. When I said I was, she laughed and said good luck.

'Paul thought I could get it all done in one week. I told him that he ought to come into the cutting room and find out what was involved. Each one of them had shot separate sequences. Ringo had done lots of stills. He should have been a cameraman instead of a drummer. John's definitely the most way out. He's full of ideas. So, I can identify with him on that level. George is the most withdrawn.

'The other day Lennon said they'd go out for lunch and leave me to fart about. I told him off for that. This is art, I said, I am not farting about. That was after I'd been working alone with each of them in turn. So it was like all these different films. I told them to leave me alone and I'd see what I could do. There wasn't really a solid idea or script behind the overall thing. I got it together in a running order and showed it to them.

'We got a film, was what they all said,' Roy flung his arms apart. 'I'm flavour of the month. But who can I get to assist me?'

I telephoned Mark.

'Now Roy is a decent chap and a friend of mine,' I told Mark, priming him. 'Can I count on you not to let him down? He's going to need help in communicating with the Beatles. Any old-guard editor would have the same problem. Roy's so unpretentious he'll get along with the group, but he'll need help.'

'Look, mate,' Mark responded. 'You're the last person in the world I'd shaft. This sounds like the chance of a lifetime. Don't you worry, I won't let you down. Now, who's this Roy geezer?'

I was at work laying in the music for our forthcoming dub on *The Burning*. We'd booked Warwick recording studio, in the basement at the corner of Carlisle Street and Soho Square. Suddenly a friend telephoned. It was a hot tip. I put the phone down and rushed out, asking Gerry to tell Lindsay and Stephen that I wouldn't be away long but that something important had come up.

I raced through the traffic along Old Compton Street and across Charing Cross Road down to Cambridge Circus. Gasping for breath, I approached the row of market stalls and tried to look casual. If what I'd been told on the phone was true, I'd have to be careful, thoughtful and sensible. What little experience I'd had with dealers had taught me that few of them were avid collectors. Most of them were in it for the money. I stopped at the new stall in the row. Sure enough it was packed and stacked with comic books. At a glance, I could tell instantly that this was gold dust. I didn't know where to begin but it was a quiet time of the day. Most passers-by were heading for the vegetable stall or for one of the barrows selling antique bric-à-brac. I was rooted to the spot, staring at the comics. The stall owner sidled over to me and got chatting.

He was lanky fellow named Bob. He had a zany swagger, a battered a top hat, a frilly shirt and tails. It was all rather worn and torn, like his lived-in young face. As Bob looked me over, I rummaged through pile after pile, picking out what I wanted. But there was so much, so many to choose from and only one pair of arms. I'd have to return with a bag.

The stock on sale was an absolute treasure trove of vintage gems, all American and in four colours, dating back to before I was born. I opened one for a sniff. Different decades had different odours.

'You snort the stuff?' Bob flopped about, narrowly side-stepping a car that swept past. 'Don't you read them? You look like a scholar and a gentleman to me.'

I laughed without interrupting my search. I was mesmerized by the array of black Dells, western comics from the late 1940s and early 1950s with luscious painted covers. I rummaged through pile after pile, and Bob kept on finding more for me in cardboard boxes he kept under the barrow.

Bob thrust another pile into my waiting hands. *Crackajack, Adventure, Famous Funnies* and *King Comics.*

'All in mint condition, and they could be quite old,' he said.

They were rare newspaper strip reprints from the 1930s. I just scooped up as much as could carry, paid, and said I'd be back.

'I'll have more of the same next week,' Bob said, stuffing the notes I'd given him into one pocket and then another.

I staggered away, regretting that I did not have longer arms to carry more. These were comics I'd only ever heard of and had never seen. Not only were they rare beyond belief but, by any market standards, they had been dirt cheap.

In the 1960s, at long last, my personal addiction had hit the jackpot. My mind was blown into the stratosphere. I was in seventh, eighth and ninth heavens. It was what life was about, at its best.

I had acquired genuine 1930s comic books which, today, thirty years on would cost thousands for one issue. They were all published before the advent of Superman, the first individual comic hero to have his own book; and the newspaper strips of the 1930s were a literature in their own right. My personal passion, though, was for the black Dells. I adored those cowboy adventures in my childhood and no less as a grown-up. Fashionable contemporary intoxicants and excitements were small beer compared to the

weight I carried in my arms back through Soho.

As I was going up Wardour Street, a black taxi pulled up alongside of me and out stepped Mark.

'Look, mate,' he addressed me as he paid the fare, 'why don't you come up with me right now? I left Paul alone with Roy up in the cutting room. Be a good chance to meet him.'

Already in a euphoric state over the comics, I wasn't going to miss the chance for yet another high. Stephen would have to wait.

I followed Mark along Old Compton Street and up narrow rickety stairs, to the second floor, past a burly bodyguard stationed to keep out any Beatle chasers, and into a crummy cutting room.

Roy was delighted to see me, looked as nervy as hell, and kept on cutting away ferociously.

I was introduced to Paul McCartney, who enquired about what I was carrying.

'I have just made the most incredible comic book score,' I said and went on. 'You just don't come across stuff like this,' I raved, breathless from the stairs and my excitement. 'It's a once in a lifetime thing.'

I flashed the brilliant painted covers of the Dell westerns, and Paul moved closer. He was interested.

'These are great,' he said, examining some *Red Ryder*s by Fred Harman.

'It's the most authentic western in the comics,' I told Paul. 'No one else can touch that kind of brush stroke or match the feel of the dialogue. Also the Little Beaver relationship doesn't come across as racist or patronising. That in itself is unusual. But if you're interested in the grammar of cinema, it would be the best western to study.' I pointed at how dramatically the angles changed

Mark Davies, the working hippie. Definitely an individual and of his time.

from frame to frame, how a page became one panel.

'The most successful western in the newspaper strips,' I declared.

I went on about the muted colours in Dell comics. They were never garish inside, only on the glossy hand painted covers. I paused to assess if my audience of one was still with me. Paul urged me not to stop. Out of the corner of my eye I noticed Roy and Mark smiling. Mark was rolling a joint.

I raved about the artwork of *Gene Autry* by Jesse Marsh.

'Marsh is said to be the most prolific of all artists in comic books. He does Tarzan regularly.'

Perhaps Mark handed me a joint but I'm not sure. My enthusiasm appeared infectious and Paul was a more than willing captive audience.

'Hello, what's going on in here?' Rosie, an habitué of the Soho streets, shambled in.

Rosie wore a faded beige raincoat and had two red roses, with their stems wrapped in silver foil, tucked behind his ears and under his glasses.

'Paul,' he grinned with a mouthful of tobacco, wine or tea-stained teeth, 'guess what day this is.' Rosie made his way towards Paul. 'It's my birthday,' he announced, 'an' can you guess what birthday it is?'

Paul reached down, picked up a guitar and handed it to Rosie. Still seated, Paul reached behind and brought out a second guitar. Turning to face me, they both began.

At first Rosie only strummed, while Paul sang. I shivered with delight as the melodious sound wrapped itself round me. I was transported into a world different to any other world I had touched. If the film was to be a *Magical Mystery Tour*, I felt then, it would be Paul who would provide the magic.

'Will you still feed me, will you still need me when I'm sixty four...?' By now, Rosie was croaking along with Paul in a rasping duet. It only made it better, and more real.

They went through the whole song facing me, except when they faced each other. After that Paul turned back to me with a polite bow, as if he

Magical Mystery Tour: Roy Benson. From David Lean and Stanley Kubrick to the Beatles.

was performing to a vast audience.

At the end of it, Rosie gave a hysterical laugh, clamped his hand into Paul's and sauntered out carrying the melody with him. Later Rosie would be at his regular pitch, on the corner of Dean and Old Compton Streets. He'd be crooning his heart out, singing the same song, ignored by the passers-by, as he always was.

'I want to hear more about these American comic books,' Paul said to me. 'So have you got time to have some lunch?'

I said yes.

There was suddenly a chilly atmosphere.

'Hello John,' Paul raised his hand slightly.

I turned round. Facing me with Ringo slightly behind him, was John Lennon in a light cream suit, looking not at all happy and narrow eyed with suspicion.

Without responding to Paul's greeting, Lennon

stared straight at me. His look was pure ice, and it was unfaltering. I stepped back, totally unnerved by the intensity of the look. Its meaning was cold and clear: who is this hustler, and how did he get in here?

Lennon kept his back to Roy and Mark, and didn't take his eyes off me. Nobody said anything, including Paul.

I could not handle it. I turned back to Paul.

'I don't think now is a good idea,' I said to him. 'Maybe we can have lunch another time.'

'Yes, another time,' Paul replied but his soft face was no longer looking at me, it was watching John Lennon.

Ringo had started moving about muttering inaudibly and Roy had his foot down on the moviola at high speed, making a hell of a din.

I gathered up my comic books and scooted out.

The moment was over but the magical memory was unforgettable. I never did get another chance to meet up with McCartney.

Equally, I could never forget the look that Lennon gave me.

Years later, Roy told me that I should have braved it out. Lennon was like that with everybody, Roy said, and he could change at the drop of a hat. He always came on nasty, but quickly softened, and was actually more genuinely interested in people and ideas than the other three. Lennon, Roy emphasized, was the most inventive and creative one. I was sceptical of Roy's flattering assessment of Lennon but I never got the opportunity to determine the truth.

A couple of years later I had one other private performance that ranked alongside the one with Paul McCartney. Only the song was of a very different kind.

I was at actor Malcolm McDowell's flat. This was at the end of a cul-de-sac in a smart part of Notting Hill Gate, behind Kensington Church Street. Malcolm's place was tucked in the furthermost corner of a dead-end street. There was almost no frontage, just enough for a door. Once inside it was like a scaled down church interior, spacious and light. Massive windows and a narrow balcony overlooked a small bank of greenery. The feel and design of the structure definitely had clerical origins.

We were messing about on an idea for a feature film.

Sitting cross-legged on the floor, I asked Malcolm to do *Singing in the Rain* for me. This referred to the very sinister scene from the recently released *A Clockwork Orange*.

Malcolm obligingly limbered up and set to. The song didn't falter and the kicks whizzed by my ears, perilously close and with full force. He was quite a kicker. As it went on into escalating frenzy, I froze. I was nailed to the floor. The performance was chilling. Up and over my head his foot sped. He was the perfect ballet dancer, and he was the perfect, vicious street fighter. He was phenomenally agile. I could detect no flaws in his body movements or in his singing. I wondered how many set-ups it had taken Kubrick to get the fluent, sinister effect that he wanted right through.

Malcolm gave me the works, all of it, from start to finish. There was no make-believe. There was no actor performing. It was all for real and I could feel myself starting to sweat as the footwear just slightly touched my hair. He was

swinging his leg closer and closer, as he hopped about. One slight miscalculation was all it would take for me to lose my head.

Then it was over, and I was relieved.

'Come on,' Malcolm said. 'Let's take Alex for a walk.' He attached a lead to the collar of his large, sleek, black dog. 'I let him loose in the park.' Malcolm paused at the front door. 'Maybe we should take some rotten tomatoes to throw at the Royals.'

A few weeks passed before I saw Mark next, in Old Compton Street. I went over to him.

'It's going great, man,' Mark waved at a passing black cab but someone else got to it first. 'I sold John Lennon some of my 8mm film. McCartney lent me a 16mm camera, and Roy's going crazy. He gets upset if anyone lights up a smoke and, all the time, we're dropping stuff right, left and centre,' Mark chuckled. 'They respect what he's making of the crap they shot, and they love hanging out in the cutting room. They're into the mechanics of film, specially Lennon and McCartney. You know what Roy does? He checks out the waste basket. Got Paul's lyrics for *Fool on the Hill*. He's building a collection. One day he'll flog it for a fortune and buy some decent clobber.'

More taxis sped by, but all were occupied.

'Guess where I'm off to,' Mark smiled. 'I got an appointment with Pat. You seen anything of him?'

Shaking my head, I said that I had not.

'I'm going to lay Alfred Bester's *Tiger! Tiger!* on him. Think he'll go for it?'

I submitted that he would make a convincing Gully Foyle, but I doubted that Pat was ready for pure science fiction, despite *Tiger! Tiger!* having been so widely acclaimed. I said that he'd probably try get something underway relevant to *The Prisoner* values, something serious. I told Mark that Pat had given me a copy of *Brand* when I had started working for him. It was what he wanted me to read, but at a later stage.

'Can't get more serious than Ibsen,' I said to Mark. 'Whatever he does will depend on how the public responds to *The Prisoner*.'

I heard myself sounding disinterested and vague.

It wasn't comfortable for me to discuss *The Prisoner*. The whole business still wrankled, and I had little desire to reawaken my disappointment.

'I'm going to turn the Beatles onto McGoohan,' Mark told me. 'They'll be chuffed to know their music's in the last episode.'

'How responsive were they when you told them about the series?' I asked. 'Have they been watching?' I'd heard that the series had started, but not in colour.

'Don't tell me you haven't got your own television yet?' Mark asked incredulously.

I admitted I had not, but sometimes I visited friends who had television.

'Lennon saw it and you know what he said? I got to think about it Mark and he's still thinking. It's not always easy to get them to listen seriously, but I'm working on Lennon. He's the number one. There's a *Mystery Tour* fancy dress party coming up. I'm going to ask Pat to give me something to wear. *The Prisoner* meets the Beatles sort of thing.' Mark looked at me quizzically. 'You know you're always welcome to see it at my place. Yvonne's still keeping the macrobiotic kitchen, and a bit of drugs won't do you no harm. Be good for you,' he paused. 'You did get to see the first episode a month ago?'

'Not on television, but I saw it at MGM,' I told Mark. 'I had some music tracks to fit, getting towards our final dub.'

'I'll let you know how it goes with McGoohan.'

'I don't know if I want to know.'

'Don't be like that,' Mark chided. 'You know he's a great guy.'

'Mark, I'm all for Pat. He gave me the break. But it didn't work out the way I thought it would.'

A taxi pulled into the kerb for Mark and he disappeared inside.

Lindsay whispered to me in the semi-dark as black repair frames blotted the screen and engulfed the dubbing theatre in deep darkness. Towards the conclusion of the mixing, with the only light coming from the flickering projection, he told me how well he felt I'd done on the cutting of Stephen's film. Lindsay talked about his next project, a script titled *The Crusaders*. It was about a revolution in an English public school. He stipulated that if I took a job cutting commercials for the next six months, he would consider me for editor on *The Crusaders*.

I told Lindsay that I had no intention of editing commercials. Lindsay was outraged. He knew that I'd been offered some lucrative jobs in that field.

'Well,' Lindsay said leaning away from me as light returned from the screen, 'you may end up a better person, but you won't end up a better editor.'

18

On the Edge of Uncertainty

In Lindsay's kitchen, I made mugs of instant coffee. I took them through to Lindsay and his writer, David Sherwin. Sherwin was effusively polite and thanked me twice. He was so nervy, he had the jitters.

'Can't you get it into your head that you're writing a screenplay, not a book?' Lindsay muttered as he scratched out part of a long speech and slapped a page on the low round table beside him.

Gingerly, Sherwin picked up the page and nodded as he scrutinized it.

Lindsay snatched the page out of Sherwin's hand and gave it to me, telling me to read it. I read it. Lindsay's trimming had made it far more effective. I said so.

'You see,' Lindsay cooed. 'If Ian likes it that means it's passable. Ian does know a bit about film.'

'But who is Ian?' Sherwin grinned at me, and fiddled with his glasses.

'Ian's just here,' Lindsay sighed. 'God alone knows what his role is. You know he turned down a job cutting commercials, against my advice.'

'Good for him,' Sherwin smiled at me, and lit a cigarette.

'Not good for him,' Lindsay said and complained about his coffee.

I said that he'd better go and make his own.

'Do you have any idea of what a commercials editor can earn?' Lindsay addressed Sherwin. 'A lot more than the piddling amounts you and I get.'

'Lindsay, aren't you two supposed to be working?' I asked.

'Here,' Lindsay handed me a copy of the script, 'you can go home and read it. We'll meet at the Curzon tonight.'

'Can I come to the screening?' Sherwin interjected.

'No, you can't,' Lindsay got out of his chair, yawned, stretched and put on a record of liturgical music from a John Ford western.

'That's for your inspiration. Forget about seeing films, and get on with the writing.'

Lindsay shut his eyes for a moment and rocked back and forth soaking in the music.

'Do you think you could write a western?' Lindsay asked me without opening his eyes and waving his arms.

I told him that the western I had written was scheduled to be on television shortly.

'When is it on?' Sherwin asked with interest, spilling ash as he aimed his cigarette at the ash tray.

'I'll be busy unless you can assure me that it's as good as a John Ford western,' Lindsay stated.

'I couldn't say that,' I laughed.

'Of course not,' Lindsay snarled. 'You're not a dope like Sherwin. He'd say something idiotic like that. Wouldn't you, David? You'd say that you could write a brilliant western, wouldn't you?'

Sherwin giggled.

I said goodbye to Sherwin. We shook hands and I followed Lindsay out of the room. 'He really can be a pain,' Lindsay moaned as he led me along the dark corridor to his front door.

Outside the sky was grey, and it was almost dark. There was a chill in the air but it didn't seem to worry Lindsay as we stood outside and chatted amidst the garbage cans.

'We don't have to go tonight,' I said.

'We must put in an appearance,' he insisted. 'Quite a coup, Stephen getting his first film on at the Curzon, and in the company of Truffaut. Mind you I wouldn't count on the Truffaut being much good.' Lindsay paused. 'Has Stephen thanked you?'

'He doesn't have to do that, does he?' I asked.

'You think the critics will write about *The Burning*?' Lindsay asked.

'I think so, and because it's on at the Curzon, critics will take note of it. It's a good cinema and the South African struggle is becoming fashionable.'

It was starting to drizzle. I hurried to the number thirty-one bus, hoping to miss the downpour.

There was a good turnout of familiar faces at the Curzon. Stephen was surrounded by people with Mary-Kay, his wife, hovering to the side and looking sceptical. Roland the writer approached me, fearful of meeting Lindsay. Karel Reisz and other worthies had turned up to support Stephen as much as to see Truffaut's *The Bride Wore Black*. I saw Lindsay going over to Stephen. People made way for Lindsay like the waves parting.

I collected our tickets from the box office and shoved my way towards Lindsay. Seeing that I had the tickets, he wished Stephen well and we went into the auditorium. Lindsay complained that, as usual, I'd got seats too near the front. I did not apologize.

It was the biggest screen on which I'd seen *The Burning*. That in itself was a thrill. Some of the film still creaked along irredeemably. But, all in all, I was far from displeased. I was convinced that it went down well.

After the screening Lindsay excused us from the crowd round Stephen, and we stepped out into the night.

'Italian?' Lindsay asked me. 'I'm paying.'

'Italian's great,' I replied, 'and your script is

nothing short of brilliant.'

'You should've seen it when it first came to me. Now, try say something more intelligent about it.'

'I don't think there's been anything like it, not from England,' I enthused. 'Did you go to a public school like that, did you lead a rebellion like in the script?'

'I only wanted to,' Lindsay chuckled as we strolled along the back streets towards Soho. It was too expensive to eat in Mayfair.

We entered Biancis in Frith Street. Elena, who'd run the restaurant for years, welcomed us and told Lindsay that there was a table upstairs. I greeted some people I knew. In their midst was Roy, evidently negotiating his future in life after the Beatles.

'Who were those people who greeted you downstairs?' Lindsay asked me after we'd taken our seats.

'From commercials,' I told him.

'Oh my God!' Lindsay exclaimed and poured me some red wine.

The critics weren't at all kind about Truffaut's latest. But, though the reviews of *The Burning* were brief, they were all praising.

Having read *The Crusaders*, I was staggered both by the fluent economy of the writing and by the whole idea. It was about rebellion and I had to be on it. But in what capacity? Stephen was going to be Lindsay's personal assistant for the shoot. Also, no production date had been mentioned.

About a month later, Lindsay intimated that his project was on the move. The script was finished and pre-production loomed close. A

production deal was being negotiated with a subsidiary of CBS. Lindsay said nothing specific about my involvement. I was on standby.

Roy Benson contacted me. He wanted to commission me to write a film outline which would be right up my alley.

'A mystic thriller,' Roy said. 'The paranormal.'

Roy's partner in the venture was John Poyner. Inviting me to his home, Poyner uncovered the Oscar he'd won as sound editor on the *Dirty Dozen*.

The ingredients were a seance, a psychic, hints of the dead returning, murder and mystery. I visited a psychic in Chiswick. He was a neat little man with a bow tie. He saw an aura round me and told me that Sir Alexander Korda was watching over me. The visit got me started on my writing journey into the paranormal.

Roy and I wanted the project one way. Poyner had other ideas. The result was hollow and tepid. I got paid, but the script went nowhere.

It was a Sunday 14 January 1968 and *Living in Harmony* was on television. I'd made no plans to see it. The memories still hurt. I didn't want to smell my failure rubbed in my face. Knowing I had no television, Roland telephone and insisted I come round.

Roland and Jim, his sunny blond Californian lover, fed me and got me plastered in their recently acquired, swish basement flat in Sheffield Terrace, off Kensington Church Street. In a well-fed, alcoholic haze, I watched *Living in Harmony*. Again, it was a painful ordeal. I felt too removed from it to have an opinion, I told Roland. All I could see was an unhappy memory. Nevertheless, the explicit sadism I thought even more revolting than when I'd seen it at MGM.

'For God's sake, what have you got to complain about?' Roland screeched. 'Your name will appear in the States from coast to coast.' Convinced that I was on my way, he poured me another whisky.

Literary agent Jonathan Clowes read my African epic, *Warriors of the Assegai*, set before the arrival of the white man in Africa. It was a folkloric epic adventure. Over lunch, Clowes told me how he'd met Len Deighton at a party and left with his unpublished manuscript. He'd got it published and acquired other writers, including Doris Lessing. That's how he got started. He offered to take me on.

'It'll take you a long time and you'll have to be better than good,' he warned me.

A deal had been struck, and the title changed. *The Crusaders* was out and *If....* was in, but with four dots, Lindsay stated emphatically. The title suggestion was made by Daph. The film was to be made by Memorial, with Michael Medwin producing.

'Tell me Ian,' Medwin asked. 'Are you going to edit *If....*?'

'I don't think so,' I told Medwin about my refusal to do a stint in commercials.

'We may have the editor,' Lindsay told me. 'You'd better meet Gladwell and see what you make of him.'

I met the bearded David Gladwell in a pub. He was keen to cut for Lindsay but was worried.

'I've no features experience, only documentaries, but it's all film. Lindsay said that you knew all about features.'

Gladwell's dour exterior, I learned later,

actually hid a mordant wit, and a sometimes willingness to laugh. Prior to film, he'd been an art teacher. He'd also known Lindsay for years but found him deeply unnerving.

It was settled. I was to be the First Assistant.

'I was over at Memorial and they talked about Lindsay as the "Master",' Gladwell shook his head. 'I can't be doing with any of that.'

I laughed, telling him that I didn't think it was essential.

'A lot of people refer to him that way,' I said, 'but not to his face.'

'That's a relief,' Gladwell polished off his half-pint and said he had to get back to the documentary he was cutting.

I went into Memorial to settle my deal with American-accented Gavrick Losey, the production manager. Gavrick's father, the director Joseph Losey, had relocated his career to England in the wake of the McCarthy witch hunt in Hollywood, in the 1950s. He'd never gone back. Losey junior was slightly built with small dark eyes, and played the big tough guy.

'You realize it's low budget,' Gavrick said brusquely.

I said that I did.

Gavrick then began a spiel about the limits of the production money.

'Nothing will be on the cheap, but everything will have to go for the minimum.'

I cut him short.

'Just tell me what you've got budgeted.'

He told me; and I said that was fine.

As I emerged from Gavrick's office, Lindsay was waiting for me. He grabbed my arm and pushed me into an empty office, shutting the door behind him.

'Now did you get a fair deal?' he demanded. 'I don't want you to sell yourself short just to work with me.'

I said it was all fine. He had a surprise for me.

'Never could make up my mind about Gladwell,' Lindsay mused. 'Can't tell what's going on behind that beard. Could be nothing and one still couldn't tell. Well, it doesn't matter,' Lindsay concluded. 'That's your department now.'

Since she'd helped me on my BFI film, Miriam Brickman had become a friend. She invited me to the Royal Court Theatre in Sloane Square to see *Twelfth Night*, with Malcolm McDowell playing Sebastian. He was under consideration for the lead in *If....* which Miriam was the casting.

Malcolm didn't walk across the stage, he swaggered and strutted. He didn't care two hoots for anything. Miriam was convinced that Malcolm was the one. I had doubts. Malcolm seemed so extraordinarily relaxed, I couldn't see him mustering the discipline for anything. It turned out that Lindsay had already made up his mind.

From the start Malcolm was talking back to Lindsay, but with an almost immediate affection. Malcolm was popular all round. There was no side to him and he possessed a fine sense of the absurd. This might have been the main connection between him and Lindsay. There was a definite electricity between them.

Having settled on most of his cast, Lindsay concluded crewing up technicians. One of the last to be taken on was the head of wardrobe,

my friend Shura.

'You sure she's not too trendy for me?' Lindsay asked sceptically; but he gave her the job anyway.

Arrangements had been made to get Miroslav Ondriceck, Milos Forman's lighting cameraman, over from Prague. This was inevitably going to complicate production: Miroslav, known as Mirek, spoke no English and Lindsay spoke no Czech.

However, even getting permission for Mirek to come over and light *If....* was no easy matter, under the closed-shop policy maintained by our trade union, ACTT. To make it possible for Mirek to work on the film, a standby British technician would have to be employed.

Lindsay had little sympathy for the trade union. They were a bunch of Stalinists, he complained, led by an arch-bureaucrat who chewed big cigars. This was my pal, Alan Sapper, ACTT General Secretary and later President of the TUC.

'If anything goes wrong with getting Mirek over,' Lindsay warned me, 'it'll be up to you to sort it out with your union connections. I don't see how you could be friends with someone like Sapper.'

Prior to the technician's union, Alan Sapper had been general secretary of the Screen Writers Guild. That was during the time when George Markstein was a prominent member. They had been friends.

One dubbing editor had made a direct approach to Lindsay. But I wanted my, old pal, Alan Bell. I'd already introduced him to Gladwell. The meeting had gone well.

'Yes, but doesn't he drink?' Lindsay had questioned my choice.

'They all do, because it's such a boring job. It's par for the course,' I countered. 'Alan Bell, at least, is more sensitive and intelligent. He'll bring something extra. You can talk to him.'

I knew I was right. Bell was about the best around. But Lindsay was also right. Bell liked his beer.

I'd spent some weekends at Bell's house on the outskirts of Rye, an unusually picturesque little town on the Sussex coast. Bell owned a large, motorized catamaran. We went for a spin along the coast in a haze of alcohol, as a result of visiting most of the seventeen twee pubs in Rye. It was the first English town I'd seen with so many cobbled streets. With us was Bell's friend, a dubbing assistant, the notorious Johnny Lee. He had a mouth like a swirling sewer and a gut to match. He was built like a tank and was continuously either on the make or on the take. Johnny was born a gypsy, and unquestionably one of the most colourful, cutting room characters around. I liked Johnny. You knew exactly what he was and where you were with him. I hoped that Bell would bring him onto the film. I was sure that Lindsay would take to him.

Lindsay had his unit; cast and crew. Set construction was underway at various locations with the minimum amount in a studio. Some of this was at Twickenham. Lindsay had no liking for the studio system and its kind of filmmaking.

Everything was ready to go.

Ten days before the camera was to turn over, the CBS subsidiary pulled out. CBS was the network that had purchased the rebellious *Prisoner*. I could not fathom why they had backed the one and now pulled out of the other. Their motivation only became apparent to me when they banned *Living in Harmony*. This, it transpired, was too rebellious for the American palate. With the unwinnable situation in Vietnam dawning, the American psyche was near incapable of sanctioning rebellion against the establishment, even if it was set in England, as was the case with *If....*

I was amazed at how Lindsay took the CBS pull-out in his stride. He wasn't surprised. Medwin was in a flap and got onto the phone to speak to Albert Finney, in New York rehearsing for an opening on Broadway.

Medwin caught the next flight out, met with Albert and went to see Charlie Bludhorn, the head of Gulf and Western, the oil company which had just bought Paramount Pictures. Something was promised about Albert doing something for Paramount and *If....* was back on schedule.

We were now under the aegis of a Hollywood major. I liked the idea of that. It made the movie seem more like a movie.

19

The Director And The Editor

There was a slight undercurrent that we would be working on something so radically anti-establishment that it could have dangerous repercussions. It was the mood of the times. It was the end of February 1968, the year of violent protest. The threat of the authorities clamping down was never far away. The memory of the Profumo scandal had not been forgotten. It had toppled a Prime Minister. The prime suspect, Stephen Ward, had met a suspicious death after his arrest. It was never openly investigated. It was brushed under the carpet in the way that I associated with South Africa and not with England. Now, here, the authorities appeared to have done as they pleased. If the film turned out as potent as Lindsay intended it to be, how dangerous would it be? How would the establishment deal with subversion in the present climate of disaffection with the state?

Lindsay wanted to cut the film safe from prying eyes and snooping visitors: in other words, away from the studios and away from Wardour Street.

After scouting round for suitable premises we decided on Sound Associates, a recently opened post-production house in Redan Place, a narrow side street off Queensway. Opposite Sound Associates' entrance was Whiteleys, then a large, run-down department store. Its only apparent virtue was that it sold proper coffee; but by now I'd got my coffee habit under control. I was down to just a couple a day.

Our cutting room was on the ground floor, along a narrow corridor right at the back. No one walked past our door. We were suitably cut off from the other productions. Our windows opened onto a small alleyway and a high brick wall. There was nothing to look at.

'Excellent,' Lindsay observed when he popped in to see the cutting room. 'Not much room for distraction.'

'Not much room for anything,' Gladwell mumbled.

'How sweet,' Ellis the second assistant remarked with a snigger as he came in. He flopped into a swivel chair and asked where the numbering room was.

'Right here,' I said slapping a low table. 'The machine's being delivered later today.'

'Going to be a bit crowded,' Gladwell muttered, as he played with the moviola.

'But it will be cosy,' Ellis laughed.

Gladwell, Ellis and I settled into our semi-isolation. For the eight-week duration of the shooting schedule, and another couple of months afterwards, this was where we'd be. Then it would be open ended as to exactly when we transferred to Soho for the dub. Lindsay had said that he wanted to prolong our stay out of Soho for as long as possible. I wasn't too happy about that. It was much easier for me to get from home to work in Soho.

Medwin came in, following Lindsay and praising our locality.

'It's got some good restaurants,' he said. 'There's a lovely Bertorelli's just on the other side of Whiteleys. There's Indian, Greek and Chinese to name but a few.'

'And what makes you think that the editors will have time for leisurely lunches?' Lindsay snapped, turning on Medwin.

'Lins, we all have to eat,' protested Medwin, backing away from Lindsay. 'You'll have working lunches.'

'No we won't, we'll be in the cutting room,' Lindsay said, peering over my shoulder at the large chart I was making. 'That's why we're not in Soho,' he said as he traced his index finger up and down the columns of scene descriptions.

'It's bound to change. Aren't you overdoing it?'

I lifted the celluloid sheet from the card and rubbed off some chinagraph writing.

'Comes off rather easily,' Lindsay complained, and then turned round as there was a knock at the door. 'Oh my God, what is this?' he demanded.

'Humphries delivery,' a man in a long, white, buttoned coat wheeled in a cartload of glistening thousand foot cans and asked me to sign for it. 'Got your leaders and spacing in the top two cans.'

As the man left with his empty trolley, Lindsay turned to me.

'We haven't even started shooting and you're already spending money.' He looked at Medwin. 'You're the producer; what do you have to say?'

'I'm sure that Ian knows what he's doing,' Medwin chortled.

'Well I don't know about any of you, but I'm off to lunch with our producer,' Lindsay announced. 'I imagine you chaps are all too busy.'

I put on my jacket and we all traipsed out, locking the cutting room door behind us. Lindsay handed me his bundle of paperwork.

'Carry that and make yourself useful,' Lindsay turned to Medwin. 'What about Bertorelli's?' We stopped as Lindsay bent to tie a shoelace.

'If Ian booked,' Medwin glanced at me.

Having tied the lace, Lindsay snatched his papers away from me.

'Of course he did, unless he's got somewhere cranky to inflict on us.'

As we entered Bertorelli's I asked Lindsay to pack it up, he was going on too much. Out of the corner of my eye, I caught Gladwell and Ellis exchanging looks. As we sat down, Gladwell murmured to me.

'Bit of a palaver, isn't it?'

'Isn't our producer looking particularly sartorial today?' Lindsay waved his hand across the table at Medwin.

I said that I liked his beige, checked jacket.

'You could do a lot worse, Ian, than picking up a few tips from our producer on how to dress,' Lindsay put a mock smile on his face and turned to the waiter. 'What's good on the menu today?'

Back in the cutting room, the lunch was talked about. Was Lindsay always like that? Did Medwin have a clue about what was going on? Gladwell had balked at the way in which Lindsay went on at me.

'Rather you than me,' Gladwell shook his head. 'I wouldn't put up with it.'

Ellis shook with laughter. He thought it was all great fun.

Filming began. Tuesday morning at six o'clock, Gladwell and I were at Humphries, to see the first rushes with Lindsay and Miroslav. Overnight, the negative had been processed and a print struck. The labs didn't usually provide screening facilities for rushes but our contact man, Les Ostinelli, had made special arrangements. Having met Lindsay and Mirek, Ostinelli had quickly got the drift of what kind of customers they'd be. Ostinelli, with his whining drawl, was the doyen of lab contacts.

As I sat waiting, I unfolded my *Magnus, Robot Fighter* comic.

I heard a squeal and looked up. Mirek was standing over me and pointing at my comic. His interpreter informed me that he was very pleased to see me reading a comic.

'Put that rubbish away,' Lindsay made a derisory noise, moaned and sat down.

The lights went down and the picture came up on screen.

Mirek was not happy. He wanted to see it all in colour and not just the master shots. Lindsay said it was too costly. As the lights in the screening room went on, Ostinelli walked in. He said he was sure we could come to some arrangement about having more colour rushes with not much added cost. Colour cost three times as much as black and white film stock.

Lindsay asked Gladwell what he thought of the rushes. Gladwell said that he had nothing to say.

'We'll have to hear how it sounds and how it cuts together,' he added wryly.

'That won't be for a while,' Lindsay said. 'I can't direct and cut at the same time.'

Lindsay turned to me and asked if I had anything to say.

I said I had nothing to say.

'Say something!'

'After it's synched up,' I said to him.

'Comics, comics!' Mirek flung his arms up and laughed heartily as he followed Lindsay towards the door.

'Ian,' Lindsay called me over. He wanted to make sure that I charged overtime for coming so early to the labs.

I said I would.

'And there's no need for you and Gladwell both to get in here so early,' Lindsay said. 'One of you is enough. You needn't take him everywhere.' Then he walked out.

Medwin appeared, disappointed that he'd missed Lindsay.

'Has Lins been giving Ian a tough time?'

'I'd say it was the other way round,' Gladwell observed.

In the second week of shooting, Gladwell and I went down to watch the filming on location at Cheltenham College. The March weather seemed oblivious to that fact that it was nearly spring. It was bitter and standing round watching Lindsay shooting the school rugby match was not fun, as Gladwell said. We'd come just to put in an appearance and Gladwell felt we'd been in the cold long enough.

'Cut!' Lindsay shouted.

The first assistant director yelled the instructions for the next set-up while listening to Mirek via the lady interpreter.

Lindsay marched briskly over to us. He greeted Gladwell politely and started criticising my clothes. I was wearing my new, thigh-length, leather jacket, and a light, florid yellow scarf. He didn't approve.

'You really go off the rails when it comes to clothes,' he said.

I grabbed the edge of Lindsay's faded tartan scarf.

'Do you call this style?' I said tugging.

Medwin came over rubbing his hands for warmth.

'That's a nice jacket, Ian,' Medwin chortled.

Lindsay pulled me away and pointed along the side of the school hall looming over us. It was a large old structure with thick sloping buttresses between long windows of coloured glass.

'There!'

I looked at Shura swathed in a black cape crouching and whacking clothes on the ground to make them look worn.

'Your friend,' Lindsay chuckled. 'Isn't she a sight? She looks like one of the witches from Macbeth,' Lindsay paused thoughtfully. 'When you first meet her she's quite impressive, but I'm still waiting to see something inventive coming out of her. Is she as intelligent as she tries to appear?'

'Isn't she working out okay?' I interrupted Lindsay.

'I suppose so, I wouldn't really know,' Lindsay laughed. 'Oh well, I'd better get back.'

Gladwell said he hoped we could now leave. As we started walking off, Lindsay called us back. Saying we should earn our keep, he pushed me towards the end of the line of extras. Gladwell and I joined the crowd of school visitors watching the rugby.

'If the camera picks us up,' Gladwell said waving an arm and pretending to cheer. 'I'll cut us out.'

'Come on chaps, a bit more cheering. Think of House,' Medwin said, sliding in behind us. 'It's what Lins expects.'

After another week of struggling to keep himself busy, Gladwell was seriously bored with just looking at film. He wanted to start cutting. I suggested that he just carry on looking at material, get to know it and avoid cutting until Lindsay said he should.

'Is that what feature editors are supposed to do?'

I said that it was not the way in which other directors might work. But Lindsay was making his film his way, irrespective of what others might think. Most directors cut as they went along. None dared, or were permitted, to wait until the end of shooting. Gladwell was bored and determined to show Lindsay what he could do.

Gladwell selected the longest sequence that had already been covered. However, what made perfect sense on the scripted page revealed no visible coherence as rushes. The daily continuity sheets had minimal cutting instructions. No one but Lindsay could comprehend the inherent dramatic structure. It was probably the challenge of this that lured Gladwell like a moth to a flame. He was confident that he could make something of it.

Gladwell worked away steadily and efficiently. He had a feel for handling film; that was apparent.

This was the sequence under the joiner:

The school cadet corps was out in full force, in uniform and with their weapons but no bullets. Boys took turns at bayonet stabbing with the fervent yell of hate. Squads paraded across the fields. The Chaplain and the new teacher dished out tea and sandwiches.

Suddenly the tea urn was riddled with bullet holes. Everyone took cover. The unarmed Chaplain strode through the grass towards the hidden rebels, calling for surrender.

Travis, the rebel leader played by McDowell, got up out of the grass and shot the Chaplain.

In the oak panelled Headmaster's office, the rebel boys were admonished for their behaviour and warned about the hairy dangers of the present age.

The Headmaster opened a cupboard drawer and up sat the Chaplain, to accept the rebels' handshake of apology.

The poetic surrealism ordering this part of the film was implied in the script and in the continuity sheets, but to realize the sequence required an insight into Lindsay's mind.

Gladwell's brazen disobedience placed me in an invidious position.

When I said that the cut didn't look good, Gladwell told me that was because it was badly directed.

'I could do better,' he insisted.

I duly informed Lindsay about the edited reel. He was livid.

'You know I don't want him cutting a frame without me,' Lindsay scowled. 'Why didn't you stop him?'

'Lindsay I did try, but he's the editor,' I answered feebly.

'So that's what it comes down to,' Lindsay raged, in full tantrum. 'Don't you have a brain in your head? Can't you do what must be done?'

'He wants to show you what he's cut,' I said.

'Is it any good?'

'You better see it for yourself,' I replied evasively.

'What?' Lindsay yelled. 'I'll see it with you, but not with Gladwell.'

Lindsay was only available on a Sunday. I made a booking and arranged for a projectionist at double time.

The cut sequence was under ten minutes long and fitted onto one reel.

After it had been projected, the lights went on in the viewing theatre.

Lindsay turned slowly to face me.

'What do you make of it?' he sneered.

'I can see that it doesn't work,' I answered, 'and I can see that it will.'

'What are you going to do about it?' Lindsay erupted in fury. 'Don't try and tell me that it's not your fault. You'll have to fire him.'

'Lindsay, it'll turn out perfectly okay,' I said. 'He can rejoin everything back to rushes. That'll keep him busy until you're ready for him. He won't let you down.'

'Well, it's your job that will be on the line,' Lindsay warned me. 'It's your responsibility.'

The door to the screening room opened, as if on cue.

'Everything all right, chaps?' Medwin's head popped in around the door. 'What about a spot of food. Brand new cuisine, called Tandoori. What about it, Lins?'

Further along the schedule, Lindsay would worry about the sword fight sequence. Malcolm, driven into a corner, slumped on the floor held up the palm of his hand. It had been cut. It was the first blood.

Lindsay gave his directions over the phone. Gladwell cut the sequence. Lindsay was impressed, though he hardly said so. Gladwell had kept his job but the chemistry between director and editor was never going to be good.

As for me, I'd flitted along, severely off balance and in constant uncertainty about every aspect of the job except one: that the film was going to be worth it. There was no doubt of this.

Frames from *If....* One of the scenes which troubled the South African Censor.

20

Shades Of Number One

A couple of weeks before the end of the two-month shooting schedule, we expanded into another cutting room on the opposite side of our corridor. This was for bushy-faced and cheery Alan Bell, the dubbing editor, and his assistant Jones.

'Where's Johnny Lee?' I asked.

'He'll be coming on for footsteps and FX. Right now he's in the pub, where we should be.' Bell laughed and put on his jacket. 'When Lindsay's around, I'll tell him that the film looks terrific. The sound's good, won't need much post-sync.' Bell laughed again. 'And that's why we can slope off to the pub.'

'It really is rather good,' Jones said.

Bell soon proved to be reliable and made intelligent suggestions. But he did spend a lot of time in the pub.

By the time the shooting schedule ended, all the floor to ceiling racks in our room were packed with film cans, meticulously labelled by Ellis. What wall space remained was covered with a pin board and a large chart of sequence summaries and file reference numbers.

After throwing a few bits and pieces Gladwell's way, Lindsay finally authorized him to get on with the cutting. Gladwell grumbled about lost time, then got on with it.

When the shooting schedule was over, at the beginning of May, Lindsay moved into the cutting room full time. His authoritative presence had a familiar ring to it for me. The cutting room became an outpost of the Village. Within its four walls, the director was a monarch. If Lindsay was Number One, I was a contender for the post of Number Two. I relished being in the heart of the battle. Number One demanded freedom of creation. Number Two ensured that he got what he wanted in his relentless, anti-establishment role.

Despite our initial bid for seclusion from the outside world, actors, critics and admirers were constantly in and out of the cutting room.

Lindsay had an extensive fan list and they were all welcome. Malcolm was around a lot. Visitors seeking an audience poured through our door; and Lindsay delighted in the constant attention.

Lindsay would swan about, making a communal venture out of the editing process, roping in all and sundry to watch the editing and voice opinions. Gut response was what he demanded. There was a complete absence of the usual film hierarchy; but you had to have an opinion and Lindsay had to know.

Lindsay claimed a space on the side of the chart where he kept a list of whomsoever he was unhappy with; this was the hate list. On reaching the top, the individual named was fired. With the film now in post-production, Lindsay was running short of names.

Gladwell's ability to concentrate in that cutting room environment was amazing. He never objected to the endless telephone calls and Lindsay's unending stream of visitors. Lindsay insisted that all visitors peer over the editor's shoulder. Gladwell never openly complained.

Almost magically, the film started coming together. It was evident that If.... was no ordinary film. Sparse though the script may have been, and low though the shooting ratio was, everything seemed to be there once Lindsay was actively at the helm. The detail of the cutting had all been meticulously predetermined.

The field day cadet sequence, with Lindsay's cutting direction, emerged perfectly understandable and effective. Gladwell had missed the logic entirely. So had I. Only with Lindsay did it all make sense.

Of all the sequences in the film, for me one stood head and shoulders above the rest.

It consisted of a bunch of schoolboys dashing along a corridor with coat tails and ties flapping behind them, all in slow motion and in black and white. The boys ran out of a school building and floated slowly, lyrical and elegiac, across the quadrangle.

Lying on the cobblestones the Matron, in a starched white nurses uniform, held up her arms out as the boys fell into her embrace.

It was the most poetic sequence in the whole film.

'I'm sorry Ian,' Lindsay said. 'I know it's your favourite, but it has to go. It doesn't belong. It slows the narrative down. It's too dreamy. Possibly it might have stayed in if If.... was *Zéro de Conduite*'. This film by Jean Vigo was considered by all of us to be a major French classic.

Gladwell deleted the sequence.

Seeing the assembly without the sequence, it became obvious what Lindsay meant. Its presence had disrupted the unity of the film. I was reminded of the scene he had eliminated from *The Burning*.

Gladwell could not relax with Lindsay. Whenever he was on the phone with Lindsay, Gladwell got the jitters. His voice rose, and he couldn't stand still or stop fidgeting. This didn't occur when they were face to face.

The film had pronounced visual limitations. It was static, as if it had been composed with the proscenium arch in mind rather than a moving camera.

One set-up, however, had precisely the right visual tenor. This was the theft of the motorbike from a showroom by Travis and his blond co-conspirator, Johnny. The sequence soared because of the way in which it was shot, but it was the only time that the film was so alive and graphically sensitive.

Stephen told me that, while assisting on the set, he had been surprised how Lindsay had questioned nothing of what Mirek did. Lindsay hardly looked through the lens. He left it all to the lighting cameraman. Lindsay wanted to concentrate on the acting; and he poured his entire being into that process. Lindsay Anderson was an actor's dream; whereas, for technicians, he was often a complete nightmare.

Filmmaking was for Lindsay, overloaded with technical demands. Stephen said that what made Lindsay's film work so significant was his impeccable sense of structure. Stephen related this to Lindsay's having taken Classics degree at Oxford.

Roy Baird, our executive producer, hit the number one spot on Lindsay's hate list. Lindsay selected me to deliver the bad news.

I hopped in a taxi and went up to Memorial Films. I found Roy in his office. He was cleaning out his desk and packing up his things. My message did not need to be delivered. He was off to a film at Pinewood Studios where, he said, he could rely on things being done professionally. Roy had found Lindsay intolerable because he had to have his finger in everything.

'He has to have control over everything,' Roy complained. 'He can't stand anyone else sharing control with him. How you getting on with the shit?'

I said I was getting on well with Lindsay. Roy looked at me blankly for a moment, then shook my hand and said that it was good to meet me.

I returned to the cutting room. Gladwell was standing beside the movieola. Lindsay was seated on one of the three swivel chairs.

"Eight minutes is a long time," Gladwell repeated a line from the sequence he had been cutting. 'It doesn't make sense to me. Does it mean anything?'

Lindsay glanced round the room waiting for someone to make a comment.

Medwin hunched his shoulders unknowingly.

Lindsay looked at me. 'You'd better explain it, Ian.'

The sequence under discussion concerned Travis and his co-plotters. Having just discovered live ammunition, they were pondering on what to do. They talked about death, their reasons, how to die and time in a mystical sense. One of the trio remarked that in India, someone died of starvation every eight minutes.

Malcolm, as Travis, holding up a live bullet, says very slowly: 'Eight minutes is a long time.'

'It means,' I said, answering Lindsay, 'that a revolution could happen in eight seconds or eight years. The span of time doesn't matter. It would happen when the moment was right. The time spent plotting was irrelevant.'

Lindsay nodded, crossed the room to the telephone and called David Sherwin, the writer. There was a pause, then Lindsay exploded.

'For God's sake, have you been drinking barley wine this early?'

Every conversation Lindsay had on the telephone was overheard. He spoke clearly and at high volume. Only the single-minded Gladwell managed not to listen. Nothing seemed likely to throw him. He was a relentless workhorse; and the cutting was going well.

After the sequence in which Travis and Johnny stole the motorbike, they stopped at an isolated roadside café. As they entered the café, the film changed from colour to black and white. Here Malcolm gave an electric performance and met his match. They selected a record on the jukebox, the 'Sanctus' from the *Misa Luba*, music which Malcolm had suggested. It accentuated the eerie atmosphere.

The solitary waitress, a girl with no name, was played by Christine Noonan. Her long black hair, voluptuous figure and huge, dark eyes lured Malcolm into her domain. This was where violence and passion intertwined. The scene was redolent with simmering sexuality.

The girl purred seductively about her eyes being as large as a tiger's. She taunted and tempted the truant schoolboy, while Johnny watched with dreamy envy.

Malcolm was not expecting the sudden whack across the cheek that Christine delivered on a first take. It nearly tore his head off, but it threw him into a suitable frenzy.

On screen, Christine and Malcolm both radiated great warmth and sensuality. All clothing vanished as, naked with passion, Travis and the girl clawed and entwined, rolling onto the floor.

Malcolm didn't fancy people catching sight of his uncensored genitals. The viewing of rushes from the naked scenes was restricted. I alerted the projectionists to make sure that no one

sneaked into the box to take a peek. Nudity could be an offence; and the film censor was far from powerless. The law had taken no notice of the wider social changes afoot.

Another sexual uncertainty involved the wife of a new schoolmaster strolling naked along a row of enamel washbasins in an empty boy's shower room. The woman was naked and shot full-frontal. In the event, this got by the censor. With male nudity, the censor was considerably less tolerant. Nevertheless, about a year later, Ken Russell's *Women in Love* made the history books. Alan Bates and Oliver Reed wrestled naked in the mud. Shura was in charge of costumes.

When Gladwell suggested altering a cut by three frames, Lindsay was outraged. All cuts had to be by even numbers, he told us. This was his intuitive sense; and nothing could deflect him. When Gladwell erred into the realm of the odd number, Lindsay would magically detect that something was amiss. One frame was only one twenty-fourth of a second on the screen; but it mattered. The initial cut, however, was not governed by the evenness rule. I was never asked to count the frames of an entire shot; but, in the changes, evenness was paramount. Oddity was out.

On *The Prisoner*, McGoohan's rather different fixation with numbers had found expression both on screen and off.

About the time that Lindsay was dropping odds for evens when chopping off frames, McGoohan was into the application of numerical mysticism. The writer of the episode *Schizoid Man*, Terence Feely, would tell this story about McGoohan's obsession with numbers.

Terence and David Tomblin had hooked up with McGoohan as writer and producer on two post-*Prisoner* films financed by Lew Grade's ITC. One was a thriller about a retired agent settling in Ireland and getting involved with the IRA. The other was to be a screen adaptation of *Brand* by Ibsen.

At one of their production meetings in Pat's office at MGM, Terence and Tomblin came in and heard McGoohan mutter something.

'What did you say, Pat?' Terence enquired.

'It's not the magic number,' Pat replied.

Bemused, Tomblin and Terence looked at each other.

'What's not the magic number?' Terence asked.

'Nine-hundred thousand is not the magic number,' McGoohan explained. 'It has to be a million,' he said emphatically.

Lew Grade had given them £900,000 to make the two films. Both men pointed out that that was enough of a budget to make both films. They didn't need a million.

'It has to be a million. Otherwise it's no good,' Pat insisted.

Terence pointed out that it was crazy. Pat should accept what they had. They didn't need more. The reactions to *The Prisoner* had not been at all good, he argued, so why jeopardize what was already in the bag? Commercially McGoohan was no longer in such a viable position. Why sink the ship with unnecessarily quirky demands?

'Lew Grade treats me like a son,' Pat said

confidently. 'He'll give me the million. He'll understand.'

In the event, Lew Grade refused to increase the odd figure to an even million. McGoohan flipped. He jumped onto Grade's desk, ranting and throwing things off the desk around the room.

Neither of the two films got made and McGoohan went to live in Switzerland.

I came into the cutting room and found Lindsay alone. He was staring intently at a copy of *The Daily Telegraph*. A huge photograph covered almost half the front page. It was of the student rebellion in Paris. At a glance, it could have been lifted straight out of our film.

I laced up the last reel of the assembly where the rebels are firing down and throwing molotov cocktails. The newspaper photo showed the French students on rooftops throwing molotov cocktails. The film and the paper could be interchangeable at this scene. They were almost identical. Even the clothing looked the same. The pitch of the roofs, the gathering of the smoke were no different. It was uncanny. What was fiction in March had become fact in May.

It was exhilarating, a feeling that I was so much a part of the world stage. I wanted that sense of being close to the pulse of events. I'd felt it on *The Prisoner*. Now I felt it on *If....* Two recent events had left me feeling uncomfortably irrelevant. In April, the government minister Enoch Powell had delivered his 'Rivers of Blood' racist speech. A few weeks before, the Rev Martin Luther King had been assassinated in Memphis.

The concern that drove me towards political

films also sent me to hear Pablo Neruda reading at the Roundhouse in Chalk Farm.

Neruda was a total exemplar of the political artist. As part of the liberal intelligentsia, he was automatically a target for Chile's dictatorial regime. Fleeing Pinochet's security forces, Neruda was helped by Chilean country people, many of whom may not have read or even heard of his poems. This experience politicized both Neruda and his writing. His lyric verses became charged by activism. Later, when the democratically elected Allende came to power, Neruda was appointed ambassador to France. A few years later, he was awarded the Nobel prize for Literature.

The setting of the Roundhouse seemed particularly suitable. The rough-hewn edge of decay created a welcoming ambience for the nonconformist spirit of the time: the perfect place for a dissident voice to be aired.

Neruda was a rotund, elegant, unassuming man who read easily and with impressively casual confidence. The place was packed and his delivery was received with rapt attention. The translations were read by the South African actor who had played the chauffeur beaten to death in *The Burning*.

After a show at the Roundhouse, what it was I can't recall, I bumped into George Markstein and his little daughter. He was as affable and chatty as ever. He'd heard about my involvement with the series after he'd left. He assured me that if he had still been around, he would have taken care of my interests. He was appalled that I had given away my residuals. He'd had similar problems with other writers on the series. He was very sympathetic and said that what had happened to

me had more or less happened to him. He was unhappy about *The Prisoner* but not embittered. Both of us were wronged, he concluded. I hadn't seen it quite like that until George made it clear. We shook hands. He went his way and I went mine.

World events, Neruda, King and Enoch went off-stage to the back of my mind, displaced by my commitment to *If....*

We had a serious problem. The very last shot of the film was of Travis on the rooftop firing a bren-gun. In every take, Malcolm just hadn't caught the right look.

'We'll have to reshoot it,' Lindsay announced. 'Rebuild the set at Twickenham Studios, get Mirek over from Czechoslovakia.'

Lindsay instructed Medwin to arrange a reshoot for this one set-up. Medwin didn't argue with Lindsay; but he didn't like the idea or the cost.

I had a suspicion that I'd glimpsed the right look somewhere in rushes. I spent some time going through the trims.

'What are you wasting your time on?' Lindsay asked caustically. 'Don't you have better things to do than fiddle with trims?'

I gathered the trims I wanted and scooted off to another cutting room. I found what I was looking for: a bit of film at the end of a take, before the final unusable flash frames. I rushed to the main cutting room and interrupted Gladwell and Lindsay at the movieola.

'We'll just have to have a look at what he's got,' Lindsay sighed resignedly. 'Otherwise he'll never leave us alone.'

I fitted the bit of film onto the movieola. It was

barely over a foot long. We watched.

'You think we can end the film on eighteen frames?' Lindsay shook his head. 'Sometimes, Ian, you really are quite mad. It is the look but it's too short.'

I said we could print it optically back and forth. Lindsay was convinced that, if we repeated the process, the smoke from the bren-gun going back and forth, from side to side, would look ridiculous. He told me to forget about it.

'I don't want you squandering money on opticals we can't afford over another half-baked idea.'

The rooftop set was rebuilt at Twickenham Studios. Mirek flew over. A full crew was engaged. Malcolm was delighted. Not only would it be fun but he'd get a bit of extra lolly.

Contrary to Lindsay's instructions, I ordered the optical.

We screened the rushes of the reshoot. None of it was any better than what had been filmed first time round. The lights went on in the screening room. Lindsay was gloomy and Malcolm was disappointed.

People were walking out of the screening room as the lights dimmed and my optical appeared on the screen.

The repetitive action of the gun juddering and the smoke wafting from the barrel were hardly discernible. With sound of gunfire and explosions, no one would notice anything.

The optical was cut into the film.

'Bloody marvellous,' Malcolm exploded with enthusiasm at my rescue operation. 'Lins, old boy,' he said, imitating Medwin, 'you could learn a thing or two from Rakoff here.'

Lindsay told Malcolm to piss off.

If.... From sexuality to revolution. Malcolm McDowell and Christine Noonan.

21

LIVING IN DISCORD

If.... was not readily identifiable as belonging to any particular category. There would be marketing problems. We'd shown a rough cut to various people in the Paramount publicity department. They were all suitably impressed with the film but they were unnerved by Lindsay's blunt and direct personal style. They cowered but, as soon as Lindsay turned on the charm, he won them round. After that there was nothing they wouldn't do for him.

The most extreme case of intimidation by Lindsay was the music composer, Marc Wilkinson. The very mention of Lindsay's name gave him the shakes. He was a jittery specimen to begin with; I had to spend a lot of time working with Marc.

'What if Lindsay doesn't like it?' Marc had cried on my shoulder, almost literally.

As the film moved towards completion, the more testy Lindsay became. Medwin was always behind me and supportive, there to soothe my

often ruffled feathers. In effect, I was given the gun but not the badge.

It was the end of a long day. Everyone had gone home. While waiting for me, Lindsay demanded to know when I intended to get rid of Gladwell.

'Are you mad?' I objected to his returning to an old theme. 'What do you want? Isn't it enough that the editing has gone well? What do you expect?'

'Yes, thanks to me. If I'd have left him alone with you, can you imagine where we'd be? What are you up to tomorrow?'

'I won't be in the cutting room. I'm delivering music measurements to your composer, that you brought out of the theatre. He's a mess because he feels that you've abandoned him,' I shook my head. 'He's petrified of you, and now he's on the edge of a nervous breakdown.'

'Really,' Lindsay rolled his eyes up towards the ceiling. 'You always exaggerate. You're a megalomaniac, that's what it is. Or is it egomaniac?' he paused. 'Now who should we get rid of next?' Lindsay went across the room and stared at his somewhat diminished hate list on the board.

'Would you like to start with me?' I suggested.

'Don't be facetious.'

I switched off the cutting room lights and we went to Bertorelli's for something to eat. I paid the restaurant bill.

'That's not out of your own pocket is it?' Lindsay asked. 'I won't have you doing that kind of thing. Money is money.'

'I claim it on expenses when it involves the director,' I told him, 'and this is yours,' I handed Lindsay a wadge of cash under the table.

'What's it for?' Lindsay asked.

'Taxi money. Even if you hardly take taxis, it's what you're entitled to.'

We strolled out into Queensway.

'Unless you're willing to have another chauffeur,' I said, looking out for a taxi.

I stopped a cab.

'Well how are you getting home?' Lindsay asked, as he got in.

'I'll also take a cab,' I replied.

'Make sure you do,' he said getting in. 'And charge for it.' He smiled out of the open window.

I waved at the black cab, sliding away into the darkness.

The next morning, a taxi collected me and the music measurements from my flat. Marc had sounded nervier than ever on the phone. Watching the streets on the way up to St Johns Wood, I wondered what I'd say to calm Mark down.

David Gladwell: a solid film editor.

'You mustn't rush away, please,' Marc pleaded as soon as I got in his front door. My visits to Marc were lasting longer as the deadline for recording the score grew closer.

Like a character in a 1940s melodrama, Marc banged away at the piano keys, with his hair flying about. Sometimes he shook his head so violently that his glasses flew off. Without them he was as blind as a bat. He often narrowly missed stepping on them.

I was spread out on the carpet sorting out what was ready for the copier. My knowledge of music was minimal but Marc seemed to have more faith in my abilities than in his own.

As he concluded playing a sequence, Marc swivelled round on his piano stool and asked me what Lindsay would say. I replied that it was magnificent and urged him to get material ready for the fixer who needed to know what was required before engaging the session artists. It was going to be a full-blown orchestra; and Marc was conducting.

'Thank you, thank you,' Marc gasped.

I left him in a state not much better than when I'd arrived.

A couple of days later, I was sprawled once more on Marc's floor. I listened, as I went through his music sheets, as if I was reading exactly what was on them. I turned pages when he changed pages. I pretended I knew it all. I was convinced that, if I had not, he'd collapse in tears and be carted away.

We were booked to record the music at Anvil out at Denham, once the studio of Alexander Korda. It was a depleted remnant of what it had been in its heyday. Now all that remained was the one sound stage, the Technicolor processing laboratories and the vaults which had been the cutting rooms. The windows were frozen shut. The doors creaked open on rusted hinges. Weeds had crept inside.

The huge music stage, one of the finest in the country, was run by Alastair Campbell, a tall, kilted Scotsman with receding grey hair, a thick accent and a powerful bearing.

Lindsay was in fine fettle. Gladwell and Medwin were also there. The four of us hovered behind the control desk, in a spacious glass-fronted recording room.

Campbell sat between two assistants, twiddling knobs, levers and an array of switches. The sound-proofed door was open. High-pitched sounds reverberated from the speakers on the stage.

Lights came on and musicians started arriving. They settled in a semi-circle facing a rostrum, under a screen suspended in mid-air. Numbers flicked onto the screen as one of our loops was projected.

The orchestra started tuning up. The fixer distributed the music sheets. Marc marched past us, grinned and ascended the rostrum. He dropped a pile of music sheets. He didn't look at all well.

The padded door between us and the stage was tugged shut.

Marc twisted his head round. His hair was all over the place and I could see that he was trembling.

Standing with his back to us and facing the thirty piece orchestra, he called out that he was ready. As he raised his baton, he was not looking up at the screen.

I moved away from Lindsay and stood towards the back of the recording booth, where the shadows were deeper.

Lindsay whirled round. He too had noticed that something was amiss.

The first loop, M1, went round and Marc glanced up. Next to me Gladwell chuckled.

'Glad it's nothing to do with me,' he murmured.

Sarcastically, I thanked Gladwell for his support.

The same loop went round again.

Marc stood transfixed, staring at the screen. He was frozen solid.

He was immobilized by fear. His baton arm

was stretched out as stiff as a ramrod. He wasn't moving and the loop wasn't stopping.

'Do something,' Lindsay swung round to me. 'Right now,' he hissed.

Without any thought whatsoever, I left the recording booth and trotted across the stage towards the rostrum.

Marc twisted his head round and gazed down at me. His lips moved but no words came out of his mouth. His whole body was trembling. All he could do was look at me. I glanced at the music sheets. They were all in order.

The first loop continued going round and round. I was sweating. I asked Marc to look at the screen. Slowly, he turned his head. I clasped his right arm carefully and waited for the first yellow line to whack the edge of the moving picture. As it did so, I pushed Marc's arm.

The whole orchestra burst forth. I got onto the rostrum close behind Marc, still wiggling his arm up and down, back and forth, from side to side, trying to keep the beat. I put my left hand on his shoulder. I stroked, I patted, I prayed and I conducted. I could feel him sinking, getting heavier and then lighter. He turned a sheet. I could feel his body softening, with me pressed up against him like a lover, and my hand was no longer driving his baton arm.

Marc moved his head round, nodded violently, and gasped.

'Thank you, thank you, you can go now. I'm all right now, I can cope, I can cope.'

I released my grip on him, spun around, bent over and scurried back towards the recording booth. I could hear Marc behind me, still going strong.

The first take of the first piece ended, the red light over the padded door turned green and I slid back into the recording booth.

Lindsay didn't say one word.

We said goodbye to Sound Associates in Queensway, and hello to the De Lane Lea outpost in Wardour Street.

We set up our cutting rooms on the second floor. Down in the bowels below street level, in the dubbing theatre Doug Turner, the mixer, would hold court with Lindsay in attendance.

The theatre was fitted out with soft, wall-to-wall carpeting, low leather easy chairs, a padded sound-proofed door, low ceiling and dim lighting. From above, behind the broad sway of Doug's mixing panels, projection beams streamed across the darkness and came to life on the screen at the far end of the basement room.

In here, daylight never ventured. We were cocooned away from that reality.

Doug viewed the cutting copy and, in his crisp, blunt manner, said all the right things to Lindsay. How to tackle the mixing process was discussed between Bell and Doug. They were colleagues of old.

Lindsay swung away from me and started to hum a hymn. Bell approached him.

'Lindsay,' he said, 'I'd like you to listen to some FX I fitted for the beating.'

I slumped down onto one of the soft sofas. I'd looked forward to cosy days in this place. The lights dimmed, though not as darkly as in a cinema, and we watched the sequence with a dialogue track and the FX.

Travis bent over a gymnasium post bar to get viciously beaten by Rowntree, the sadistic prefect. The sequence went on for three and a half minutes, cutting across to the three other boys anxiously waiting their turn beyond the swing doors, out of sight but not out of hearing.

The sound of the cane on Travis's bum was incredibly effective. I told Bell how good I thought it was, and asked him what the sound was.

'It's Johnny Lee whipping fresh lumps of steak from the market,' Bell guffawed, stroking his beard. 'Anybody want some slightly tender meat?'

Lindsay got up, folded his hands behind his back, glanced at me, then addressed Bell. The effect was too severe for what he wanted.

Film was ferried up and down over the ensuing days. More than once, someone got stuck in the rickety old lift.

I was going through the dubbing charts I'd roughed out with Doug when Lindsay butted in.

'Now Doug, you mustn't encourage him. Give him a chart to do and he'll happily avoid dealing with anything else.'

'Lindsay, this is not your concern,' I objected.

'Everything you do is my concern,' Lindsay snapped back.

Doug joined in. Like a seasoned double act they went at me. Like the proverbial cavalry, Medwin arrived and asked Lindsay to come to Paramount and meet Michael Flint, the new head of Paramount UK.

Lindsay acquiesced grudgingly. Medwin, Lindsay and I made our way up Wardour Street. Lindsay bitched about the waste of time it was meeting executives.

At Paramount, a reception guard summoned a lift for us. We zoomed up to the top floor.

Lindsay sniffed at the smell of fresh paint and ground his heel into the soft pile underfoot.

'Can you imagine what this cost? They wouldn't spend this much on *If....*'

'Please, Lins,' Medwin pleaded, as the door in front of us swept open and we entered a large office, still spick and span from recent refurbishment.

A small man with glasses darted out from behind a massive desk and approached us with an outstretched hand and a smile. A phalanx of vice-presidents scurried aside to make way for Flint as he drew closer to us.

'Mr Anderson, what a great pleasure,' Flint said, grabbing my hand and pumping it vigorously.

'Do you mind?' Lindsay seethed with indignation. 'I am Lindsay Anderson,' he said, pushing in front of me and introducing Medwin.

I stepped aside, swallowing my laughter.

'But who is this?' a perplexed Flint asked, glancing at me.

'That's nobody you'll have heard of,' Lindsay replied, with a dismissive wave in my direction. 'His name is Ian Rakoff.'

'Not the Ian Rakoff who wrote the western on *The Prisoner*?'

As we walked back down Wardour Street, Lindsay was still fuming about my being mistaken for him. I teased him and Medwin told him he needed a drink.

As we passed the alleyway entrance to St Anne's Court, Alan Sapper emerged, bent over like a beetle. He wore a grey suit, not expensively tailored but not cheap. He carried a leather briefcase and was chomping a cigar. He halted when he saw me.

'Well, my friend, seems you've done something with *The Prisoner*,' he grinned. 'Said in *The Observer* that the western was the best of the series so far.' Sapper patted me on the shoulder.

Sapper gave Lindsay a perfunctory nod and hurried on his way.

Lindsay wanted to know how I could be friendly with a specimen like Sapper, 'and what is it about the fucking *Prisoner?*'

'Ian, do you want to choose a nice restaurant for a spot of lunchies?' Medwin asked me.

'No!' Lindsay answered. 'You choose,' he told Medwin.

Lindsay found Johnny Lee playing cards in his cutting room. Lindsay told me to fire him. I said it's inconvenient and too costly to replace him. Lifting his nose, Lindsay said that I should find it convenient as soon as possible.

Lindsay and Johnny had been getting along extremely well. Crude and rude, Johnny met his verbal match in Lindsay's loose invective. What had annoyed Lindsay was that, when he walked in, Johnny had carried on playing cards with a chap from an adjacent cutting room and ignored Lindsay.

The news of the Russian invasion of Czechoslovakia sent Lindsay into a spin. At least his friends like Miroslav and director Milos Foreman were safe in America.

'You'd better arrange a meeting with our union General Secretary...your friend,' Lindsay said sarcastically, refusing to mention Sapper's name.

Sapper wasn't keen but he made a booking to have lunch.

Lindsay, Gladwell and I set off to meet with Sapper.

We'd hardly got seated before Lindsay started.

'What is the union going to do about the Russians?' Lindsay demanded to know. 'What will your official statement be?'

Sapper asked Lindsay which wine he preferred.

The divide between Sapper and Lindsay was irreconcilable. Gladwell squirmed in silence and I said little. The two men parted with poorly concealed acrimony.

Sapper had found Lindsay rude and intractable, as well as politically naïve. Sapper's solution was to fob Lindsay off on an underling. Lindsay said it was an insult to be offered a meeting with union representative Les Wiles to discuss the Russian invasion and plot an official statement.

Despite the worsening conditions in Czechoslovakia, Lindsay refused to deal with anyone other than the head of the union.

We received a summons that the European head of Paramount, Bud Ornstein, wanted to see *If....* and was keen to meet Lindsay. We'd have to do a rough mix for the screening. Lindsay did not like the idea and felt pressured.

'But Lins,' Medwin implored, 'it is important and a day in Paris will do you good.'

Grudgingly Lindsay acquiesced and told me that I was included.

'One of us has to wear a tie and it's going to be you,' Lindsay informed me.

I argued. I hadn't worn a tie in years.

With the cutting copy and the accompanying magnetic sound boxed up on the back seat beside me, I directed the driver to Greencroft Gardens. I fumbled with my tie and unbuttoned the collar of my shirt.

As I was opening the door, Lindsay came out. He sat in the front and made conversation with the driver as we headed for Heathrow.

'So what do you make of the Russians invading Czechoslovakia?'

'Bloody terrible and we're doing nothing about it,' the driver replied.

'It's worse than that,' Lindsay said jerking his hand back in my direction. 'And that person has a trade union friend who won't take a stand because he's a fucking Stalinist,' Lindsay said and turned round to me. 'Isn't that so?'

'Do you know which terminal?' I asked the driver.

'Did I mention that's a nice tie?' Lindsay said sweetly. 'Did you buy it specially?'

'No.'

'Pity, you could've charged it to the production.'

Lindsay, as ever, wore his black leather jacket and red shirt.

We flew first class and sipped champagne.

'It won't make you drunk, will it?' Lindsay asked me.

'Not on a couple of glasses.'

'What makes you think you're getting a second?'

I took out a comic.

'Oh, for God's sake!'

I put away my comic, and Lindsay refilled my glass.

If there was any trouble with customs, Lindsay informed me, I would have to assume full responsibility.

We had trouble getting through customs in Paris. The representative who was supposed to meet us and take care of things that end hadn't shown up. Lindsay almost blew a gasket.

At the Paris HQ, a rather smooth Frenchman in a dark green suit was going spare. The man he'd sent to meet us had gone astray, he blustered, and it was my fault. In broken English, he started to attack me over the condition of the film. Then Lindsay let loose. The Frenchman didn't know what hit him. First, Lindsay raged, he had no right to pick on me and, secondly, I was not in the habit of making mistakes. Lindsay then went on to give him a dressing down in impeccable French. I couldn't understand a word but, as Lindsay finished, the smooth Parisian was visibly rattled. His tone changed, he apologized for everything under the sun and tried to get away from Lindsay in one piece.

Medwin arrived and, with his usual social skill, poured oil across the troubled waters. The French executive assured us that he'd booked a fine restaurant for our lunch.

After lunch Medwin flew back to London.

'Well, that's out of the way,' Lindsay said. 'At least we don't have to worry about watching out for Medwin.'

We were invited to the Hôtel Georges V to meet up with Ornstein. He'd seen the film without us; or rather, almost without us.

Lindsay and I had been lurking out of sight in

the projection booth for the ending. In the rough mix Lindsay had been dissatisfied with the volume of the explosive ending. Doug refused to push it beyond the maximum before distortion set in. So I whacked up the volume on the projector. Through the projection window I saw Ornstein, a very large man, lurch up in his seat, as I turned up the sound. I could feel Lindsay smiling as he watched from the other projector window.

The Georges V was rather grand. Ornstein insisted on taking us into his bathroom to show us a vast tub on clawed feet. He ran the water, took a pull on his huge cigar and asked what we thought of the bath. We both said admiring things as we followed Bud out of his bathroom. His wife appeared, an equally large lady. They were so loose and friendly that I felt I should kiss Mrs Ornstein.

Bud thought *If....* was great and assured Lindsay that he had his full support, though he wasn't sure quite what the film was.

I said that it was easy to categorize.

'It's going to be a masterpiece,' I declared.

Lindsay gave me a dirty look. Ornstein puffed at his cigar and said I was probably right. Showing us to the door he clamped a beefy arm across my shoulder.

'Rakoff, that's a great name for the movies,' he opened the door and repeated my name.

In the lift, Lindsay told me that I shouldn't be saying the film was a masterpiece. We couldn't take anything for granted.

Back in Soho, Lindsay made a point of telling everybody how I had kissed Mrs Ornstein on both cheeks.

WINDING DOWN

The contrast was sudden. On a Friday the dub was over. The cutting rooms were emptied out. Much of the film was dumped and the rest was shipped to the vaults at Denham. This would accumulate rust for whatever the statutory period required by Paramount.

I was left to oversee the rest of the post-production, assisted by Lindsay.

Gladwell had wished me good luck. He said I was going to need it.

Our shrunken operation moved into a cutting room at John and Marlene Fletcher's Dateline. The building's decrepit ambience and its seedy entrance in the Flaxman Court alleyway suited Lindsay to a tee.

'At least we'll be safe here from being pestered,' Lindsay sniffed at a fresh puddle on the doorstep. 'Be a bit like the old days,' he said, referring to his years in documentary filming, as he ascended the narrow, bare, wooden stairs carrying cans.

We unloaded onto the rewind bench. I started placing the cans on racks.

'We should make our producer carry cans,' Lindsay said, handing me more cans. 'I'm sure it would be good for his soul, if not for his clothes.'

I said that I should have kept an assistant.

'Not one of those dopes,' Lindsay remarked. 'There's no need, I'm here.'

Marlene popped in to see how we were settling and whether everything was okay. The movieola had just been serviced. Her husband, John, shuffled in and went into a monologue on recording for Lindsay in the Free Cinema days.

Somewhat irritated, Lindsay said that we had to go out.

I told Marlene that Lindsay wanted privacy. Marlene assured me that we would be left alone.

The days and nights sped by. The chores were endless, and Lindsay was always at hand discussing, resolving, dealing with Paramount, talking to Memorial and the labs. We functioned as a double act, with Medwin taking the steam out of it when necessary. Journalists hovered round for interviews. Stars and producers invited Lindsay out to offer him projects. He was the flavour of the moment.

'When do we see the first answer print?' Lindsay asked as we strolled up Wardour Street carrying yet more cans.

'Soon,' I replied.

Lindsay told me that Jocelyn Herbert, the art director, would be on hand to help with the grading. I said, thank God.

'What's that supposed to mean?'

It means, I said, that her being around could give us a rest from arguing.

'We don't argue,' Lindsay argued. 'It's simply that you can be so difficult.'

I stopped in the middle of the pavement.

'Me, difficult?' I yelled. 'What do you think you are?'

People walking by stopped to stare at us.

'Oh, calm down,' he shouted, and then changed the subject. 'How much further? I suppose it'll have a hundred stairs and no lift.'

'Basement.'

Representatives from the Cannes Festival flew over from France. We projected the cutting copy with the end volume at full blast. They were overwhelmed and Lindsay was assured that *If....* would be accepted for competition, provided a married print reached France by the prescribed date.

There had been talk of disregarding Cannes and going for the Oscars; but the dates were impossible and Lindsay had not thought it a viable prospect.

'Too European for the Americans,' Lindsay said.

'Bud Ornstein liked it,' I reminded him.

'He's different.'

Our West End opening was set and the pressure went up a few degrees. The venue was to be the Paramount Cinema.

Lindsay was edgy and I was strung way out. I could feel my eyes sinking with the prolonged strain, but I kept on having to take on more and more. Lindsay wanted me everywhere with my finger in everything.

Paramount constantly wanted screenings for selected groups, newspapers and magazines. The demand for previews was constant. Everyone wanted to publicize the forthcoming Lindsay Anderson film. I kept on turning up the volume at the end of each screening to boost the final sequence into distortion. Occasionally someone staggered out clutching their eardrums. Nothing could please Lindsay more. Drinks and snacks were laid on.

Sherwin dropped into the cutting room. Lindsay berated, bullied and wore him to a frazzle; but Sherwin kept on coming back, shaking nervously, grinning and smoking non-stop.

Strolling along Shaftesbury Avenue, Lindsay was going on about Sherwin.

'He's been utterly useless,' Lindsay complained. 'There's hardly a line in the film that Sherwin wrote. I wonder if I should take the credit of screenwriter.'

My heart sank. I bit my lip. I thought about what happened to me on *The Prisoner*.

'I don't think you're being fair,' I said to Lindsay. 'Besides, you don't want to be a screenwriter. Let Sherwin have it. It's not going to cost you anything.'

The subject was not raised again and the credits were not changed.

The first married print was a fiasco. The colour was horrendous. Lindsay was livid and attacked the senior grader, Bob, with unrestrained venom. Even Ostinelli was taken aback. Bob was a veteran colour grader of consummate skill and knew what was wrong with the print. He didn't need Lindsay to rub his nose in it; and he couldn't deal with Lindsay's acerbic manner.

After the screening at the film labs, Lindsay, Gladwell, Jocelyn and me went to a café in Rathbone Place. Lindsay was annoyed with my rushing the group of them out of the labs.

Gladwell mumbled how awful the grading was.

It was all my fault, Lindsay said. I was the one that had recommended Humphries Laboratories in the first place. I lost my rag. I said that, if Lindsay didn't stay out of the labs and leave the graders alone, we could kiss our completion schedule goodbye. The graders were petrified of him, I said. Lindsay got up and, flinging his arms apart, cried who did I think he was, Jesus Christ? I replied yes, and that I'd brought the nails. I jumped up and hammered at his wrists.

At these histrionics, Jocelyn and Gladwell made some excuses and left. Deprived now of an audience, I went into the coffee shop next door and asked for half a pound of Blue Mountain.

'Can't you be satisfied with instant, like the rest of us?' Lindsay asked loudly from behind me.

The little old lady serving me looked askance at him.

'Oh, and I'll have some of the same too,' Lindsay said politely.

Out on the pavement I remarked that I'd not seen Lindsay making fresh coffee.

'It's a present for my mother,' he told me.

Lindsay did keep away from the labs; but the number of regraded prints reached monumental proportions. First they'd get one thing right, then lose it next time round. A new type of grading machine created havoc in the labs. There was no end to the teething problems.

I had more to do than I could handle alone. I asked Marlene to get me an assistant for a couple of days.

Mary Brown, whom I hadn't seen since *The Burning*, was available. She seemed to have disregarded our past conflict.

By the evening, I was surprised at how well Lindsay had taken to Mary. I told him that I wanted to keep her on. I was also fed up with being alone with him. Amused, Lindsay said that I could do as I liked.

'But you do that anyway,' he laughed.

Mary stayed on and turned out to be efficient, reliable and able to take Lindsay in her stride.

Getting the titles right was a major chore. Getting the opticals done was a nightmare. The titles designer had never done a film before. I now got involved, laying out the titles and overseeing the shooting, which we did at Axtell-Hall, a new company around the corner from Dateline. The optical shoot of the titles kept going increasingly wrong. Only after innumerable reshoots was Lindsay satisfied.

'Shouldn't you have a bigger credit?' Lindsay said to me, as we were carrying cans up Wardour Street.

I was taken aback. How could he make such a suggestion at this late stage? I wanted a better credit but, after all the troubles we'd already had with the titles, it wasn't possible. I pointed this out to Lindsay. We didn't have enough time for yet another change to the titles. It would jeopardize our schedule.

Lindsay agreed. Too much fuss was made out of titles, he said, and then added 'besides, everyone will know that it was you and I who made *If....*'

By now it was 1969, in the month of March. Apprehensively, I kept a precise log of the differently graded prints. Reel one was good in one version but not in another. No decision had been made by Lindsay as to which print we would use. In the morning before the first afternoon screening we were going to project the last print.

I collected the last print from Humphries. We screened it in Paramount in Lower Regent Street. The first, 2000-foot double reel was superb. The sepia-tinted titles, the school buildings in sunset silhouette, were just right. What followed was not good. Some of the reels looked like recycled rejects.

'I will not allow a print like that to be shown,' Lindsay announced as we assembled in the area adjacent to the projection box.

There was absolute silence. The chief projectionist was astonished. The heads of Paramount were horrified. The end leader of the last double reel slid off its spool and continued round and round, slap, slap. It was like the sound of a whip.

The projectionists replaced the reels in their cans.

Mary arrived lugging more hitherto rejected answer prints. We formed stacks of the different graded prints.

Medwin, panting from running up the stairs, gasped that the box office had already opened and that it was pelting with rain. The queue for tickets had been building up for ages.

'Lins, they're selling tickets right now. They're queuing round the corner...' Medwin urged Lindsay to make a decision.

Lindsay took no notice and walked out.

Everyone looked at me. I was flitting from one pile of cans to another, writing on my Asprey pad different possibilities of combinations. I was sweating and shaking. It was as bad as when I conducted the orchestra at Denham.

Could I manoeuvre what we had to make it acceptable?

'Well?' Lindsay was back and he was glaring at me. 'Have you come up with anything?'

'How about keeping the new first two-reeler and then going back not to the last answer print, the one before where you felt it was almost good enough and...' I said pointing at the different lists of combinations I'd written on cards.

Lindsay was appalled by my first offering but less indignant about my second. The third he said had possibilities. However, I'd better try another combination which obviously, he said, I had not considered. He snatched a card from my

```
        S T E R    F I L M S    ( P T Y . )   L T D .

COUNTRY: SOUTH AFRICA              DATE CENSORED:  30/4/69

PICTURE TITLE:  "IF"

CENSOR'S CLASSIFICATION:  "D"    No persons 4-18.  Whites only.

REASON FOR CUTS:
_____

NO.:     DESCRIPTION AND LOCATION OF CUTS:               LENGTH:


        All Measuring from No. 3 on Academy Leader

1.  In scene where the three older boys sit together in
    room and one reads from "Woman's Own Magazine",
    eliminate all dialogue referring to sex.
        Cut from:  1608 ft. +  8 fr. to 1629 ft. + 15 fr.    21 ft.
                   1642 ft. + 10 fr. to 1662 ft. +  6 fr.    20 ft.

2.  Eliminate talk about "making love once and then die".
        Cut from:  1708 ft. +  5 fr. to 1727 ft. + 10 fr.    19 ft.

3.  Eliminate scene of boy licking picture of naked girl.
        Cut from:  1734 ft. +  7 fr. to 1739 ft. +  2 fr.     5 ft.

4.  Eliminate full length nudity in shower scene.
        Cut from:   172 ft. +  4 fr. to  193 ft. + 10 fr.    21 ft.
                    209 ft. +  4 fr. to  213 ft. +  1 fr.     4 ft.
                    226 ft. + 12 fr. to  240 ft. + 10 fr.    14 ft.
                    247 ft. +  3 fr. to  251 ft. + 14 fr.     4 ft.
                    258 ft. +  5 fr. to  285 ft. +  5 fr.    27 ft.
                    304 ft. +  5 fr. to  306 ft. + 5 fr.      2 ft.

5.  Eliminate scene of girl and Travers in naked scramble
    on floor of roadside cafe.
        Cut from:  1753 ft. +  4 fr. to 1767 ft. +  3 fr.    14 ft.

6.  Eliminate pictures of naked girls on wall during
    target practice with pistol.
        Cut from:  1628 ft. + 12 fr. to 1673 ft. + 12 fr.    45 ft.
                     34 ft. +  3 fr. to   40 ft. +  5 fr.     6 ft.

7.  Eliminate scene of Wallace and Phillips in bed.
        Cut from:   426 ft. + 10 fr. to  443 ft. +  0 fr.    17 ft.

8.  Eliminate whole scene of naked women in corridor and
    in washing room.
        Cut from:   731 ft. +  2 fr. to  761 ft. +  2 fr.    30 ft.
```

**The South African Censor's deletions from If....
Note that the film had been passed for
screening to "whites only" audiences.**

hand.

'The most obvious thing you left out,' he said disparagingly. 'Just swap that with that,' he continued, making swift marks with his pen, 'and we've got a presentable print.'

Lindsay walked out. I sorted out the cans for projection and Medwin thanked me profusely.

The cinema was packed. Lindsay was somewhere in the auditorium, prowling about in the dark and watching the audience.

For the last reel I was in the projection booth again, belting up the sound.

As the audience poured out, Lindsay was in the foyer surrounded by admiring, shell-shocked schoolboys. He could not be prised away. The Paramount noteworthies had to wait.

We'd made the West End screening in time, and the film was officially accepted for Cannes. As soon as the grading was all resolved, I would ship a print off.

Both the critics and the public took to the film. Its chances in the Cannes Festival were encouraging. We expected to pick up something. The hot favourite was *Z*, the film by Costa-Gavras, about the Junta take-over in Greece.

Lindsay and Malcolm flew off to Cannes, along with Medwin. Before they went, Lindsay told me that I was lucky not to have to undergo the insincere festival glitz. I would have liked to have been asked.

I reckoned that *If....* had a chance of winning.

The day before the Cannes' awards were declared, I received a postcard from Lindsay. The buzz on *Z* had got stronger. To quote Lindsay's words, he was standing by for compromise.

The next day, the festival's top prize, the Palme d'Or went to *If....*

I wondered about Lindsay wanting so much to win? Did that undermine the establishment? Was it because he needed a power base to make more films, freely, in his way? Was that what it was about? And was Lindsay disappointed in not being decried and vilified publicly, like *The Prisoner*? Would such vociferous attacks have made Lindsay happier? Unanswerable questions; shades of *The Prisoner*.

RUNNING ON EMPTY

Once again the pattern of my life had altered. Lindsay wasn't around to pummel me, nor Paramount to pester me, nor Memorial to console me. Without all of that going on, life was strangely empty. I missed the furore of being so involved. But I was seriously burnt out. I had no desire to go back into the rat race. I was running on empty and standing still. I felt that I had to press on at the typewriter, generate something of my own. Foremost in my thoughts was my very first venture, *Warriors of the Assegai*. This was my epic saga of life in southern Africa before the white man.

A girl named Mitzi moved into my neighbourhood. We'd met back at British Transport Films when she'd been a secretary. She was zany, skinny and fraught, with a nervous energy. She'd been married to Paul McDowell, the deadpan singer of The Temperance Seven. It wasn't my sort of music, but Mitzi was my sort of person. Through her, I met Richard De la

Mare. He'd produced a documentary feature on Algeria with narration by Richard Burton. De la Mare was the grandson of the poet, Walter. He'd also moved into a powerful position in Rediffusion Television. He asked to read *Warriors*. I sent him a copy.

Over lunch, De la Mare exuded enthusiasm and offered to send the manuscript to a publisher.

A week later, I got a call to meet the wunderkind of publishing, Tom Maschler. In his office at Jonathan Cape, Maschler told me that my book wasn't viable. He did not clarify what he meant. I did not ask. Nevertheless he'd wanted to meet me because of my association with Lindsay Anderson, which is all we talked about. I drank coffee and left with my rejected manuscript. I wondered if some awful pattern to my life was underway, generated by *The Prisoner*.

I showed the manuscript to a Hollywood producer, Sandy Lieberson. He was laid back and charming. I was impressed by the fact that he'd been instrumental in the making of *Performance*. Sandy praised *Warriors* lavishly but said I would have to incorporate some white characters to make it commercial for the cinema.

I gave up on showing the manuscript to any more people. I contemplated shipping it off to McGoohan. Though we'd had no contact whatsoever since I left MGM, I thought he might be responsive and not be clouded by commercial bias. Then, I heard that McGoohan had funded Kenneth Griffith to make a film in South Africa. At this time the film union, ACTT, was about to impose a ban on its members working in South Africa. I was appalled at McGoohan's financing a film in South Africa. For me it was tantamount to supporting the apartheid system.

I desperately wanted to sink my teeth into something, but what? Macrobiotics had become a governing discipline in my life. I learned to bake bread. I submerged myself in that kind of food. I drank jasmine tea.

I got a post card from Monument Valley. Lindsay was skedaddling round the States, publicising *If....* Malcolm was doing the lecture circuits and, apparently, referring to how I saved the ending of the film with an optical. I missed being with Lindsay yet, at the same time, the whole business of *If....* had left me unsure about our relationship.

My legacy from the year on *If....* was a remorseless, low period in my life. It had given me an ulcer. Having spent a year without a sniffle, I suddenly got flu. My body was going on strike. I felt terribly low.

I had a few local remedies guaranteed to buoy up my waning spirit. The most reliable one was strolling along the nearby riverside, watching the dirty water, the bobbing houseboats, the people spilling out of the pubs and the greenery of Battersea Park across the Thames. I often strolled along the river en route to the NFT. Sometimes I stopped at the Tate Gallery where I saw 'Whaam!', the Roy Lichtenstein painting based on a comic book. I also saw the Magritte exhibition. I was startled by the precise mind behind the surrealism. Magritte might have had a hand in creating Portmeirion, I thought.

My favourite haunt for solace was the V&A. I dreamed of getting my collection of comic books into that museum.

Another haunt of mine in the search for calm, about a ten-minute stroll from my flat, was the Brompton Cemetery. The unkempt stones overgrown with weeds, the mausoleums cracked with age and neglect, and the frequent emptiness drew me and soothed me. Often I'd find a broad stone to sprawl on, following the clouds' slow movement and mulling over the universe searching for myself. At other times, when there was a soccer match on at the adjacent Stamford Bridge stadium, it was a very different picture. The whole cemetery reverberated with the roar of the crowd. In the failing light, the brilliant stadium lamps burned across the skyline, appearing to hover in mid air, seemingly unattached to the ground, glowing like flying saucers. These visits amply recharged my batteries.

I'd popped into Memorial to have a coffee with Daph and a chat with Barber. As I was getting into the lift, Albert joined me. He asked me if I was going to the BAFTA awards evening at the Grosvenor House in Park Lane. I said I wasn't.

'If.... is in the running, it's been nominated,' he looked at me quizzically. 'You should be there,' Albert insisted. 'I'll pay for the renting of a tux,' he offered.

Smart events had never been my forte. I doubted that any such activity would enhance my career. Birds of my feather didn't have to wear suits or ties.

Nevertheless Finney's sensitivity to my predicament was exceptional. I wondered if he'd hurried to catch me in the lift to get me alone and make his offer. I wouldn't put it past him. His acting ability could fool anybody, including me.

I answered my phone. It was Roy Benson.

'Where've you been? I've been trying to find you,' Roy said excitedly. 'Can you meet me?'

Roy wanted to commission me to write about the then fashionable and popular interest in extra-terrestrial life, flying saucers and arcane belief. He wanted an outline for a screenplay on contemporary theories of creation and human development. Roy was sure that he could get George Harrison involved; but I wasn't sure that the Beatles were committed to anything.

'John Lennon raved over *The Interrupted Journey*, the account of the couple abducted by flying saucer,' Roy told me.

We agreed terms for a treatment and I plunged into research. I frequented the Cecil Court bookshops off Charing Cross Road and met up with steely-eyed ufologists. One of them was exactly the same type as the Moral Re-Armament producer for whom I'd worked. The ufologist sat in my flat holding my hand. The fire of truth burned in his eyes as he imparted to me the essence of saucer belief. I attended a John Michel lecture and was intrigued by his theories.

The title of my treatment was *Galaxy*. It would be a documentary feature tackling human enlightenment from outer space, the pyramids, the Aztec temples, ley lines and geomancy. I steeped myself in paranormal and mystical phenomena. I devoured the books of the 1950s, when reds were under the beds and people were kidnapped and observed by benign aliens in saucers. I read up on the secret Blue Book project: sightings of UFOs kept by the US Air Force. I devoured the classic EC comics on extra-terrestrial visitors. I followed the story of Kaspar Hauser growing up in a space vehicle.

Galaxy was to be a summation of the popular sky-gazing sentiment so all pervasive at the time. Roy and I were both pleased with the outline.

This is the way in which it kicked off.

FADE IN... to an outer galaxy; before day was day.

'In the beginning at a time before our memories began - before we were.'

A ball of flaming matter broke away from a disintegrating dying star.

Out across the endless ocean of space it travelled aimlessly, without direction from galaxy to galaxy. Its wandering came to an end when it succumbed to the power of the sun and

Performance. Breaking down many barriers and prejudices, including gender. James Fox and Mick Jagger.

took its orbit as the third planet.

Gradually the flaming surface burned itself out and was covered by a thin rocky crust. The only climate was rain; rain and more rain, endlessly wearing the hard granite down and carrying the dust to the valleys between the high cliffs of steaming earth.

For the first time the sun's rays broke through the cloudy layer that surrounded the planet.'

A silver disc moves in through the cloud gap and travels over the bleak face of the land.

'Lifeless. Absolutely dead.'

'A good place to dispose of our dirt.'

And so on.

We met with George Harrison and he said how much he liked it. However, Roy got nowhere when he cornered Harrison about money to develop the outline into a screenplay.

It was never rejected; just never accepted. It was too big, too ambitious, even for the Beatles. If they didn't go for it, there were few other places to turn. Roy tried, but to no avail.

I was soon back to visiting Memorial.

'I'd like a word with you,' Paul Joyce, another first-time director in cahoots with Memorial, stopped me in the middle of the broad corridor beside the wide window. As he spoke, he tapped a set of keys in the palm of his hand. He told me that he'd noticed my name on *The Prisoner* credits. He complimented me on my good effort. He was well meaning but he came across in a peculiar way, almost patronising. Over time, as I got to know him, I found this to be misleading; he was a really straight guy.

Daph couldn't make up her mind about Paul Joyce. Barber worked closely with him on *The Engagement*, which was scripted by playwright Tom Stoppard. It seemed that Barber had at one stage found a soul mate in Paul.

Nevertheless Paul seemed somewhat out of key with the general tone of Memorial. He looked as if he'd dressed in a hurry and was wearing borrowed clothes. There was something bleached about him.

I was fed up with things not coming off. I was fed up with swinging close but not getting the brass ring. I was pretty down in the dumps and then I received a phone call from Paul Joyce. He'd telephoned to tell me that he'd recommended me for an editing job.

I made the call to arrange an interview with Nic Roeg.

WRAPPING IT ALL UP

It was late summer in 1970. The new decade was palpably different to that of the 1960s. I could almost feel the values receding. The radical was in decline. Something unpleasantly different was creeping in. Materialism and hard ambition were back in the ether. I assumed that Nic would be a product of the 1960s. *Performance* with Mick Jagger was another venture that kicked over the traces. It had disregarded the supposed norm and presented an eclectic, morally ambiguous and sexually ambivalent portrait of the contemporary London scene. In some respects that was not dissimilar to *The Prisoner*. It, too, challenged the establishment and posed uncomfortable, critical questions.

Getting up to Cricklewood in North London was a pain. My heart sank when I got to Samuelson's, the film equipment hire centre. Its vast conglomeration of soulless buildings and its furore of activity did not endear me to the place. A klieg lamp strutted past me on four puny legs.

Chomping a ham roll, a burly man at reception, pointed me to some stairs. It all reminded me of Humphries.

As I ascended the stairs, I looked down through a cracked window pane and watched the loading of pantechnicons with the Samuelson logo emblazoned on their sides. I glanced at my watch. I was early, but had no intention of delaying. I didn't reckon that I had much of a chance landing the job. The impact of *Performance* and *Walkabout* had made Nic one of the most talked about directors on the scene. I was keen to meet the so-called 'golden boy' of filmmaking.

In a poky, windowless room, I found Nic Roeg with two pasty-faced assistants. The anaemic-looking pair greeted me indifferently, almost coldly.

Nic moved towards me jauntily and gave me a warm handshake. His producer, Si Litvinoff, came in and stood hunched over, looking antagonistic. Nic introduced me as if we were old friends.

'This chap Rakoff has come highly recommended,' he said simply.

Nic then led me out of the room with Si following at a distance. Si didn't look at all happy. As we walked, Nic inclined toward me.

'Who did you say recommended you?' he asked in a lower voice. 'Doesn't matter,' he added before I could answer, 'those things are always nonsense. Here you are anyway.'

We went through a maze of dark, narrow corridors until we emerged in the soft, fine Autumnal light of a broad rooftop terrace. I leaned against a low railing. Beneath stretched the bleak concrete vista of overcrowded North London. Despite the sun, it was a cheerless spot to be located.

Without looking at me, Si started asking questions. Nic cut him short.

Quite apart from his shielding me against the producer, I felt relaxed with Nic. He conveyed the sense that he was a person at ease with himself. As I learned later, he was concerned about the state of his film; but everything he said had a touch of light humour about it.

Nic enthused over what he'd been shooting. He'd covered the Glastonbury Festival and it had been magnificent. The gathering said everything that there was to say about the 1960s, he maintained. Every fad and fashion that had made the 1960s what they were put in an appearance at Glastonbury.

'The atmosphere was quite remarkable,' Nic told me. 'There were no bad feelings or any friction amongst this army of thousands from different values and different beliefs. It was a coming together. It was tolerant and peaceful,' Nic spoke in a gentle, undemanding ramble. There could hardly have been more marked a contrast between this first encounter with Nic my interrogation by McGoohan before I wrote *Living in Harmony*.

'I'm not even sure that it's a film,' Nic said. 'I really just walked round with a camera crew picking up whatever took my attention.'

'We nearly met a couple of times,' I informed Nic, 'at the Sugdens.'

'Teddy and Catherine?'

'And Al,' I added. 'Mulock.'

'Used to drink with him in the Bunch of Grapes in Old Brompton Road.'

'Yes, Al took me there a few times,' I said.

'So what credits have you got?' Si interrupted us. His impatience was turning into anger. 'What features have you cut? What was the last thing you worked on?'

I gave Si a look and for a moment I froze.

'I have no credits,' I told Si, 'and I haven't been working on anything.'

'Si,' Nic addressed him firmly and clamped a hand on my shoulder. 'His credits don't matter. This is the man for the job.'

The dialogue was perfect 1960s. It all worked on instant trust, irrespective of fact. Suddenly I was set to cut a Nic Roeg film. Then, I couldn't imagine doing anything better.

Samuelson's was mushrooming and acquiring a reliable reputation for supplying any film equipment to any place at any time. However, I disliked working in the middle of a vast depot devoted to servicing the bulk of film locations in the UK and across Europe.

Si had schmoozed a special deal out of Samuelson's. They had supplied all the equipment for the Glastonbury shoot. The cutting room was a congested afterthought transforming one windowless overgrown cupboard into a working space that housed the minimum of editing equipment.

Nonetheless, I settled into sifting through the mass of footage. I narrowed it down according to Nic's selection even though, as we'd gone through the material together, he'd kept insisting that I choose the shots.

I chopped off the heads and tails, and joined pieces together, deliberately avoiding any initial search for coherence. I wasn't too happy at working with the tiny spaghetti-like 16mm shots. I hadn't touched the gauge for years. With 35mm I could hold a frame up to the light and see what it was. With 16mm I had to screw up my eyes and peer intensely. I didn't like the stuff, but it was film.

I was assembling to enable the shot material to determine its own identity, to speak for itself and find its own level. It was the way in which Lindsay would have tackled such an abundance of film without an obvious centre. Nic said nothing to deter me in how I was going about it.

Si got us a place in Soho. We moved into two adjoining rooms in a building on Wardour Street, up on the second floor. Our rooms overlooked a narrow courtyard with cars parked higgledy-piggledy. Facing us was the back of a building with its entrance in Dean Street. We had big windows with good sunlight but most of the time the shades were fully drawn, giving the continual shadow necessary for a decent screen image.

First assistant Joe Gannon left and the crew was now down to Falcon Stewart and me. It was his first time in editing. He'd been one of Nic's roving camera crews at Glastonbury. Nic also came in every day. I felt easy enough to bring in a stash of comics. Though Nic had a childhood deprived of comics, he possessed a curiosity about them. The stylish sharp-edged graphics and documentary flavour of early *Dick Tracy* intrigued him. I found a ready audience. I could talk freely about my passion for comics. Nic was insatiably curious.

Things were coming more together. The assembly was being pared down to a cut. I needed a movieola. Si complained about the money but Nic insisted that we get one.

We were beginning to define the Glastonbury perspective. The different groups in the film were cut to make their points. There were the zealots who charged their spiritual batteries on ley lines, hilltops and tors, and those who believed that Jesus was coming back in a flying saucer. John Michel voiced his theories on sacred geometry to the camera. Sufi dancers and oddities from all sectors of the youth-oriented community were documented. There was much music, incidental, spontaneous and arranged. What had registered on Nic was the unexpected harmony amidst such disparate cultures, cults and identities. Crucially, there was an absence of proselytising. For different reasons and different aims, different people had simply gathered to worship in their own way.

Nic also said that rampant sexuality was absent. Neither was there any sign of the typical

1960s concert hustle he'd anticipated. Nothing disruptive occurred; neither aggression, alcohol nor drugs. All three were present but to an unusually lessened degree, considering how many thousands were in attendance. It was an inspiring event; but could it all hang together as a film?

Nic came in with some cans.

'I brought some film I made of Borges. I had nothing specific in mind, but I wondered if it could have a place in the festival film,' Nic said. 'He belongs in a commentary of the 1960s doesn't he?'

I told Nic that he definitely belonged. The blind Argentinean writer, Jorge Luis Borges, had maintained a relatively small literary output but he had a growing readership. I was amongst those who read Borges avidly. Nic's footage consisted of the writer speaking against a black backdrop. I thought it could be dispersed in sections through the film, like a Brechtian or Greek chorus. It was an excellent eclectic addition to the project.

We had a visitor.

'Donald,' Nic rose from beside me to greet a tall, slim, lightly and loosely dressed gentleman. The man, Donald Cammell, had a decidedly aristocratic mien. A decadent sensuality oozed from him. Donald pulled a chair up beside us and settled in, at ease and patient. He was soon keenly interested in what we were doing.

Nic explained how we'd cast everything up in the air and we were just catching what we could wherever it fell. This, Nic postulated, was film living and breathing as it should, free of preconception. Something natural would emerge, he argued.

'Of course it could all come to nothing,' Nic laughed. 'Our producer's already biting his fingernails.'

Donald put his hands behind his back. Nic would invite him to give his opinion whenever he felt he had one. Donald was present frequently in the cutting room in Soho because he was collaborating with Nic on another project.

Some days later, Donald invited me over to his flat in Old Church Street off the Kings Road.

A sphinx-like part-Ethiopian, Myriam, welcomed me warmly. Donald had told her all about me, she said in a soft and easy voice.

The decor was speckled with things near-Eastern. Everything was draped, flowing or flung. It was like a film set, dressed and designed in a hurry but with an unmistakable flavour. I could see where much of the visual hallmark of *Performance* had originated. Although it all seemed hurriedly makeshift, there was nothing tacky. In the apparent casualness, there was something quite studied.

I took in the detail of Donald's flat and reflected on his relationship with Nic. I was curious about their collaboration when they'd directed *Performance*. They were opposites in many ways. Nic was a more earthbound sensual figure, more solid. Lofty Donald soared upwards into a mystic stratosphere. Both were refined, articulate and equally alert, though Nic had a sharper eye. When Nic tended to overembellish, I had noticed, Donald would nail him down; and *vice versa*. They complemented each other with some manner of mental and spiritual balance. Donald had a certain rigidity about him, or perhaps just a rather good posture.

As I assessed and compared the two directors, I slumped onto a cushion and removed my shoes. Donald paced about a bit before settling into a high-backed fan wicker chair from Morocco. It was the same as the one that Shura had in her living room. Myriam wafted about, her thin long dress waving and trailing behind her as she floated past. She was fifty per cent Ethiopian and a hundred per cent exotic. She was about to sprawl on a cushion when something Donald said annoyed her. She snapped at him before withdrawing and leaving us alone.

'Tell me,' Donald began 'who do you think did the most in directing *Performance?*'

I nearly slid off my cushion.

Nic had, more or less, asked me the very same question. My opinion of the film was that they had both equally contributed. Six of one and half dozen of the other, as Number Six would have said. I felt it unwise to probe deeper. There was a frisson between them, and that simmering conflict of energy was apparent on the screen, making it all work.

I had, more or less, given Nic the very same answer.

Donald had a script which had been dormant for some time. If he could get Malcolm McDowell to star, there was a good chance that a production of his old project, *Ishtar*, could get underway. Set in North Africa, it was a mystical piece. Without being tempered by Nic, it was probably considered too weird. Its irreverent attitude seemed similar to the works of the enfant terrible of the American underground, Kenneth Anger. Anger's 1963 *Scorpio Rising* had made considerable impact across the world of cinema. This avant-garde child of the Hollywood bore a distinctive but indiscernible similarity to Donald. Strains of the mystical and the occult infused both men, according to what I heard and what I saw. Indeed, I learned that Donald was planning a film with Anger.

Donald was apprehensive about having Malcolm round and asked if I could also be there. I said I would.

I was at Donald's well before Malcolm got there. I had a coffee while Donald sat at his kitchen table, clipping his fingernails. The pieces fell onto a plate with a few slices of abandoned toast on it.

The doorbell went.

Malcolm clapped me fondly on the shoulder and dropped onto the chair where Donald had been sitting.

'Ah some toast, just what I wanted,' Malcolm said and, before Donald could get a word in, Malcolm had taken a bite.

'What's that?' Malcolm mumbled with his mouth full as he caught sight of the rest of the clippings strewn across the plate.

Still standing, Donald backed away, quite speechless.

'It looks like fingernails,' Malcolm said incredulously.

'It is,' I handed Malcolm a screwed up napkin.

Malcolm and Donald appeared to get on famously. Subsequently Malcolm said he wasn't really interested in the *Ishtar* project but didn't want to disappoint Donald, as he seemed a really nice guy. Malcolm gave his word that he would do it, but doubted that his name would be sufficient to get it off the ground.

Ishtar didn't go into production and Donald moved to California. For years, he drifted disappointedly in the miasma of the Hollywood struggle. Then he chose his own way of leaving it all, and shot himself in the head.

Back in Wardour Street, I was enthusiastic about the concoction that was emerging. The disparate elements were seamlessly joining into a piece. However, we hadn't yet incorporated Borges.

'Things are a bit sticky on the financial side,' Nic warned me. 'Nothing to be alarmed about, but Michael Flint who's now the co-producer wants us to screen the film for Bernard Delfont. I know it's a bit early, but we can't miss the opportunity to get to someone like him.'

Nic asked me what I was laughing at. I told Nic that Flint had once mistaken me for Lindsay.

'Lindsay was furious,' I shook my head from side to side with recall, 'but Flint handled the situation well.'

The assembly was tidied up and the booking for Delfont was made. There wasn't enough time to insert Borges.

Nic had not met Delfont, and neither had I. His brother was Lew Grade. I have no idea why their surnames differed. I was curious to come face to face with the brother of Number One, the brother who had an equally awesome reputation for achievement. Not having met Lew Grade, I hoped that meeting his brother might provide some insight to the family. I'd never

forget McGoohan's raging at me after he'd had a session with Grade. To get Number Six so rattled, Grade had to be quite something. But what? All I knew about Lew Grade was that he had stepped nimbly from the title of World Champion Charleston dancer to success as media impresario par excellence.

'He'll probably arrive with full entourage and be quite difficult,' Nic reflected, as we waited in the screening room on the first floor in Paramount House. 'I know nothing about him, but he must be some kind of a monster. So brace yourselves,' Nic addressed Falcon and me, then glanced at the clock. 'And we might be waiting here for ages.'

There was a slight cough from the doorway. A large man in a nondescript grey suit stepped in, puffing at a cigar. He politely apologized for being a few minutes late. He was not escorted by anybody. He glided across the room, noticeably light on his feet, carrying his bulk effortlessly. We all shook hands and sat down for the film.

At the end of the running, Delfont made a few nondescript remarks with a few pleasant observations. He said he'd like to see the film when it was completed.

He walked out leaving the three of us stunned.

'What a decent, nice person,' Nic observed.

A week later on a Friday evening, Michael Flint appeared in the cutting room. He handed out our last paycheques. He told us that, for the time being, the well had run dry. Nic assured me that we could put this project aside and return to it later. He was off to Hollywood to set something up. I was to wait for him.

I didn't wait.

The next morning I was in Ireland working on John Boorman's *Deliverance*.

I recently went to see Nic and talk about our mutual past. I asked why he never made a film such as *Scandal* whose events and characters had been so much a part of Nic's life. He'd known most of the people in the story which the film was about through the Sugdens. The main players had all been recipients of the hospitality in that Malvern Court flat. It was the perfect vehicle for a statement on the 1960s, which he could have made, and made well. 'I couldn't make a film about people who'd been such close friends,' Nic said emphatically.

Nic had to get some videos for his kids and walk the dog. He said we could stroll and talk.

Outside it was already dark. It was almost March and bitterly cold as we crossed Westbourne Grove. I asked Nic why we had got on so well while cutting the film that was never finished.

'That was because we both loved film,' Nic reflected, 'in a way which isn't as common as we'd like it to be. You understand the nature of film,' he stopped to unleash his dog. 'Film is a living thing which always changes because one can never tell in advance what'll happen. That's why I don't like rehearsing. It undermines any natural spontaneity. Film is an extraordinary, magical thing. It has nothing to do with literature or theatre.'

Nic voiced his puzzlement at the prevailing disdain for the 1960s.

'Why are people so mean-spirited about that period? Why did it have to slip back into complete materialism?' he demanded, recalling some of the characters of the time. 'They'd found something of value and turned their backs on it.'

Fondly he went back to the film we almost made.

'That summer festival at Glastonbury was an historical event,' Nic recalled. 'Besides the summer solstice it marked the spirit of the times which had passed, the end of tremendous spontaneous personal freedom. By its second year it faded into a self-serving venture.'

I waited with the dog outside the video store while Nic went in.

On the way back Nic continued his reminiscences.

'You remember Joyce the voice? She got up and sang and it was wonderful.' He smiled and then added sadly, 'I tried to find her but she'd disappeared.

'Remember the boy guru with his Rolex, which he kept on trying to cover with his sleeve?' Nic changed tack. 'There was religion without being religious. The English Hell's Angels arrived in full force and just melded in. That's what it was like back in those days.'

Nic's incomplete film encapsulated and closed the 1960s for me. The producers sold the unedited footage and a documentary feature was made. It was a shame that our collaborative venture never reached fruition. It would have made a fine counterpoint to the rigour of *The Prisoner*.

Irrespective of how I finally assess or analyse the 1960s, they spanned by far and away the most interesting period of my life in England. The most important aspect was that, at last, I belonged in my adopted home. I felt less alien. I had actively participated in projects which spoke freely and critically, and which were of substance. *Soort soek soort*. I was finding the creators of value with whom it was worth working.

I want to recap what I have tried to write about those now rather distant times.

I've skimmed through the decade, meeting again characters of comparable power and position. I've trawled outside events and witnessed their affects on the film and television media. I've traced the highs and lows, followed achievement and disappointment; common cause and common ground intertwined with different driving forces. I've examined the making of rebellious film and television, and gauged their levels of impact.

Yet through all the broad range of activities and encounters, I never escaped the shadow of *The Prisoner*. It was the essential morality of *The Prisoner* which provided a sense of direction. It had remained my yardstick for assessment, not as a work of art, but as a guide to values for which it is worth striving.

The Prisoner was a journey to save an individual from moral decline into the anonymity of the melting community. It was the battle of the 1960s.

With the testing of time, it is *The Prisoner* which has prevailed, through continuing to intrigue with unanswerable questions.

What is the ongoing appreciation of a piece of art, literature, film or television beyond the aspects of its construction? It is termed by some as a cult. Of its time, and ahead of its time, *The Prisoner* remains beyond category. The series was, and remains, more than the sum of its parts. Its durability has proved its potency to stay in the mind.

Despite its sometimes inadequate realisation, the series has lost none of its impact. Cinematically, much of it is somewhat dated; but this cannot diminish the appeal that provocatively reaches within, beyond the apparent. At the heart of it is the question: what boundary can or should exist between the individual and authority? It strikes a chord and appeals to a sense of responsibility still denied in our daily lives. It provides a clear cut delineation between what is right and what is wrong. It defies the wanton demands of commercialism. It's about repression but it speaks, across the years, with the voice of freedom.

SHAPES FROM ELSEWHERE

It's the look of it all, where it's set and what it is that provides the distinctive background. It is the background that enhanced the enigmatic and intriguing ambience brought to the screen by McGoohan. It is a film set made real. It is something real made into a film set. It is an idiosyncratic amalgam of buildings past, tricks and all: stairs that lead nowhere and windows that will never open, curls of plaster and walls enclosing imaginary inhabitants.

This is Portmeirion, situated on the coast of North Wales. Tourists flock to enjoy the oddity of the place, to savour its strangeness and to smell the plethora of flowers. All is surface, yet it is thick with atmosphere. Beneath the circus façade it lends itself to substance, to ideas that only the mind can reach. It is in effect a museum of the mind, writ large in architectural terms. It cannot easily be categorized, consigned to an era, or exemplified by a particular style. It is more than the sum of its parts. It is shapes from elsewhere and is at peace when all footsteps are absent. It could be encased in glass with perennially falling snow, to be admired and never touched, never lived in. Its form never followed function, a folly in all the word's true meaning.

Above all else, Portmeirion is where *The Prisoner* was located.

In the thirty years since my *Prisoner* days, I had always known that eventually I would have to visit Portmeirion. This was the day.

I was apprehensive about going to Portmeirion for the first time. Besides what it represented in the series, it all harked strongly back to my youth.

At the University of Cape Town, I enrolled in the architectural faculty. I was soon disillusioned. The students were all white. Other faculties weren't so exclusively restricted. I had serious misgivings about my long-cherished dream.

The tradition of the university expected that all first year students wear badges. The badges were about the same size as those worn on lapels in the Village. My refusal to wear a badge was noted disapprovingly. The badge, for me, was another symbol of control by the white society.

One day I was alone in a classroom. Three senior students came in. Two grabbed me from behind while the third tried to pin a freshman badge on me. In the ensuing scrap, one of them got a bloody nose and that was the end of my architectural aspirations. I enrolled in another faculty but still I did not wear a badge. The failure to make a go of architecture always rankled.

Going to Portmeirion involved a double dose of apprehension. The publisher of this book, Richard Reynolds, was astonished that I'd never been to Portmeirion. He was going to take me there.

On a chilly October morning we set off from Holland Park in brilliant early morning sunshine. With us was Steve Edgell, friend and copy editor of this book.

Slumped in the back seat for five hours, I had time to mull over the need for my going to the Village. Would the magic of the place open some doors of insight for me? Would my thwarted architectural dreams and fantasies be reawakened? Would that uncomfortable memory of my working on the series be mollified? Would some further essence of *The Prisoner* be revealed to me?

We arrived in North Wales to find it eerily shrouded in mist. By the time we hit the coast, the mists had lessened, revealing a backdrop of steep overgrown hills encased in dark-green forests.

As we entered a canopy of rain-drenched greenery, I felt a chill that was harsher than the weather. The drizzle ceased and the surrounding silence seemed preternatural. The air had a sting to it and the mist had a distinct taste of its own. There was an almost tangible atmosphere of enforced calm. It elicited memories of childhood on the Cape Peninsula when it, too, was shrouded in mist. I half-expected that Cape Town foghorn to boom forth across the encircling Welsh hills. The last of the haze lifted as if to cue our arrival. I drew slightly back behind my two companions. Richard generously paid the entrance fee and we advanced towards the first arch over the road.

I strolled at a cautious pace, defensively clutching my unopened camera case. Pictures of the series entangled my mind and I suspected that monsters lurked amidst the dripping greenery that was everywhere.

The lens looks down on a clean, grim-faced man marching forcefully along a corridor. There is the sound of echoing footsteps. He is heading for confrontation. Angry, impatient music pounds the sound track. The man pushes aside doors and bursts into an office. Everything about him is explosive. A pink-faced, bespectacled bureaucrat listens, without saying a word, as the man, McGoohan, hammers his fist on the desk and rages volubly. We hear no words but the fury within McGoohan is matched by a violent storm on the sound track. Indifferent to the bureaucrat's lack of response, McGoohan storms out. Thunder and lightning reverberate.

A mechanical pincer's arm withdraws a file with McGoohan's picture on it. A staccato of Xs defaces the image and registers McGoohan's resignation.

Whizzing along in his low-slung, Lotus Seven sports car McGoohan arrives at his apartment, a mere stone's throw from Buckingham Palace.

Outside, a hearse draws up. A tall,

cadaverous man wearing dark glasses, a stove pipe hat, black suit with tails, gets out of the car and ascends the steps to the front door. The gaunt, funereal figure is an ominous relic from a Victorian melodrama.

Inside his flat McGoohan, in a state of rage, begins to pack. An ominous hissing sound permeates the sound track. A stream of gas engulfs the room. McGoohan struggles to resist, stiffens and collapses to the floor.

McGoohan regains consciousness in the familiar surroundings of his flat. On raising the blinds to look out, he sees that he is in an icing-cake village, the stuff of dreams. The ornate, Italianate architecture has a whiff of *Alice in Wonderland*. People appear on the hitherto empty streets. Their ice-cream van clothes appear to be more uniform than costume. The inhabitants respond to McGoohan with anodyne remarks and mindless prosaic observations, like dehumanized automatons.

A Mini Moke with a striped canopy taxis McGoohan around the Village but its range is limited. There is no way beyond the perimeters of the Village because, it is implied threateningly, no one could possibly want to leave. The Village is perfection.

A telephone kiosk provides only local calls. Everything is on credit, or bought with tokens, in the cashless Village. There are no high walls or fences around the Village, only natural boundaries. There are unscalable mountains and an uncrossable ocean.

Watching eyes are all around and everywhere. Camera lenses, embedded in the eyes of statues, follow McGoohan's every move. He cannot learn where the Village is located. His frustration mounts.

A disembodied voice addresses the newcomer, McGoohan, and allocates him the number six. Defiantly he rejects this. He is a person not a

number. McGoohan is driven by principles or possibly by some kind of madness, neither of which will accept being stamped, categorized nor filed.

I examined the impressive vista but neither saw nor felt touched by much of anything. Nothing quite resonated inside me. I noticed the door to *The Prisoner* shop. I decided to delay things and momentarily escape facing the Village by taking refuge inside.

Ensconced in a dwarfed position behind a bank of memorabilia, Max Hora watched over his domain. He'd been there fourteen years, selling badges, stills, publications and assorted souvenirs from the series. Without moving he looked at me and grinned.

'So you made it,' he muttered shaking his head and wobbling slightly on his low chair behind the high counter.

We had met briefly in March 1997 at the Great Western Hotel in Paddington. We were there for the celebration of the thirtieth year since *The Prisoner*'s first transmission.

A few days before setting off for Portmeirion, I'd telephoned Max to say I was coming up to see the Village. I had told him about the book I was writing.

'What size will it be?' Max asked. 'Like this?' He picked a book off the counter and waved it.

I said that I had no idea.

Having walked in during our conversation, Richard pointed at a smaller book than the one Max had picked up.

'You could do with fifty copies here, or a hundred?' Richard asked.

'How far have you got,' Max addressed me, 'or are you still researching?'

'I have a contract,' I replied cautiously.

'Your first visit to Portmeirion!' Max exclaimed incredulously and asked me to sign his visitor's book.

I did so, followed by Richard.

'I live over the bookshop,' Max informed us, twisting round and pointing through the window, across the chess lawn beyond the free sea. 'There!'

Max's obsession with the series had taken him from being a van driver into *The Prisoner* appreciation society and brought him to live full time in the Village. Hardly anyone else actually lived full time in the Village.

Steve came into the tiny shop. The exterior of the shop had been used as the front of number 6's home from home, McGoohan's domicile in the Village.

Richard wanted to see Rover. The three of us moved to the counter as Max stood up and laid a deflated Rover across the counter. It was a grubby, magnolia, rubbery thing as flat as a pancake. It was about two feet wide at its diameter, was symmetrically round except for the long protuberance that served as an elongated nozzle. Blown up, it would be six feet in height. In the series, the sizes varied.

In the birthing sequence of the first episode, the Rover balloon was the size of a ping-pong ball that popped up and bounced on top of a fountain of water. As it vanished, a larger-sized Rover appeared simultaneously over a building, before commencing a slow ominous descent.

The property master shot the little Rover with a pellet gun from a distance of twelve feet. He accurately hit the target spot-on for nine takes. The tenth he missed. McGoohan made a caustic remark. The property master was appalled.

The initial conception of Rover had been entirely different. The early model was a kind of low go-cart that carried a shape resembling a blancmange. On the thing's top was a blue light. It was the sort of contraption which one might expect from the BBC's *Dr Who* series. It functioned perfectly on the flat studio floor but it dealt clumsily with the multitude of steps and changing levels of Portmeirion. The mechanism was noisy and played havoc when the sound crew was recording anything. Squeezed into the device, its operator had only a small window through which to see. It didn't steer easily and was suffocating. It also tended to break down and couldn't move on water.

Someone, probably Bernie Williams the production manager, averted the impending crisis with some amazingly quick thinking. He'd remembered seeing balloons used at a horse show and suggested that they might provide the answer. Pat grabbed at the idea. Henceforth, Rover was a meteorological weather balloon.

Even the replacement Rover posed considerable problems. Filled with helium, it rocketed up into the air. Filled with air, it became a sluggish, heavy pudding. Either it was too light or too heavy. Eventually the right mix of air and helium was ascertained. Also, at times during shooting the demand for Rover was so great that one had to be blown up every five minutes. An additional problem was the Alouette helicopter's down draft,

The ebullient publisher Richard Reynolds (left) and thoughtful copy-editor Steve Edgell in Portmeirion.

which blew Rover away; a heavier air and helium mix was then used. The neck of the balloon was patched over so as not to be caught by camera.

Getting Rover up over and down a building was solved by two invisible wires, pulled up by one prop man and down by another. One wire would lie slack while the other end was pulled and vice versa.

I thought that Max was going to blow up Rover there and then with his own breath. He was getting excited. I'd heard that Max was the wayward son of an academic family. Now *The Prisoner* was his family.

'How did it move?' With curiosity Richard fondled the limp rubber.

Deftly Max tied the neck of the nozzle.

'When Rover appeared, everyone had to be standing dead still. Rover had a wire tied here,' Max said, whirling a finger round the flat Rover's neck. 'It was pulled along backwards, keeping this part out of sight. Then the film was reversed. If people moved, they'd be on screen moving backwards.'

Delighted, Richard wriggled about, flapping his elbows slightly and giggling.

'What was the sound of Rover?' Richard asked.

'McGoohan wanted no electronic sounds. Music themes were tried and rejected. McGoohan wanted a sound half-human. Finally, three sounds were combined to act as Rover's signature. A slowed-down scream in an empty lecture hall. A monk's chorus played backwards. And slow breathing. Quite brilliant,' Max enthused.

'Like the Gregorian chant to summon up the dark forces,' Richard interrupted with great pleasure. 'Devil worship.'

Without a pause Max went on.

'And heavy breathing. Birthing. Rover came out of the free sea fountain.'

'What gender was Rover?'

'It had no sex,' Max replied seriously.

I asked Max about the oval egg-shaped chair, squeezed between the counter and the window. It was a familiar shell but differently coloured. Outside, its orange surface glistened. Inside, it was lined with heavy, black, corduroy-covered cushions. *The Prisoner* chair: a constant feature in the series. It could itself also be considered part of the cast; of the inanimate kind.

'He's been here, in the shop,' Max was pleased to inform me. 'Mr Eero Aarnio, the Finnish designer of the chair. He's signed the visitor's book.'

Outside the shop, I felt in quite a mixed-up state. I felt I needed to keep on my toes. I was looking for, and expecting, something but I didn't know what. Something was disturbing me. It wasn't my companions. It was Portmeirion and its explosion of colours and curves. It was an arch, Victorian melodrama churned in with high camp. It looked like a crazy Hollywood quilt; but it wasn't kitsch. The emptiness behind the false façades and spiral stone stairs leading nowhere had an inner meaning. The place was all of a piece, despite its disparate elements. It was an aggregate of styles that emerged as something else. Superficially the cacophony of pink and blue walls, peppered with green domes with spires, steeples, towers from different eras and places, looked like the perfect setting for Charles Dodgson's celebrated fantasy. Pale pinks and yellow fronts were dotted up and down the hilly circumference of the Village.

I couldn't make sense of it. Could I, would I, within the space of a few hours be able to assimilate and decipher the nature of the Village in which my thoughts had dwelt for so long?

Mark, my fellow assistant editor on

the series, had lent me his Pentax camera. I've never been much of a lens buff but Mark had been confident I'd be able to cope. His instructions on the camera were clear and easy. Steve, snapping away, would make up for what I failed to catch. I opened the camera, and looked through the lens. I waited for some strolling Japanese tourists to clear the view. They looked as if they belonged in the Village; as new arrivals. I closed up the camera without taking anything. I could not see what I'd take any pictures of; yet that was what I needed to do.

'You have to take pictures,' Richard had stipulated.

The flowers were still in bloom and it all looked pretty, but on a scale smaller than it had been sized in my imagination. I wondered if that was my failing memory or the deception of the screen. But I reminded myself that even a return visit to somewhere well known is often a shock, after a long absence. The selective memory is almost always out of proportion and all things tend to loom larger in the mind than in actuality.

Richard was quite bubbly. He called out details of whatever he observed. He read aloud from a plaque. Steve was silently concentrating with his camera. I was counting on his pictures being good in case mine were terrible.

The overcast sky was burned aside by suddenly brilliant sunshine. Autumnal light drenched our stage and I began to take photographs. I picked out low angles of tall shapes suspended in blankets of rich dark greens. I avoided any signs or trappings of people. I wanted a feeling of atmosphere that any human presence would disfigure. I sought exquisite façades glistening in the sunlight. I wanted to evoke mysterious circumstance. Could the camera in my hands capture any such intrigue?

I was drawn away from the architecture and towards the water. I saw no endless expanse. To the naked eye there was no open sea, only water and sand, ending at the far shore. There was no confining sea. Yet it had been on the screen. How could that be possible? How did they so convincingly make this water seem to be the imprisoning sea?

Wherever I pointed the camera, I could not avoid the verdant hills on the far side of the estuary. A close view of several episodes reveals that the hills on the other side are often visible but very thinly. On screen the estuary could, convincingly, be a part of a sea; but not to the naked eye or the ground-level camera. The answer was that the film camera was operated from a higher angle that diminished and illuminated the distant, hilly horizon.

I gave up and went back to watch what the buildings were doing. I was preoccupied with analysing the rift between my screen memory and the reality confronting me. The varying gradients and levels had not registered. What stretched out all around me seemed to me as if it had once been flat and considerably vaster. There was a distortion in my mind in the correlating of what I had viewed on screen and what now confronted me. What stood before me resembled the aftermath of giant hands, scooping and squeezing buildings and soil into a tiny space, pushing the lot upwards creating hillocks where flatness might once have been.

A plethora of azaleas, rhododendrons, camellias and other exotic shrubs, encircled the free sea, drooped over walls and crept up columns. The terraces were giddy with flowery colours.

Richard indicated an azalea bush It was flourishing, despite the lateness of the season, in a climate where it shouldn't even grow, at least not outside a hothouse.

'This is amazing,' Richard declared.

'This isn't the climate for those kind of azaleas. It's too temperate here. And they certainly shouldn't be flowering in October. Look at it! It's part of the mystique of the place.'

We strolled for quite a while before I felt ready to take more pictures. I was concerned that time might not be on my side. Again I took care to excise sign posts, vehicles and the bands of passing tourists. I focused on the lofty architectural skyline. I was striving to penetrate the conglomerate of divergent styles, to find out what was behind the often non-functional falseness of the buildings, the trompe l'oeil. What was the architecture inside itself trying to convey? I did not just want to see the setting for what it said in the series but for what it said for itself. I wanted to assimilate its intrinsic nature. Was there one, or was I wanting what wasn't there? Perhaps it was just frosting with nothing under it, no cake of substance beneath the icing. Was it nothing more than the transparent folly of a Victoriana-loving dilettante?

This open-air architectural museum was conceived by Clough Williams-Ellis in the 1920s and added to over the years. After the First World War, Williams-Ellis designed satellite towns to decentralize the London slums. The movement for a protected green belt encircling London was underway. In the process of demolishing buildings, Williams-Ellis accumulated bits and pieces, façades, sections and entire buildings. His background as a son of the landed gentry gave Clough a certain aristocratic taste. Whatever caught his eye was salvaged and reassembled in Portmeirion. The imposing façades crept up the slopes of hillocks. Bas-reliefs from distant faiths glinted with gold leaf.

Today the Village seems to demand a certain calm respect. The few tourists I saw were all circumspect. There were no noisy children in sight.

People strolling about seemed quietly spoken. I found myself talking more softly than usual. I felt we were being watched. From amidst the multitude of nooks and crannies, anyone could suddenly jump into your path. It could be Rover.

During the filming of *The Prisoner*, Clough was to be seen wandering the periphery of activity, sporting lurid, yellow, knee-high socks with his crumpled trousers tucked into them. Puffing his pipe, he was at home in his museum, on the search for litter, stooping to pick up bits of paper and other discards. His Village had to stay clean. The exotic fresh flower in his lapel; had he picked it there or bought it somewhere else? Perhaps he didn't allow himself the right to pick his flowers because they belonged only where they grew? Was he that kind of gardener? My own father was scrupulous in not allowing anyone to pick his wonderful roses, including my mother. Perhaps Portmeirion's flora too, was too sacrosanct to permit the cutting down of a flower. It had been reported that Clough seemed not to mind the intrusion of *The Prisoner*. He could well not have known about the real nature of the series. On seeing it, did he comprehend the strange overlaps of identity? Could he have foreseen that Portmeirion would no longer be just an open-air museum, that it would also be the unforgettable location of *The Prisoner*. I suspect that the association between the two would be very much to his liking.

In 1971, post-*Prisoner*, Clough was knighted for his contributions to architecture and the environment.

Richard announced that we should start thinking of getting back. I was not happy. I had not found what I'd been looking for, though I could not say what it was. What could I have missed?

Our last stop before driving away was a visit to the Portmeirion pottery shop. Richard wanted to buy his wife a gift. Steve drew my attention to a rack of postcards. I turned the rack round indifferently until I was drawn to a card with a photo of two venerable-looking, aged men. At a cursory glimpse I had thought I recognized the stately figure under a broad black hat, standing alongside Clough. I pulled out the card and apprehensively turned it over to read who it was. Sure enough, it was none other than the first live hero from my childhood. It was the American master architect, Frank Lloyd Wright. He had visited the Village in 1956.

What could a man like that have made of the Village? What would his reaction have been? Possibilities raced through my mind. What could I recall about Wright's motivations that could link him favourably, or unfavourably, to Portmeirion? I tried considering what drove Frank Lloyd and reached a conclusion that he was probably entranced by the place and sympathized with the idea of an architectural museum that was Portmeirion and which was in keeping with the nature of its role in *The Prisoner*. I felt there was a logical connection, a leap from *The Prisoner* to Lloyd Wright, via Portmeirion. I would have to dig and something would be unearthed. So I hoped.

One could only describe Frank Lloyd Wright as a political animal in the broadest sense. He was motivated by the conditions of living space and how that encapsulated the human being, and how it could dominate our existence. He objected to architecture that imprisoned people in ill-suited boxes. He aimed to free the spirit and enhance the soul with his designs. A home ideally should be designed in harmony with the natural environment and the needs of the individual. In this sense, his sentiment was not far removed from *The Prisoner*. He designed for freedom and not for imprisonment. He offered his designs as a solution to the human condition, albeit packaged within the scope of his taste and sense.

He'd been in Cardiff to receive an award. His ancestry was Welsh. Clough had met him by chance on a train across Europe and invited Frank Lloyd Wright to visit Portmeirion. He did.

Apparently he'd approved of what he saw and had commended Clough. How would Frank Lloyd Wright have assessed such an assembly of diverse styles into the cohesion of one museum, as accumulated by an eclectic collector? It was what it was, but also something somewhat greater than its components. It had the appeal of unfettered freedom. It offered every possible comfort for life. All one had to do was be there. In effect, it was the perfect seemingly open prison camp.

From this it is a short step to what Portmeirion did for *The Prisoner* and vice versa. Though Portmeirion was in itself a reflection of free, open thinking, it also formed a perfect setting for lulling, seducing and imprisoning the mind. It offered an irresistible feast for the mind looking for comforting, cushioning, unthreatening security. Designed to take the visitor off guard, it lends itself adroitly to social engineering and manipulation. Seemingly a place of refuge and retreat, it is a padded prison without fences or handcuffs. If there were trains anywhere in the vicinity, they would certainly have run meticulously on time.

Birds of a feather. Number Six, Clough and Frank Lloyd Wright exuded a commonality of the idiosyncratic. All cared about the human condition and were committed, in their separate ways and manners, to bettering the lot of their fellows. On the other side of the coin is the quirky, questionable stability of

Number Six contained in the Village: Portmeirion as an asylum for the mentally deranged and the excessively inventive.

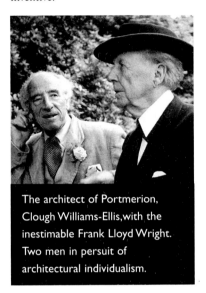

The architect of Portmerion, Clough Williams-Ellis, with the inestimable Frank Lloyd Wright. Two men in persuit of architectural individualism.

Either way, *The Prisoner* single-handedly put Portmeirion of the map, dragging it out of backwater obscurity. In April 1977 at the age of 92 years, shortly before he passed on, Clough declared that the series showed Portmeirion to its best advantage.

IN CONVERSATION

In the late 1980s when I first thought of writing about *The Prisoner*, I did a number of interviews. Equipped with my Sony, spare batteries, tapes and a readiness to drink tea when offered, I set off to talk to people who had contributed to the programme and to the times that produced it. Since then I've intermittently been on a quest in search of what lay behind the series. In checking through these interviews, I felt part of them to be valid and relevant to my ongoing search. Selections are presented here.

JACK SHAMPAN WHO CONCEIVED THE VISION

I had telephoned Jack Shampan, the flip side of the Portmeirion coin. Jack was the art director who had devised the futuristic look of sophisticated technical wizardry to go in tandem with the deceptively charming allure of the Village: the guts that ground the duped citizenry into line. The doors with no handles, the windowless control centres, the hydraulics that pushed and pulled seats to come and go at the press of a button; these were all his doing. Jack had not only to conceive the vision, but to make it function efficiently.

On the phone, Jack was unfriendly and reluctant to meet anyone interested in the series. He changed when I reminded him that I'd assisted on two episodes and written another.

'You worked on *The Prisoner*,' he said with audible relief. 'They keep calling me,' he moaned, referring to the programme's many active fans. 'They must be nuts, liking all that codswallop. Yes, come and see me. Maybe you can tell me what it's all about. I'll be home, I don't get out much. I'll be here.'

I caught a bus from my place in Holland Park to Kilburn in North-West London.

It was a bleak, wintry day with a gloomy, overcast sky. I rang the bell and heard shouting for me to wait. After a long shuffle and fiddling with the locks, the door opened.

'You the bloke that phoned?'

I said I was and the door opened just wide enough for me to slide in. I followed Jack as he shuffled down the dark, narrow corridor, led me into his sitting room and lit the gas fire. His slippers were worn, his cardigan had holes at the elbows and his baggy trousers were crumpled.

'Sit, don't stand,' Jack ordered me. I gave him a fresh loaf I'd baked. 'What's this, a bribe?' He chuckled and left for the kitchen.

I glanced round. Odd pictures and drawings for sets dotted the walls. They were in disposable frames, interspersed with family pictures. The decor was unashamedly ordinary, somewhat unassuming in effect.

I set up the tape recorder and Jack returned with tea and biscuits. Jack was certainly a bit quirky but somehow he epitomized the type of technician on the series.

There was an East End lilt to his accent. Jack sounded as if the hairs of his moustache were catching in his mouth. He spoke as his ideas leapt in, crowded and jumbled. We chatted about various people on the series. Jack was insistent that McGoohan owed it all to David Tomblin.

'David was, in a lot of ways, Pat's right-hand man. He was the spiritual support. He's a very experienced film man. He's done First Assistant Director on *Ghandi* and *Cry Freedom*. The Richard Attenborough films. David's not a show-off, in fact he's there, a real professional.'

Jack complained about the 1984 documentary made on *The Prisoner*. 'I didn't think much of it...' he paused to summon up the right expression. 'I hated it.'

He shook his head disapprovingly and recalled being pushed about by the director. 'He made me sit, get up, and walk. My feet aren't my best feature.'

I asked him what influences were behind Jack's concept of *The Prisoner*.

'Actually, in the old days, I used to go to a little theatre in Shaftesbury Avenue where they used to show those old German films. The photography was out of this world. They haven't improved on the technique.'

Jack mused over these early cinema memories. He recalled the films of Fritz Lang and other German Expressionists of the 1920s and

A Christmas 'Be Seeing You' from **The Prisoner.**

1930s. The masterpieces, as Jack referred to them. He talked of the shadows, the mood and the depth, before sound came to the screen.

I asked how he got onto the series.

'The reason Pat wanted me was because I did the last batch of *Danger Man*, the hour ones, not the half-hour ones,' he replied. 'The Americans called it *Secret Agent* because *Danger Man* was too subtle,' he added.

Jack maintained that *The Prisoner* was a direct and straightforward continuation of *Danger Man*.

'There was no room to manoeuvre,' he tried to explain. 'They used to have these ideas overnight. I had the expertise,' Jack shrugged.

Jack repeated that it had all begun with *Danger Man*. His views on *The Prisoner* fluctuated between derision and praise for its style. He admitted to being bemused by the fervour of later years in response to a series that had been so disliked when first broadcast. The earlier series, he felt, had the greater influence.

'They all came out of *Danger Man*. *The Saint*. Even *Bond* is only a very expensive *Danger Man*. Of course, Pat would never have any women business. You know, none of this smoochy moochy like the Americans...'

I encouraged Jack to say a bit more about what he thought of *The Prisoner*.

'Very heavy going...' he started but then changed the subject. 'With Bond, they take weeks and weeks. They spend millions and we had a very limited budget. But bigger than what they usually give in television.'

Jack began talking about George Markstein, and again cut himself short. He referred to Pat and George having a big fall out. I asked to hear more about this but Jack could not comment.

'Don't ask me. I was only the boy there.'

Jack told me, by the way, that McGoohan was the first to be offered the part of James Bond and that on a film in Pinewood - Jack couldn't remember the title - Pat and Sean Connery had worked together.

I pushed again for his opinions of *The Prisoner*. He told me that he had some drawings lying around for a science fiction film that never got off the ground, so he'd used them for *The Prisoner*.

I asked to see the drawings. He said it was too much of a business to locate them. Rapidly changing the subject again, Jack referred to John Osborne and the 'angry young men', the big symbol of the youngsters at the time.

'The people who liked *The Prisoner*, and still do, are mostly university types, people who want to save the world. I mean, the ordinary bread-and-butter, cor-blimey blokes like me, they don't know what it's about.'

Abruptly he leaned forward and snapped.

'You can come again, but it'll cost you,' he paused. 'Another loaf of that bread. Now I got to give you something.'

He shuffled about rummaging through papers and pages looking for something suitable. I said it wasn't necessary to give me anything. He insisted. He had to. He gave me a 1967 Christmas card he'd designed for *The Prisoner*.

'Did you like MGM as a studio to work in?' I asked.

'Of course. I knew the studio because I'd worked there on *Danger Man* and I was doing the impossible then. I was building whole towns and God knows what - harbours - all on the stage. They had all the facilities there and, of course, we used to work seven days a week. Although my boys all got overtime, I used to work seven days and I never got overtime. But that never entered my mind.'

Jack spoke about the fundamentals of set design.

'The background mustn't fight, it must enhance...it's aesthetic. It's not the thing.'

Jack lit up and I helped myself to one of his cigarettes. He talked about the underworld he'd built on the MGM stage, the complexity of the hydraulics and the expertise of his crew. He complained about the way acting was going, losing the sense of communication. Now, actors swallow their words instead of sharing them.

'In front of the camera, you underplay. The camera will do all work. You just relax. You know Pat McGoohan was voted top young actor of the year for Brand.'

We talked about the absence of rank around Pat.

'This is why we got on so well, because with the blokes who worked for me, it was a real team. And if they were pulling their weight, they weren't just slaves. I valued their help. Now this is the whole crux of the matter. There's too much of the megalomaniacs about. Everything could happen. Even the cleverest of people need a backup.'

MGM was also, he said, the only studio equipped for something like *The Prisoner*, with its demanding schedule and variety of scenarios.

'Scott Elliot, the supervising art director at MGM, wouldn't throw anything away. I'd go round with a bit of imagination and take the boys out with a low loader and bring in the stuff and plonk it on the stage and you'd got all the carcasses. It might take a few days to complete.' This was easier, Jack said, than working from scratch. 'You can't make it in two weeks, all the stuff we were using.'

This applied to the design for *Living in Harmony*.

'The western I revamped on an existing French village there with *The Dirty Dozen*. The church I made into the Western saloon.'

There was just one exception. Jack wasn't allowed to use anything that Stanley Kubrick had thrown away, which it had cost Kubrick a bomb to make. Jack was convinced that *2001* had been financed by the American government in order to ready the public for the space age. Kubrick was a very expensive director. Jack said he didn't think much of the film, but added that he was probably talking out of turn.

It was time to leave. A jolly handshake and I was gone.

Outside it was still grimly overcast but no rain was falling.

I thought about Lindsay's art director the stylish Jocelyn Herbert. From a literary background, she was cultivated with an illustrious design career in film and at the Royal Court Theatre. She drove a swanky, 1940s, beige roadster that looked as if it had come straight out of the film *Isadora*, which she designed. I don't think she ever touched television.

Looking back at Jack's house made it apparent that in his career Jack had not been one of those to feather his nest with the generous help of production money. He was good at what he did; and loved it. There was a tinge of disappointment. He was a

modest man and it had come through despite some rude remarks and occasional invective. As a character he was no weak-kneed conformist. If he had been a Village citizen, I would guess, he'd have helped Number Six design the boat in which he almost escaped.

LEWIS GREIFER WHO CLAIMED TO BE THE GENESIS

It was still winter when I went to meet Lewis Griefer. He'd sounded civil on the telephone but I was somewhat apprehensive.

I made my way to another terraced house in North London, on a main road thick with traffic fumes. There was no rain but the sky looked dark and ominous.

Lewis let me in. Grey and leonine, he wearily led me into his sitting-room off the corridor. The layout was similar to that of Jack Shampan's house. Despite the lighting, inside it was as grey as it was outside. No amount of artificial light can ever quite dispel that looming darkness in the middle of the day that comes with a London winter.

Over a cup of tea, we launched into Lewis's friendship and history with Pat.

'I used to go drinking with him,' Lewis told me. 'He drank a bit more than I did but we had discussions over booze. Actually, I came in an odd way to be the genesis of *The Prisoner*. I'll tell you how.'

At the time Griefer was well on his way as a professional screenwriter. He also worked on a local newspaper in Hampstead. McGoohan was acting.

Pat had told Lewis that he was looking for a script editor. Pat had started writing and he wanted someone to work with, person to person. Unfortunately Lewis couldn't do it, so he'd recommended George Markstein, an out-of-work colleague

from the paper.

'I was the editor,' Lewis remembered. 'George was a reporter of mine going back to...in the 1950s, even.'

I remarked that I'd found George considerate, enthusiastic and had been very nice to me.

'Not everybody will give you that opinion on George,' Lewis informed me.

Lewis told me about George's idea, which he hugged to himself for a long time. After the war George had worked on *Stars and Stripes*, the US armed forces daily. Its editor had CIA connections. From these, George learned about a secret wartime camp in Scotland. George had written something and then showed it to Pat.

'Pat took it to Lew Grade and Lew, at that stage, would have said, 'Yes,' if Pat said, 'Listen, I want to dance naked on the moon.' He'd have said, 'Go ahead, you've got my blessing'.' So George's idea went ahead.

Lewis described Pat as a non-political animal. Pat was totally instinctual, he said, both as an actor and as a thinker. His later talk of the allegory and ideas that elevated the series to a cult status had occurred only on reflection, Lewis suggested.

'Post hoc!'

Lewis further argued the programme's particular appeal to youth. It wasn't political, he contended, it was spiritual and psychological. It was a reflection of the times. People felt helpless under the political developments and the Atom Bomb.

'The political situation marginalized people and made them feel manipulated and fairly impotent,' Lewis cited Gian Carlo Menotti's opera, *The Consul*, in which the Consul's Secretary sings the line 'Your name is a number' repeatedly. 'Pat assimilated all this agitation and paranoia, as you say, of the times.'

Lewis spoke about how well Pat and George had got on to start with, but that this turned to an absolute hate relationship, despite the closeness between them that began on *Danger Man*.

'While *Danger Man* was going on, I did actually write a script for him,' Lewis recalled. 'It was about a guy without any commitments just roaming around, didn't want to have any ties, a free agent, a free spirit. So you can see the sort of thinking that was going into Pat before *The Prisoner*. I think the script was called *The Outsider*.'

Pat had liked the script, Lewis said. At that time Pat wasn't driving and, as a mixture of payment and kindness, he had given Lewis his Volvo.

I asked Lewis what else in his view had influenced Pat. Without elaborating, he referred to Pat's working in the theatre with Orson Welles on *Moby Dick*, where he played Starbuck opposite Welles's Captain Ahab.

I asked about McGoohan's relationship with Lew Grade.

'Lew gave him total power and Pat gradually began to feel that he had to shape the series in his own way, whether it was directing, writing, anything at all. He wasn't prepared to have a series produced in the conventional way. Series are normally departmentalised. If it weren't like that it wouldn't work. The series vanished up its own backside because Pat had gradually taken over the situation, and how long can you go on like that?'

The series was initially rejected by the wider viewing public because it was too confused, Lewis had decided. People already had enough confusion in their lives. He also felt that the series contained immature ideas which appealed to the younger elements of its audience, who felt they'd be warped and twisted by the system, and no longer free souls. His own episode,

The General, was about subliminal education and rote learning. At the time, young people were dropping out of universities left, right, and centre.

'I'm not a number and all that sort of thing really expresses their views,' Lewis maintained. 'Pat was a bit of a tortured man, and still is I think. That's why the series is so perennial. And also there was some very good writing in the series, by the way. People wrote better than they'd normally do.'

Lewis pointed to Franz Kafka's stories as an unconscious influence on the making of the series.

'Kafka really explores a man lost against social forces which confuse him, which are intangible. Some of that was in *The Prisoner* but not as an intention. It was there because Pat felt like that.'

I left Golders Green perplexed by Griefer's reference to Kafka. I thought back to my horrific meeting with McGoohan over my scripts. If Lewis had spoken accurately, why had Pat been so outraged by my initial writing? What I'd written evidently fitted what he had been doing and what he wanted. *The Application Form* was bleak enough to be considered Kafkaesque. Try as I might, I still could not divine what really lay behind McGoohan's behaviour at our meeting in his office at MGM.

My last thought, before switching off the subject was Lewis's contention that all the writers did far better writing on *The Prisoner* than they normally would have done. This is a view with which I would come to agree wholeheartedly.

JOHN S SMITH WHO SAID HE WAS JUST A JOBBER

Still in the late 1980s, I visited John S Smith at his home in Middlesex. He owned a spacious house surrounded by lots of greenery, with a huge back garden. We'd not worked together

since *The Prisoner* but, over the years, our paths had crossed. We'd kept in touch intermittently. Whenever we met, we were always pleased to see each other.

John had a definite point of view on the calibre of technician employed on the series. He was circumspect about his fellow workers but, when encouraged, he would not flinch from being critical. Overall he felt that McGoohan had been saddled with unimaginative technicians.

As he poured tea, John described the 'chemists', as Pat referred to the sound technicians. McGoohan had spent the minimum of his time with them.

On the first showing of the fine cut of *Arrival*, McGoohan had not been happy about the sound. A door slamming had been fitted with the literal sound of a door. It was not good enough.

'When you have a door slam, I want to hear thunder,' Pat had told the dubbing editor.

Later the editor put it to John that the governor had gone mad. It was taken as further evidence of eccentricity.

'We all thought Pat had a screw loose, satisfying his actor's ego,' John reminded me, 'but he was trying to stimulate the brain.'

We moved onto how John had got the editing position on *The Prisoner*.

'Lee Doig gave me the job. I'd worked with him on other TV series. I was engaged as an editing mechanic to keep up with the schedules. It wasn't until you actually confronted Pat that you realized something more was expected.' It was a situation faced by everyone.

'I think all of us were square pegs in round holes,' John declared, admitting that a lot had gone over his head. He had not been alone in this.

David Tomblin, we felt, was of the same ilk, a good jobber. Tomblin, he said, was a puppet producer, Pat's sidekick only. Pat was not good at delegating any authority and had taken on all responsibility, creating a position for himself that was independent of other controls.

'It was autonomous. Pat was the governor.'

John criticized the overall television lighting which allowed nothing shadowy, no mood or atmosphere. *Dance of the Dead* was different because so much was filmed on location.

John argued that what made the series substantial was the creative chemistry between director Don Chaffey, actor Leo McKern and Pat. Originally, McKern had been slated to do the entire series as Number Two.

'It was like putting a match to a powder keg because they all had strong personalities which overlapped. The chemistry lasted for the earliest episodes, until the three geniuses broke up.'

This was when Chaffey crossed swords with Pat and left under a cloud. Leo McKern had a nervous breakdown. The tiny clique was gone and McGoohan was alone. Markstein, too, had departed under a cloud, John noted.

Our tea tray was replaced with a bottle of chilled white wine and a couple of large, friendly glasses. Conversation veered back to the cutting rooms.

John remembered that Geoff Foot was by far and away the best editor, with impressive credits. He was capable of the fast turnover needed but he was unhappy doing it. Lee Doig had been incredibly fast. He could be finished by four o'clock and be off to deal with his properties: buying, renting out and decorating. Doig was more interested in these, John said; he just used the industry to make a living.

'Pat had the best of both worlds. He'd got a classy editor and also one who could keep up with the schedules,' John opined. 'He was trying to do something different and we had all been schooled in the other method of filmmaking so consequently we weren't particularly sympathetic. The only good thing about it was it was getting us a longer duration of employment. We didn't spend that much time with Pat or at least I felt we never got to know him, in a funny way, working in the cutting rooms.'

John recalled Pat's working regime. He'd be up at five a.m. He'd take a swim in his pool at the end of his garden before heading for the studio on his bicycle.

'He was totally dedicated to his directing, his scriptwriting and his acting. The editing, of course, came last. In those days too, studios worked in what I considered factory conditions. You got there at eight-thirty, had a tea break at ten, you resumed work until lunch time when you had an hour for lunch. You sometimes had to give part of that lunch hour to see your rushes. You went back to work at two o'clock, broke at three-thirty for tea. You didn't have it at the bench. And at five-thirty you went home,' John smiled. 'Well, that's a long way behind us now.'

John sympathized with McGoohan having to work under such restrictions, at a project on which he had a mainly intuitive grasp.

'The problem was, the poor bloke was struggling with all us philistines, trying to create something he couldn't express.' McGoohan, John felt, knew exactly what he wanted but he just didn't know how to say it. However, it was an opportunity that McGoohan, himself, had engineered.

'It wasn't that Pat was given the freedom, it was that he took the freedom. *Danger Man, Secret Agent,*

was transmitted coast to coast across three time zones. It's unique.'

I pointed out that *Danger Man* had no cult following.

'It didn't, but it made a lot of money,' John grinned, returning to McGoohan's dismay at the industry. 'On one occasion I was waiting with Pat to get into the theatre. He was saying how he loathed the studio system and how he would much rather gather a nucleus of people round him and get an old stately home or a castle way up the country. No factory regulations and tea breaks, no artificial sets, but real rooms. He was never particularly happy with the end result of *The Prisoner*. He was frustrated and I was very sympathetic. I was a little bit nervous but he usually put me at my ease.'

John shook his head over the first episode we did. *The General* was so pedestrian.

'There was little camera movement and very, very square shooting indeed.' In regard to the actual cutting, John said, it was another matter. 'Pat taught me that you can manipulate film. It doesn't have to be squarely cut.'

John's recalling this really surprised me. I had no recollection. I remember Pat being acute and perceptive, but not that innovative, in the actual editing. Or had this kind of lesson occurred while I was out of the cutting room or preoccupied with my BFI test sequence for *The Application Form*?

John talked about Pat's stint in Hollywood on *Ice Station Zebra*. On the one hand, Pat had been spoilt rotten by the lavish treatment in the star system. On the other, Rock Hudson had been the star, not Pat; and Ernest Borgnine was also a star of considerable stature. On Pat's return to *The Prisoner,* something had changed with him.

John reminded me of the feeble end-of-production party we'd gone to in the MGM restaurant. The cutting crew arrived late and stood, as a clique, in a corner.

'Pat came in with his Cheshire cat grin saying, "Enjoying yourself?" and not interested in us. He was more familiar with the people who were working on the floor with him. He breezed on down the room and out.'

We chatted about the ritual of visiting the other studios in the Elstree vicinity. Every one seemed to have a television series on the go. There was an aura of mystique about us, however. Rumours had built up around *The Prisoner*; that Pat was off his rocker and anyone working on it had to be vetted and sign a secrecy clause. John had treated this with some credence.

'I scanned my contract to see if there was anything like that,' John told me. 'It didn't exist but Pat was trying to hold onto an element of secrecy, in fact, because he hadn't quite found the vehicle for the series yet, the direction. And so we all knew we were either working for a nutcase or else something a little bit out of the ordinary.'

We talked about some of the other episodes. I asked John how finally he rated *Dance of the Dead*.

'What I liked about *Dance of the Dead* is the style. Pat filming totally in situ. He shot with the sun going down on the beach, and Mary Morris looking quite bizarre dressed in a Peter Pan costume with grotesque lines on her face, and tremendously long shadows. I don't think it was by design. I think it was by luck more than anything else. He captured something there.'

Before leaving, I took a stroll round John's garden. He showed me where he planned to build a cattery. The film industry kept on shrinking and he was thinking of his future. Both he and his wife adored cats and they had decided to go into business taking care of other people's animals. What else

could a retired film editor do, he asked, run a pub or a video store? He'd bumped into features editors who could no longer get jobs. They'd looked lost and prematurely aged. Without the thrill of filmmaking, their lives were empty. John wasn't going to let that happen to him.

ALEXIS KANNER, CLOSE TO NUMBER SIX

It was 1988. I was over in the States editing a feature on location in Texas. As soon as we got to Los Angeles, I telephoned Alexis Kanner. I told him who I was, what I'd done and asked him if I could talk to him about *The Prisoner*. We made an arrangement and he came to see me in my hotel room. The conversation immediately centred on our footwear. Kanner was wearing a pair of beige British Knights, a style of heavily upholstered trainers. I was wearing exactly the same. He sat, cross-legged, in the corner of my room. It was midwinter and he squeezed his eyes against the brilliant Hollywood sun streaming in from the balcony.

We kicked off with stories about Kanner's start in films. When he was fifteen, he'd lied about his age to get work. He did a police series for the BBC, *Softly, Softly,* and acquired notoriety.

One day he got a call from David Tomblin. 'I'm doing this strange series. Feel like being in a western?' Tomblin had asked. He was talking about *Living in Harmony*.

'I went up MGM on a Sunday morning,' Alexis recalled. 'The place was empty, just Dave in the office. He said, "I'm going to make it archetypes," the quintessential bad guy and all that. We sat around and I made up this character out of all the characters I'd ever seen. We called him The Kid, not a name. Put together a costume from old stuff out

of the wardrobe department, as though he'd stolen it from dead men, a top hat, pants too big and two absolutely exquisite guns. Clearly a psychopath from the word go. About a day or two later, I got a cable from Patrick in California saying he was taking gun lessons from Steve McQueen and Sammy Davis Junior. I proceeded to practise for the better part of two weeks.'

He had to solve some safety problems.

'I did wire the trigger back. Robert Mitchum had blown part of his leg off once that way. On the single-action guns you have to cock it and fire,' Kanner demonstrated the process of fanning, going from cock to fire. 'My hands were bleeding 'cause I always miss and the hammer would chew into my fingers. On the day it worked all right.'

In the meantime, McGoohan had returned and the filming of The Kid's confrontation with Number Six had become a matter of great anticipation among the on-set crew.

'When Patrick and I had our showdown, lots of bets were laid on the side. Much money was wagered,' Kanner said. 'There was a lot of pent-up tension and release being poured into this event.'

Tomblin asked him to hold back on his draw. He wanted Pat's gun out and then the camera to zoom in on The Kid's gun being drawn.

'"You mean let him draw first?" I said, "Dave, give me a break!"'

There were three takes in a row but only one shot in total was fired. Both had fired seemingly simultaneously. They wouldn't know who won until the rushes were screened. The rushes wouldn't lie.

'Patrick had drawn in about two-thirds of a second, start to finish. I had drawn in eleven frames,' Alexis maintained.

I was sceptical that Kanner was the

quicker on the draw.

While filming the shoot-out, he recalled seeing a moth-eaten, cheaply-costumed monkey waving a sort of bone. It was the hairy hand having discovered a weapon, the last shot of 'The Dawn of Man' sequence in Kubrick's *2001*. This information and change of subject Kanner volunteered, unasked. The idea of the monkey and the first weapon, and of his own fast draw, had made a lasting impression on him.

He remembered arriving at the studio at four-thirty every morning and seeing Pat at the top of the stairs, waiting in the dark and saying that it was going to be a day of indescribable brutality. The dressing room next to Alexis was occupied by a *2001* leopard. There was a sign across the door that read: 'Dangerous Animal - Beware!' It was another 'Dawn of Man' creature. The first leopard hadn't been dangerous enough, according to Kubrick, and was sent back. Another leopard was auditioned and it had the dressing room next to Kanner's for the next week or two.

Kanner flipped back to *Living in Harmony*.

'With the collusion of Dave, I stole the death from *Vera Cruz* in which Burt Lancaster replaces his gun, as he always has all through the picture, before he falls down.'

Kanner told me about a tremendously intelligent film critic who was a devotee of *The Prisoner*. He held gatherings to discuss the series, attended by serious people of intelligence, Kanner assured me. He talked briefly about the local Los Angeles interest in the series and then moved on to the making of the final episode.

'*Fall Out* is the most expensive single hour of television ever made,' he started, then told me that McGoohan had begun work on it immediately after *Ice Station Zebra*.

'Patrick had written some of the trial for *Fall Out* while flying back to London from Hollywood.'

The episode was constructed bit by bit. Kanner and McGoohan had been discussing a director who wanted to do a buddy movie in Africa with both of them.

'Patrick said to me, "Beware of that fellow, Alexis, because his hipbone," he said, patting his hipbone, "isn't connected to his thighbone exactly the same way as yours is and mine".'

The phrase then evolved into The Kid singing several bars of 'Dem Bones' while on the run from the militia.

Kanner was taken aback when he saw the final script.

'Patrick,' he declared, 'there's every indication here that we blow the place up and he said, "That's right." We shoot everybody too. He said, "That's right." And I said, "Pat, isn't this a pacifist programme?" He said, "Fuck it. Do you want to keep coming back here month after month?"' It was, literally and figuratively, the series' last hour. 'People were totally cracking up. And so Patrick's general response was, "Screw it."'

The first assistant director, Gino Marotta, was in a mental institution for nine months, Kanner said. Leo didn't want to ever see McGoohan again at that stage.

'These were very tense times. But they were wonderful times,' Alexis paused thoughtfully. 'It's rather like a war you all got out of and don't want to go back to.'

I asked Kanner if he knew much about the relationship between Pat and Lew Grade. What did he make of the script concepts?

'Lew never read any of them. When we ran out of money, Patrick would make a date to meet him alone in the Tower at Marble Arch, on the top floor in Lew's office, seven a.m. Saturday morning when the whole

building was empty, and he'd act it out.

'I'd say to him, "How did it go Patrick?" and Patrick would say, "Oh, he loved it. I grabbed him by the lapels, and Lew loves that when you grab him by the lapels and get him involved in the action" and got a cheque. There was nothing ever on paper between them. There was just Lew's faith in Pat. I guess it was a sort of tax loss for Lew and to please Pat, who was his favourite son. Lew would get his own private performance and then Pat would get the cheque.'

Kanner summed up Lew Grade.

'He's the only man in the world who's allowed in the First Class section of an aeroplane with a cigar. He has a gadget and the cigar smoke goes into the gadget. That's Lew.'

I asked how come Pat had been comparatively inactive in his career for some years.

'For a number of years he devoted himself to curing his daughter. She had an incurable illness. He became an expert in it, totally cured her, and filmed it. He's extremely happy. He's a grandad now, happy with his family. And for a man who's always been difficult around actresses and females, it's always bemused me that, until the birth of his grandson, he's been totally surrounded by women. All daughters, a wife, even the pets were female.'

We'd been chatting quite awhile and Alexis was drawing to a conclusion. He summarized McGoohan. A very generous man. A great sense of irony. A good sense of contradiction. Very bold for a shy man. Very violent for a pacifist. Believes in excellence and strives for it. Icy blue eyes and incredible danger.

'Quintessential Bond,' Kanner added, 'because Ian Fleming wanted a gent, which Sean never pulled off. Sean was wonderful and charismatic, but a gent he wasn't.' McGoohan had that quality.

'Pat could have done anything he wanted, you know. Pat turned down *Butch Cassidy and the Sundance Kid*. To play the Kid with Paul Newman playing Cassidy. They offered all of England, a good part of southern France and the isle of Jersey if he would play Bond.'

ALAN SAPPER ON ESPIONAGE AND MATTERS OF SECRECY

I always thought of Alan as a politico through and through. As General Secretary of ACTT, confrontation had been a way of life for him, fighting on behalf of the workers he represented. His responsibilities covered the film processing laboratories, the television networks and the freelance technicians that kept the feature film industry going. I remember going into his wood-panelled office in Soho Square and watching a crowd of grown men and women cowering in his presence. Despite being unpopular, his position was unassailable. He got things done and he was highly effective in protecting his members' interests. He was determined, uncompromising, and he had his finger on the political pulse. He was considerably more intelligent than most of the ambitious characters under him. He'd repeatedly outmanoeuvred innumerable attempts to topple him.

We'd kept in touch, infrequently but regularly, over the years. Talking to him heartened me. It reminded me that I, too, was once an active politico, though a long time ago and in another country. In some sense he lived out the struggle to which *The Prisoner* aspired. I had little doubt the substance and content of the series had rung some bells. Like Lew Grade, he was another cigar chomper. He knew Grade and had once been offered a million pounds by Bernard Delfont to take over the running of

Elstree studio. As the offer included taking on the studio debts, Alan had refused.

Sapper had never met McGoohan but had heard plenty about him. He remembered that there had been some union problems during the shooting at MGM but he couldn't recollect what it was all about. He'd gathered that it was not a happy unit and that McGoohan was not the easiest man with whom to get along.

In 1967, Sapper had been responsible for pulling the plug on broadcast television. It was a Sunday and *The Prisoner* was one of the programmes blacked out by the ACTT action. The dispute was over the introduction of new technology being imposed without negotiation.

In 1988, I visited Alan at his newly bought home in Chiswick, just out of hearing of the busy Hogarth roundabout. We retreated upstairs to his eyrie, the one place where his doctor wife allowed him to smoke his cigars. He didn't offer tea. He opened a bottle of fancy red wine and I set up my tape recorder, ready to switch on.

He launched into the subject of isolation achieved by certain individuals.

'A powerful person who is not understood and doesn't communicate becomes very isolated and is considered eccentric. If you imagine Hitler as a great communicator, he was. But he could equally have been an eccentric and, considered as such, put away. People understood what he was saying and responded, but also he was used by the industrialists of the western world at the time. They saw in him a mechanism to responding to the Soviet threat, as they saw it.'

I pointed out that Hitler did what he said. In his perverted way he was honest.

'Honesty,' Sapper contended, 'is no virtue in many circumstances. When you are part of a confused,

downtrodden mass and somebody stands up and speaks with a coherent commitment, it's very often the words of insanity.'

Then Alan turned things around. He was asking the questions, interrogating me about *The Prisoner*. I described Number Six opposing the power structure, knowing what was surrounding him bit by bit and then finally being seduced by it, and becoming the leader, though ultimately redeeming himself by destroying it all to establish a more humanistic society. Sapper wanted to know why he wasn't killed straight away. I explained that he was too valuable. Although it appeared that his value was the information that he kept secret, it was in reality that he possessed qualities of leadership they, the powers that be, needed to incorporate into their system. He was not an automaton; he was a human being, a rare commodity. He was a precious object to experiment on but too important to lose. He was their prime investment. I said he was less a man to break the system and more a prophet to awaken the masses not just to change the system, but for people to be less concerned with comfort and more concerned with caring.

'The whole *Prisoner* thing was antidemocratic,' Alan interrupted me emphatically. 'Nobody elected these people.' He refilled our glasses.

Alan's attitude to the series was ambivalent. He expected me to convince him. He complained that Number Six seemed remarkably ignorant at times.

'He was astute, but not particularly intelligent. He didn't try and organize people.'

I said that he had tried but, in that society, it would be stupid. He had the sense to know that subversion isn't something you announce from the rooftops, especially when no one is likely to listen.

We moved onto the nature of secrecy in government and in society. Alan had a slew of ideas.

'MI5 and MI6, though set up to defend democracy, were actually eating away at it with the blessing of the government of the day. Thereafter the 'enemy within' acquires a new meaning. Secret agencies, with their masters, become a government within a government.'

I agreed that England was an excessively secret society and that had a considerable impact on *The Prisoner*.

Alan seethed about the infiltration systems in capitalist societies. He described how the anti-apartheid movement and CND had been extensively infiltrated. England, once a complacent, negotiable society, had seen more internal trouble because of provocation from agents sent by the secret services, Sapper claimed.

I asked if this was something new.

Alan said no.

'They've been doing that ever since the misinformation campaigns of the postwar period and during the war.' He added that he'd found bugs planted in his Soho Square office.

England, he said, suffered from xenophobia.

'Germany, that's the other great xenophobic country. It's got roots in the landed gentry. It's integrated with the aristocratic system.'

I asked if Alan could tell me about any brushes with the secret services other than the bugging of his office.

'I was in Portugal at a meeting of our international with our new affiliates, the post-revolutionary union of audio-visual workers, post Salazar.'

This was the occasion of a conference and a reactionary, open-letter campaign.

'I had information that money was being passed on to the open-letter campaign from the American State Department, through a solicitor's office in Munich, and I said this to the press. It got headlines in Portugal.'

Back in London, Sapper had been invited to an embassy luncheon club. The German embassy was the host. There were people from Belgium, Canada, New Zealand, France and other nations. He referred to one of the guests seeing him at the TUC and in a Labour Party action. Sapper got suspicious. He heard from a friend who worked at the German Ministry of Information.

'She saw my file with the word, "Closed" on it and the comment, "He is too well-known to take further action against" in German. And that's how it all connects up. It's incredible how you sometimes find real evidence of it happening, and it seems quite small beer. More wine?' he offered, smiling.

I asked Alan why *The Prisoner* had stuck in his mind after such a long time.

'I remember *The Prisoner* because it was so exceptional. It was perhaps the only television series that dealt with a basic situation of our society, both twenty years ago and now. It transcends contemporary relevance.'

He referred to its relevance to an autocratic society such as the Soviet Union. This was prior to the dissolution of the Soviet bloc.

'In the Glasnost period, now, they might even show it,' he said.

Alan felt that, in time, the Official Secrets Act would be withdrawn in Britain.

'Supposedly for the benefit of more openness. But the more open they say society is, the more closed it will become, and I think the society will be extraordinarily controlled by secrecy.' Alan cited an incident called the Christmas tree factor, involving BBC organizers.

'It was discovered that people they were politically suspicious of, or had their doubts about, had a Christmas tree printed on the corner of their file, so that whenever they were considered for promotion, they saw that they didn't get promoted.'

The old guy in charge of it, according to Alan, was a run-of-the-mill MI5 bureaucrat.

'This came out and the BBC agreed to withdraw the MI5 symbol, the Christmas tree, but from one section it didn't. It said we must preserve the Bush House operation. Now, the Bush House operation is the overseas operation of the BBC which spreads misinformation against the Soviet Union and its allies.' Alan lit the cigar that had gone out and leaned forward conspiratorially.

'And what's very interesting, in 1946, Reuters was owned by the security services. The head of Reuters at that time was Denis Healey. He was MI6 and head of the world misinformation service, against the Soviet Union. That originated from black propaganda during the war, supposedly against the Germans but also against the Soviets. That's what caused Blunt to give information to the Soviet Union. The Foreign Office black propaganda organization was not telling our allies, the Soviet Union, where the German armies were massing. They would have walked into a trap deliberately helped by the British side not telling the Russians what they knew. And so Anthony Blunt told them. A lot of those spies were resisting the xenophobic, racist Foreign Office.'

Alan was convinced that the secret services would never be disbanded in Britain.

'The Times reported nine years ago that, when they refurbished the Communist Party HQ in King Street, they found a bug in a table leg.'

The secret services' field of operation was highly advanced.

'They're qualified and expert at intervening. With the instruments they've got at their disposal now we can be overheard by a device in that window there,' Alan indicated the window behind me overlooking his back garden, a high wall and a dark church, 'because every time I speak there is a minuscule disturbance in the surface tension of that glass which can be interpreted. They can put a whole cable round the house without us knowing and pick up everything we're saying. They can pull it down the street, they can put it in the gutter, they can bury it in telephone wires, they can do anything they like, and the great thing is not to care.' Alan reflected for a moment. 'But that's what the Prisoner couldn't do. He had to care.'

We talked about my coming from South Africa and relating it to *The Prisoner*. Alan rejected my contention that South Africa was a close facsimile of the Village conditions. He said that the mass of oppressed people there weren't lulled by comfort. He felt the Hitler and Stalin regimes were better suited for comparison to *The Prisoner*. To illustrate my point I described the inhuman working conditions of migrant workers in the Johannesburg gold mines.

On arrival the workers would strip naked for examination. In this procedure, the naked youths were slapped and hit by black and white overseers and mine officials. Intimidation and subjugation were order of the day every day. Each man's penis was slapped and twisted during inspection. Thermometers were frequently inserted up the anus. On signing the standard yearly contract, a miner was issued a number. For the next year he would live by that number alone. Names were absolutely not be used under any circumstances.

Underground, it was forbidden to leave off digging even to urinate or get a drink of water. The control regime was as rigid as it was absolute. Death, which was frequent underground, was swiftly and carelessly handled. No disruption of the digging schedule was tolerated. The only delay was that of clearing the debris following an accident.

The workers were confined to hostels with the minimum of facilities. There were concrete bunks, little light and little ventilation. Food was slops, mostly of boiled cabbages and potatoes, mashed indifferently together. No radios were permitted. There were no newspapers and no women. Men were segregated according to tribe with rivalries cultivated. Strict curfews were violently enforced. Prison camp conditions were maintained.

At the other end of the scale, I argued, the whites enjoyed incomparable privilege as the ruling élite. At school they were conditioned to believe in their own superiority. Black people were taught to accept their inferiority. History books were designed to facilitate and justify the apartheid regime. Censorship was rife. The regime was committed to social engineering.

'It's this which makes *The Prisoner* applicable to apartheid South Africa,' I concluded to Alan.

On leaving, I felt I'd done well with Sapper. I found his information a chilling postscript to *The Prisoner* themes. My thoughts were drowned by the roar of traffic on the Hogarth roundabout.

LINDSAY ANDERSON, THE THINKING REBEL

I'd decided to visit Lindsay and discuss *The Prisoner* for a number of reasons. I knew he'd not been impressed with the series but I wasn't convinced that he'd actually watched any of it. In other words, I suspected it was a biased opinion. He felt it wasn't any good, so it just couldn't be any good. Nevertheless he'd agreed to have a look at an episode or two and discuss the subject of the book I'd told him I was intending to write.

As I've already indicated, Lindsay and Pat were the two most powerful and forceful characters with whom I'd worked. The one led on, in a way, to the other. Both were morally intelligent. Both were political animals to some degree. Both had rather large egos and lofty creative aspirations. I wondered what would have happened if they had ever met.

When I visited, it was still the late 1980s and Lindsay had moved from his dark and gloomy flat in Greencroft Gardens to a spacious, light, second-floor flat nearby in a small block close to Finchley tube station.

I arrived five minutes before I was due and Lindsay made a big point of my never being on time, of always arriving early. We snapped at each other in his kitchen and, with instant coffee and digestive biscuits, we drifted into his L-shaped living room. He drew the blinds and popped into his video player the first episode that I had brought.

He sat down next to me with his legs stretched out and crossed at the ankles. He groaned, touched the tips of his fingers together and shook his head.

'You're a bit batty, you know. You're writing about a popular medium like television. I mean, you don't watch it.'

'I know,' I replied.

It wasn't very long before Lindsay began commenting. I asked him to please keep quiet and watch. He did for a while and then he seemed to nod off. I prodded him.

'Oh, was I asleep?' he asked, suddenly alert, and zapped the remote to run the video back.

We got through the first episode and he whizzed through snatches of a few others.

He declared that he needed a drink and sent me to fetch the bottle of Bells he kept in the kitchen. As I poured drinks, he read through a draft of an introduction to my proposed book about *The Prisoner*. To my amazement, he said that he thought it quite interesting. He remembered that the series wasn't a success when it was first shown and that this didn't surprise him. Then he picked up on the cult appeal.

'I think the mark of anything that becomes a cult is often an extreme of absurdity, but has the eccentricity as well of a single, bizarre imagination. It doesn't add up, it never added up, to anything that could be successful. But when you revive it, it becomes so extreme it even has a certain exotic quality.'

Lindsay commented on the poor design and costumes which he described as kitsch.

'Perhaps that's all part of the camp appeal,' Lindsay suggested.

'You mean it's like saying anybody can create it?' I asked. 'The cultists feel a tremendous identification, that something of a superior quality would be just alien to them?'

Lindsay took a sip and nodded sagely.

'I think McGoohan had certain ideas and certain obsessions which couldn't add up to a satisfactory whole - he couldn't work it through - but it is sustained by his obsessive power. It really is a bit mad. That madness is always in a way rather compulsive. It can attract people. It can give a personality a certain forcefulness, a certain dynamic which can be attractive or intriguing, shall I say.'

I talked about secrecy, mentioning some of the ideas Sapper had spoken about and their obvious overlaps with the substance of *The Prisoner*.

'I think you've got a rather far-fetched connection you're making here but, of course, you might be right. Are you saying that McGoohan was visionary?' Lindsay closed his eyes, yawned and spoke on. 'If you do have

a kind of paranoid vision behind it, that can be very forceful. But you have a slightly paranoid temperament yourself, don't you? I mean a character like McGoohan is one that has a certain attraction to you.'

Echoing John S Smith's assessment of Pat, Lindsay suggested that I might be seeing more than McGoohan was conscious of or could express.

'Perhaps you've got to draw a distinction between the conscious intention of *The Prisoner* and its unconscious.'

I said that was very much what I wanted I wanted to get across. The distance between the apparent and the motivation behind it all, what was implied, and what the series stirred, how it worked almost in spite of itself, not because of it.

'Yes, it does make sense,' Lindsay said, quite encouragingly. He thought I was onto something interesting. 'I think you're an ideal person to write about it since I suspect that you are paranoid in rather the same way as McGoohan. It's a weird project.'

He then related his story of the one time he had met McGoohan.

He began by describing the type of acting he attributed to McGoohan.

'It's not a question of identifying so much as of advertising the acting. It's not the kind of acting where you don't notice that he's acting. It announces itself. I always remember a very funny story typical of McGoohan. When I was going to direct the first full-length play I did at the Court, *The Long and the Short and the Tall*, I had proposed Bob Shaw as the Sergeant because I knew Bob, he needed a job, and I liked him. They got a bit nervous and they thought perhaps we needed a name, which McGoohan was at that stage. I was very much against this, but George Devine said to me, "Look, can we meet McGoohan?" It was not a question of insisting that he played the part, more let's see what impression he

makes. I said all right and we met him. There was George, Oscar Lewenstein and myself in the pub next to the Court. I don't remember the conversation particularly well except I didn't take to McGoohan because he was being very sort of 'big'. At that time, they were playing Beckett's *End Game* in the theatre which George had directed and was also playing in. McGoohan started saying, "This thing they're doing at the moment, they're doing this *End Game* by Beckett." He said, "Appalling production, badly acted and quite dreadful". I sort of grinned to myself and when McGoohan went off, George - he had some humour about it - said we needn't worry about Mr McGoohan for the part. And that was the last we heard or saw of Patrick McGoohan. He did, even in that meeting, behave like an idiot.'

McGoohan's condemnation was, for me, not so offensive. He was attacking the culturally esteemed Beckett on the very doorstep of bourgeois taste, the Royal Court. In another mood, Lindsay might easily have admired such risky iconoclasm. I told Lindsay about my experience when I was first interviewed by Pat and how large I felt his presence was.

'It is a very big presence but it's a kind of presence I resist. I'm not absorbed by it, I rather don't like it very much and I think it's neurotic, really. I don't think it's just the size. Not much charm there.'

Listening to Lindsay's appraisal of McGoohan was unnerving. Lindsay could only view Pat the actor, not the writer and director. Nor could Lindsay consider what drove Pat. In fairness to Lindsay, he perceived that there was a substance to the series. Also, like John S Smith, he felt that McGoohan had chosen his technicians poorly; which, I suppose, applied to me as well.

WHERE TO NOW...

McGoohan's promise that I'd have four episodes in the next tranche of the series was perhaps not seriously meant. It was probably only a well-meaning apology for having abandoned me in order to be free to go to Hollywood. However, the figure four stuck in my mind.

It's an awkward task, certainly difficult, and probably impossible. Nevertheless, there's no earthly reason why I shouldn't take the plunge into presenting my idea of how a resurrected *Prisoner* would appear in today's climate. *Living in Harmony* took the Village into another realm. This opening up would continue.

The series ended with the destruction of the Village and the escape of Number Six. Let us accept this as given. Number Six has prevailed and must resume some kind of life, as victor and survivor, within society as we recognize it. Number Six would therefore require a new life and a new role. As a character of many parts, he would be able to choose for himself how he would integrate and adjust; but what might he do and what might he be? He could not return to being what he was prior to his imprisonment in the Village community: a government official or secret agent. A polymath, his choice of occupations would be extensive. He had clearly many qualifications and degrees to his credit. Additionally, he would only be attracted to something that had a social relevance and that afforded some measure of power. He could not easily be a voice that had no outlet. Yet, by his nature, he would reject most institutions and bureaucracies. It would need to be something legitimate, or at least to possess a legitimate façade. His integrity and his intrinsic make-up would have to be sustained. Although he destroyed the Village, he is no nihilist. Yet, undeniably, he was and

needs to engage in radical activity. Underneath it all he remains an irreconcilable dissident.

As a façade he might become a test pilot, or a design engineer in a scientific field. Perhaps he'd be an enormously popular actor in a powerful commercial position, secretly compiling his memoirs to make an exposé of the Village regime. He might retire into a rural idyll and wait for his next call to action or for a suitable cause or situation to arise.

Perhaps he could be a professor of philosophy at London School of Economics, lecturing on Authority and the Individual while quietly preparing a polemic for publication. He could assume any number of roles and he could not be taken for granted. He also would have to be on constant alert. Some government in some place would inevitably find him threatening; including his own government, whichever that might be.

Emotional blackmail, social concern and moral issues would stay as part of the underlying ethos. Any situation, any time, any place could be incorporated, provided they included the moral tone: the passion and caring of what is right and what is wrong. Humanity would remain indefatigable and indestructible as represented by Number Six, no matter what the odds. Privilege and prejudice would persist as humanity's abiding enemies, closely accompanied by greed.

The significance of individualism would remain paramount and the dangers of the mass mentality would be a constant concern. Excessive obedience and conformity would continue to be tantamount to slavery. It would be the unfettered, thinking outsider who endures as best able to elevate people, or to transcend and transform society.

Here the historic example of Nelson Mandela could provide an excellent model of character. Throughout his

years of confinement, Mandela was a prisoner only in name and number. Within himself, his spirit was always free.

However, one of the first, thematic concerns would be the resurrection of the Village, somehow and somewhere.

Let's flirt with the idea of Number Six as a philosophy professor. While he is researching in the British Museum, the professor is approached by a journalist who knows a great deal about him. Her bold, forthright honesty wins the professor's attention. She understands his reluctance to discuss his past or have anything to do with the people behind the Village. They were not all destroyed and have been lying dormant. Now they have plans to resurrect the Village, irrespective of government assurances that such a thing is impossible. People are still frightened by what he might have to say. If he was writing his memoirs, it could be fatal. The Professor insists that he accepts his political retirement and has no intention of resuming any political activism. He admits to being well aware of the continuing machinations of numerous power-hungry governments. He thanks the woman for her interest in him and takes his leave. She urges him to consider her offer seriously. She says she has powerful media connections enabling his memoirs to be published on a massive scale. The professor tells her that she's a bit too pushy for his liking but he suspects she might be sincere. Nevertheless, he insists that they need not meet again.

While strolling along Whitehall on his way to address a parliamentary select committee, the professor is accosted by two men. They demand that he accompanies them and they threaten to shoot two unarmed policemen who are approaching.

As the police disappear, the professor turns the tables. The woman journalist appears with a gas gun. As the unconscious professor is bundled into a vehicle, the police return. They are murdered on the spot. Inside the vehicle, the professor's jacket is replaced by the familiar piped Village blazer. He is given an injection.

The professor awakens to find himself once again back in the Village, which is as it was before it was destroyed, down to every detail.

Subsequently it emerges that the reconstructed Village is a cleverly sustained, huge-scale hologram. The illusion melts aside, revealing a bizarre construct of disparate elements in a futuristic mode, located somewhere isolated but scenically beautiful. It is a Portmeirion transmuted into a cacophonous, hybrid, science fiction idyll. All time spans are architecturally evident; past, present and future. I envisage the new Village to be an extraordinary city of high technical innovations, floating, moving, suspended in the Himalayas, over Siberia, or nestling on the Sahara. Number Two would be a Captain Nemo with unlimited horizons.

I'm also stirred by and refer to the vintage classics of the American comic book industry at its commercial and cultural high point, during the late 1940s and early 1950s. I used this process of development the first time round in *Living in Harmony*. Now I'm throwing my hat into the ring again with the same intention, the same conviction. I'd used Gene Autry as a source, so why not do the same again? In the comics, Autry had a sentiment and nature that was easily identifiable with McGoohan's Number Six. Autry wouldn't flinch when knives were thrown at him. Though he worked for the law, it was always on the edge with an independence so that, if needs be, his hands aren't tied by law or officialdom. Autry's fearless character was once described by two badmen.

'That Autry would face a rattler

and he'd bite first.'

However, I can't just superimpose *The Prisoner* onto any unsuspecting comic book; but, as with Gene Autry, I have to find a figure with a dimension and an identity not dissimilar to Number Six. Rummaging through my memory, I can identify one which I consider lends itself to the inventiveness of the series and which retains a certain gut relevance.

This time, the comic of my choice falls to *Airboy* circa early 1950s. The character Airboy was a moral force and he flew high. This is what Number Six did once, and should do again. The Airboy stories were a seamless heroic blend of the ordinary and the extraordinary, the fanciful and the solidly down-to-earth. Airboy was a whiz pilot with a phenomenal aeroplane, Birdie. He was a intrepid, blond, teenage hero, willing to leap in where others would fear to tread. Birdie was remarkable. Remote controlled and jet-powered, she had manoeuvrable wings which could flap and hold her as steady as a helicopter. Birdie could hover on a dime. The stories occurred in wildly differing places and circumstances. The panoply was huge. Yet, out of the disparate elements, something special emerged in these Hillman publications. When the comic began in 1942, the main character was Birdie. Airboy was secondary and a lot of the action was not in the air, but on the ground. In the meantime, Airboy grew up a little; by 1950, he'd lost his mid-teens image and had become a youth.

The stories mixed past, present and future, mythology and science fiction. The comic created an entirely credible world of its own. Like *The Prisoner*, *Airboy* was widely popular, and its distinctive qualities were unforgettable. As for Birdie, there's no reason why, at some stage, Number

Six might not pilot an equally wonderful mechanical aide. Surely Number Six's moral endeavours should encircle the globe.

While considering this choice, I originally homed in on *Airboy* because of what I regarded as its distinctive excellence. Although this was initially a purely instinctive reaction to the comic's inventive and compelling storytelling, as I reread my copies of *Airboy*, aspects of it relevant to the character of Number Six soon became evident.

Airboy's grandfather was an English government official though Airboy was American born and bred. His father, who entered the story after years of no family connections, was also an American. Like Number Six, Airboy landed in plenty of seemingly inescapable scrapes and he always overcame his adversaries without sacrificing his moral integrity. Airboy was a sensitive, clean-cut youth with a kind disposition. I never saw him depicted smoking or drinking, or with a foul mouth. It had also been the same for Autry. Gentlemen rebels were all well-mannered. Airboy's protagonists were evil to epic dimensions. His villains tended to be tyrannical, dictatorial, and aiming at world domination.

Airboy's field of activity was more extensive and international in scope than were most other comic book heroes and heroines that flourished in the public imagination during the post Second World War period. Europe, Mongolia, North East Africa and other far flung places entered *Airboy* scenarios. The problem of foreign languages tended to be glossed over, or else Airboy proved to be fluent in a multitude of languages and dialects.

Graphically, the *Airboy* landscape was less inclined to detail and more inclined to atmosphere. Although drawn by different artists between

1950 and 1954, *Airboy*'s pages conveyed a continued impression of thoughtful consideration for the blurry margins between right and wrong. Villainy in the comic was rarely one-dimensional, often the result of early tragedy. Frequently there was also in the stories a suggestion of intellect, invariably drawing some level of sympathy.

Airboy, then, could fly effortlessly in close formation with Number Six. The two characters make natural companions. Both had histories as individuals with the merest speckling of family relationships. They stood alone. They spoke out. They fought back. They both strove to make the world a better place.

From the wide range of *Airboy* stories, I have selected four which I feel lend themselves to use as starting points for the development of further scenarios on *The Prisoner*.

Airboy volume 9, issue 12, January 1953

Airboy vol.9 no.12: a view of aristocratic decay.

An explosion reveals a hitherto unknown entrance to a gigantic tunnel in Italy. At the same time, a number of eminent leaders and scientists disappear across Europe. Airboy is asked to investigate the huge tunnel, broad enough for Birdie to fly inside. Airboy flies into the maw of the tunnel and follows a labyrinthine course through the underbelly of the European continent. He is captured and imprisoned inside a monstrous tank-like vehicle, comparable in size to the Titanic.

The landship is the brainchild of a geriatric Lochivelli, the descendent of a sadistic Italian aristocrat or possibly a man who had lived through centuries. Decrepit and ancient, dressed in the courtly costume of the seventeenth century, Lochivelli has to live in a hermetically sealed room containing specially treated air. Visitors can only bear the searing mustiness for a few moments.

Lochivelli has plans for world conquest; already he has a throne. The eminent personnel who had been kidnapped are his prisoners. Most have joined him in his plans. In disguise, Airboy escapes to Rotterdam, alerts the authorities and coordinates the battle against Lochivelli's almost indestructible, earth-burrowing, armoured vehicle.

When Airboy finally reaches the sealed room, all that remains of Lochivelli on his throne are a pile of aged, crumbling clothes and a pile of dust.

Airboy volume 8, issue 9, October 1951:

Winging his way at high altitude across the desolate Arctic peaks,

Airboy sees the smoke of a small fire. He descends and finds a pilot, Tundra, who had crashed in the icy wasteland and survived at that high altitude for ten years. Airboy can hardly breath the rarefied air. Tundra has developed massive lungs. He owes his survival to a large black condor and the ability of his lungs to enlarge. Back in civilization, Tundra has difficulty breathing the impure air and adjusting to the foul society. Airboy leaves Tundra to his own devices and wonders about Tundra's megalomaniac tendencies. Airboy dislikes the superior way in which Tundra sees himself.

Airboy hears that Tundra has been evicted from different countries and finally has got a great building scheme underway, with the help of a munitions industrialist. Tundra, an architect as well as pilot, constructs a gargantuan tower, resembling London's present-day Post Office Tower except that it is intended to be higher than Mt Everest. Living at the high altitude, Tundra plans to become master of the universe. The army of builders are divided into three sectors corresponding to the altitude at which they work. Over time, they have changed physically. The Depth Men are those employed underground on the 3000 feet deep foundation that taps into subterranean heat and power; all these workers have grown squat and stolid. Those in the Sea-Level category may ascend to 15,000 feet. Above are the aristocratic, privileged Higher-Ups; they have acquired great lung superiority. With these strata of people in his thrall, Tundra plans to launch attacks on all countries and truly become the universe's master.

Airboy, formerly Tundra's rescuer, becomes his destroyer.

Airboy volume 8, issue 11, December 1951:

Airboy is in London. He notices a suspicious-looking man fiddling with his watch. A lamp post explodes. Airboy chases the man across some railway tracks. The man is killed by an oncoming train. Airboy finds the man's watch. Soon a man asks him the time and tries to snatch the watch. The would-be thief escapes.

Airboy takes the watch to a local watchmaker. The owner, Dorf, declares the watch to be rubbish and offers to replace it with one of a far better quality. Airboy refuses. Dorf offers him a hundred dollars for the supposedly useless watch. Airboy refuses. The thief emerges from behind a curtain. He has a gun. Again he asks Airboy the time.

Airboy is tied up and secured inside a grandfather clock He hears about the plot to bomb London by packing explosives into all the major clocks and triggering them with the special watch mechanism. Time is running out.

Airboy severs his bonds on the clock's pendulum and escapes.

When Airboy returns with the police, the shop has been transformed. Dorf presents himself as a respectable watchmaker and claims convincingly that he has never seen Airboy before. The police leave, not believing Airboy's fantastic tale about subversives determined to destroy and loot the city.

Airboy doubles back to the shop and follows the plotters down into the sewers. They emerge in a derelict, bombed-out wasteland and leave in a sleek, black jet. Airboy summons Birdie and gives chase. He forces the jet down and it crashes into a bridge; but the plotters escape unscathed.

Airboy goes to Lord Amberly who believes him and, using his influential connections with the government, arranges police cooperation.

Time is still running out.

Airboy tracks down Dorf and some of his cronies. Airboy had correctly assumed that Big Ben would be the main target. Flying low in Birdie, Airboy lassoes two of the plotters. He lands and chases Dorf plus another

crony inside Big Ben. Among the clockworks, Airboy despatches one of the pair. Airboy fights him on a catwalk and the plotter plunges to his death.

Dorf gets away and climbs out onto the face of the clock. Airboy follows. The time of detonation, ten-thirty p.m., is close. Out on the edge of the minute hand, Dorf refuses to come in. He intends blowing up himself and Airboy. The minute hand moves and Dorf slips. The clock strikes ten-thirty but there is no explosion. Dorf's watch had broken in his fall to death.

Airboy volume 7, issue 8, September 1950:

Flying over the Great Wall of China, Airboy lands in a remote town in order to get some food. He finds the local people in a state of panic. A horde of Tartar bandits is expected.

An army of horsemen descends on the town. Chained to their saddles, the fierce riders are led by the mad Professor Attica on the back of a centaur. Resistance is futile and Airboy is captured for trying.

Inside a vast cave in the surrounding hills, Attica, wanting the heroic Airboy to join his ranks, tells him how he found the centaur. While researching at Potsdam University, Attica had discovered proof that a tribe of centaurs had migrated from ancient Greece across Asia Minor to the barren steppes. Attica had found the last remaining centaur, half-retarded and hiding in the Great Wall. Attica had enslaved and chained him, forcing him to obey and lead the army he'd built up and controlled by use of an ancient horn.

Airboy refuses to join Attica's mad campaign and is chained to a horse.

A convoy of Chinese tanks approaches Attica's hideout. But he is unafraid and has a plan to trap the convoy. A landslide traps the tanks.

As the bandits descend, Airboy takes his chance and snatches the horn from Attica. Events move fast. The centaur snaps free of his chains and Attica is dislodged from his back. The whip-wielding Attica is trampled to death by the vengeful centaur.

Then the centaur takes over leading the attack on the trapped tanks. Airboy tackles the centaur and they battle on the edge of a cliff. Airboy sends the centaur flailing to his death.

The Chinese convoy is saved.

Riffling through my collection of *Airboy* comics, the inventive possibilities for integration into the Prisoner seem limitless. However, short of full scripting it is tricky to explain how I'd transfer and implant the stories I've selected. I'm going on a sense of what could be brought out of the subtext of these stories to supplement what I can only term as an inspirational source. The first appeal is the scale. Number Six is only equipped to tackle big issues, not the mundane or the small. A morality play requires a vast stage and life and death situations. Number Six is a big concept, demanding big opponents. Each of the stories raises a moral question or dilemma with which Number Six may be faced. I would introduce racism, gender prejudice, environmental issues, scientific abuses and other contemporary concerns as an issue of focus for each episode.

Well, that's the plunge, and I've taken it four times, as prescribed. Though I've presented a cultural source, *Airboy*, as a possibility to start from, the deciding factor would have to be that which is most timely, that which stems most from a contemporary moral dilemma; which are what make *The Prisoner* perennial.

EPISODE SUMMARIES

ARRIVAL

on the conflict between authority
and the individual

MAIN ACTORS

Patrick McGoohan as Number Six
throughout, Guy Doleman (Number Two),
Paul Eddington (Cobb), Virginia Maskell
(Cobb's girlfriend), George Baker (new
Number Two), Angelo Muscat as the
Butler in most episodes, likewise Peter
Swanwick as the Supervisor.

A man, assumed to be an unidentified
but significant government official,
resigns for no apparent reason and is
kidnapped by an unknown authority.

The man awakens in a fairy-tale
Village. His every attempt to leave or
learn his whereabouts come to nothing.
The location is secret and the people are
unwilling to answer his questions. In
effect, he is a prisoner and under
merciless scrutiny. A process of extreme
conformity rules the Village and is
administered by a figure titled Number
Two. There are no names in the Village,
only numbers. The newcomer is

Number Six.

Number Two escorts Number Six
around the community. It is a
supposedly perfect environment, though
stringently regulated with surveillance
at every nook and cranny. The pleasant
façade of Village life masks a dire
reality. Out of sight is an array of
sophisticated devices created to watch
and to control. Of these, the most
sinister are the vast, malleable Rover
balloons, the Village's lethal guardians.

Nothing is as it seems but the
subservient community is conditioned to
behave as if it is the beneficiary of a safe
and solid normality. To his cost,
Number Six learns that he cannot trust
anyone. He is a man alone.

Number Two reveals that he has
every detail of Number Six's life at his
fingertips. Documents and photographs
include innumerable private and
personal records but they do not
contain specifically what Number Two
wants to know: why did he resign?
However, Number Six won't cooperate,
collaborate or conform.

Number Two accepts that Number Six
is not ordinary and must be dealt with by
extraordinary means. He must be
manoeuvred, tricked, or coerced into
revealing the motivation behind his recent
decision to reject authority. Number Six
is dangerous because of his intransigent
individualism. He has to be brought into

line. His values pose a potentially serious
threat to the Village order.

In hospital, Number Six meets Cobb,
a once close colleague and one of the few
characters not assigned a number. Cobb
has also been abducted.

Soon after, Number Six is informed
that Cobb has committed suicide in
suspicious circumstances. Number Six
goes to confront Number Two over
Cobb's death. There is a new Number
Two, a harsher character.

At Cobb's funeral, Number Six meets
his late colleague's girlfriend. She reveals
that Cobb had planned to escape and
offers Number Six an electro-pass that
will get him safely out of the Village.

Number Six manages to bypass Rover
and reach a helicopter. Once airborne,
he finds that he has lost control and is
returned to the launch pad, where Rover
awaits him.

Cobb, we discover, is very much alive
and part of a plot to manipulate
Number Six, the prisoner.

Key technicians: Written by David
Tomblin (series producer) and George
Markstein (script editor for the major
part of the series), Don Chaffey
(director), Lee Doig (editor). Jack
Shampan (art director), Ron Grainer
(music), Rose Tobias-Shaw (casting),
and Brendan J Stafford (lighting)
worked on all episodes.

THE CHIMES OF BIG BEN

on learning to mistrust

MAIN ACTORS

Leon McKern (Number Two),

Nadia Gray (Nadia)

Number Six steadfastly refuses to become a part of Village life. He refuses to participate in an innocuous art and crafts show.

A new resident arrives and is allocated the cottage next to Number Six. She is Nadia, Number Eight, an Estonian who has also resigned from an official position. This arouses Number Six's interest but he is suspicious of her, as she is of him.

A champion swimmer, Nadia makes an attempt to swim to freedom but is captured by a trio of Rovers. Number Six is taken to watch the torturous interrogation of Nadia. She tries to kill herself. Number Six bargains to spare Nadia. He offers to participate in the arts and crafts competition.

Number Six builds an abstract artefact and plots to escape with Nadia. She knows that the Village is on the Baltic coast in Lithuania.

Number Six's entry wins the competition. His creation is in reality the elements of a boat. With Nadia, he sets off into the night to rendezvous with a colleague of hers. As his watch is defunct, he swaps it with that of Nadia's colleague. Number Six and Nadia are concealed in a packing case and shipped via Danzig and Copenhagen to London.

A couple of Number Six's old colleagues release them from the packing case. Many questions follow. Number Six offers to co-operate with

the authorities if Nadia is guaranteed protection. The chimes of Big Ben reveal to Number Six that no time zone has been crossed. He rages around the office, tearing at cupboards until he finds a tape recorder playing the London sounds.

Disgusted Number Six leaves the office. He is still in the Village. Everyone involved was part of a conspiracy against him.

For the second time, Number Six has been betrayed by a woman. This episode depicts the extraordinary level of sophistication deployed in the attempt to manipulate Number Six.

Key technicians: Vincent Tilsley (writer), Don Chaffey (director), Spencer Reeve (editor)

A, B AND C

on scientific intrusion into the mind

MAIN ACTORS

Colin Gordon (Number Two), Katherine Kath (Mme Engadine), Sheila Allen (Number 14)

The authorities have designed a drug which enables one person to enter another's dream and manipulate it. The dreams can be projected onto a screen.

Number Two, under pressure from above, believes that this innovative process is needed to probe Number Six's inner secret.

Number Six is medicated and strapped to an operating table by a doctor, Number 14. Electrodes and wires are attached to his head.

A cassette is produced and inserted into a machine linked to the electrodes. It recreates, on the screen, a party attended by Number Six at a Madame

Engadine's mansion in Paris. Three people from Number Six's past were known to frequent parties at the mansion. Number Two is convinced that Number Six sold out to one of the three characters, A, B or C.

As the experiment gets underway, another cassette is introduced. It has encoded on it an ex-colleague of Number Six's, A, known to have become a double agent.

In his dream, Number Six treats A with disdain. Nothing is revealed. The session ends.

During the recovery period, Number Six notices the pinprick in his wrist and has vague dream recollections of what happened to him.
Out in the Village he notices the doctor. She is strangely familiar.

Within twenty-four hours, Number Six has been sedated and medicated and is back in the laboratory, unconscious.

A woman, B, an old friend, is introduced to the dream. Number Six and B dance in friendly fashion. Again nothing is revealed and the medication's potency is diminishing. Words are implanted into the dream and B asks the pertinent questions. Number Six becomes suspicious and, even though in dream trance, he reverses the situation and departs.

Back in his cottage, on waking Number Six finds two needle marks. He finds and stalks the doctor, following her to the secret laboratory in the woods.

Number Six breaks into the empty laboratory. Investigating, he discovers what has been going on. He takes the syringe used in the procedure and replaces the drug it contains with water.

Once again, Number Six is sedated in the laboratory. Number Two confers with the doctor. They know C exists but they have no picture. It is a gamble as to who at the party could be C.

This third session is in an out-of-kilter, topsy-turvy world. Number Six adjusts a mirror mounted askew. As he straightens it, the room tilts and levels off. In the gaming room, a blonde woman gives Number Six her earring to bet at roulette, on number six. It wins and Number Six is given a key.

Madame Engadine appears with a matching key. Number Two is convinced that success is close at hand.

Madame Engadine drives Number Six to a secret meeting with her superior. Number Six has brought an envelope supposedly containing the information, about his cause of resignation, which Number Two desperately seeks.

Number Six meets her superior, who remains in impenetrable shadow. Number Six refuses to reveal his secrets to a faceless shadow and demands to see who is there. The figure enters the light but is masked. A struggle ensues and, under the mask, is revealed Number Two. On the screen, Number Six walks away then, still in the dream, he enters the laboratory in which the experiment is taking place. He hands over the envelope to Number Two. The papers within are innocuous travel brochures.

The cordless communication telephone from Number One rings. Number Two picks it up and listens. He has failed.

Key technicians: Anthony Skene (writer), Pat Jackson (director), Geoff Foot (editor)

4

FREE FOR ALL

on the process of democracy

MAIN ACTORS

Eric Portman (Number Two), Rachel Herbert (Number 58)

Number Six is approached by a new Number Two to participate in a democratic election. Should Number Six win, and himself become Number Two, it is implied that the mystery of the ultimate authority, Number One, will be resolved. Number Six refuses to commit himself but delivers a speech in which he tries to expose the iniquitous structure of the Village and its hostility to personal freedom. He then declares that he will stand for election. The crowd is enthusiastic, reacting to the cue cards held up by the Butler, the dwarf who is Number Two's right-hand man.

The press and publicity machine for Number Six's candidacy are waiting in readiness. Reporters ask questions and print fabricated answers. Number Six is allocated a personal assistant, Number 58, who only speaks an unintelligible foreign language, which in no way mars her excitement.

Number Six is bemused by the rapidity of his campaign machine. He is summoned to appear before the outgoing Village council. Every member has been assigned a variation of Number Two. They all wear Number Two badges. Number Six asks probing questions. The responses are those of orchestrated clones.

Accused of a breach of etiquette, Number Six is forcibly subjected to a regime of enhanced indoctrination and disorientation. Subsequently he hits the campaign trail with suitable vigour,

promising everything and actually saying nothing.

Hints of genuine communication between Number Six and his assistant start to appear. At this point, Number Six launches an escape attempt. He is chased to the beach. He overcomes two men in a speedboat and races for freedom. He soon discovers that the boat is no longer under his control and that Rover is waiting for him.

Number Six is hospitalized and subjected to yet further treatment. On his release, he resumes the inane campaign trail once again. In a public debate, he gets the better of Number Two.

In a night club, Number Six demands genuine alcohol. His personal assistant takes him to an illegal drinking place. Present is an intoxicated Number Two. Number Six consumes a spiked drink and collapses. Number Two, suddenly cold sober, is behind it all.

Drugged into near-infantile compliance, Number Six wins the election and takes his residency in the control centre. His assistant abruptly becomes a person of authority. She slaps Number Six repeatedly and with immense ferocity. Recovering his wits, Number Six immediately commandeers the Village public address system. He urges everyone to escape and be free. Then he makes his own attempt at escape, which ends in a subterranean cavern where mindless denizens worship Rover. They all turn on Number Six and beat him into submission.

Back in the control centre, Number Six is confronted with a new Number Two, his former personal assistant, who now speaks perfect English. Yet again, Number Six has fallen victim to a trap laid by the authorities. He is carried back to his cottage.

The old Number Two flies off in the helicopter. In the last communication with his replacement, she asks him to take her regards to the homeland.

Key technicians: Patrick McGoohan

(writer and director) under the name 'Paddy Fitz', Geoff Foot (editor)

SCHIZOID MAN

on the futility of control

MAIN ACTORS

Anton Rogers (Number Two), Jane Merrow (Number 24)

Number Six participates in a card test with the telepathic Number 24. As she takes a Polaroid of Number Six, she knocks over something that bruises his fingernail.

Over a period of time, Number Six is subjected to drug-enhanced conditioning. He awakes in strange surroundings. His hair is a different colour and he has a thick moustache.

A series of orchestrated incidents indicates that he is not Number Six, but Number 12.

In the control centre Number Two informs him, as Number 12, that he has to convince Number Six that Number Six is not who he thinks he is. The purpose is to undermine Number Six's identity and thereby render him vulnerable. The new Number 12 is told that he is almost identical to Number Six. To complete the deception, Number 12 must remove his moustache and change the colour of his hair.

The new Number Six and Number 12 meet. They are completely identical. The two engage in competitions and tests of skill to determine which character is which. Each time, the imitation Number Six proves to be superior. Number 12, the authentic Number Six, has been altered by programming.

Determined to prove his identity and scupper the farcical ploy, the authentic

Number Six, now Number 12, summons the telepathic Number 24. The telepathic tests consistently verify that the imitation Number Six is the real one. The authentic Number Six, now Number 12, is visibly shaken.

Surveillance indicates that the deception has deeply confused the subject. On waking the next day, Number 12, formerly Number Six, notices the bruise on his fingernail. Examining the Polaroid, he notices that the bruise is not in the same position. He realizes that something is amiss. Looking in the mirror, he has flashes of recall of his ordeal of the previous weeks. Hints of the programming surface in his mind. To reverse the procedure, he subjects himself to an electric shock. He starts to deprogramme himself and successfully resumes his former right-handedness.

Number 12 confronts his imitation double and beats the truth out of him. The double escapes with the authentic Number Six in pursuit. They are both confronted by Rover. The authentic Number Six has the sense to remain motionless. The double panics and makes a run for it. He is caught by Rover and smothered to death.

Number Six sets about impersonating his impersonator and, after reporting failure of their mission to Number Two, arranges to leave the Village.

A disappointed and shocked Number Two is suspicious, but can't put his finger on the reason. As a result, he is powerless to stop his colleague from leaving.

As Number Six is about to get into the helicopter, Number Two sends his regards to Susan. Number Six says that he will convey the message. Number Six is blindfolded before flying off.

When they land and the blindfold is removed, Number Six is back in the Village. Number Two's regards were sent to a woman who had been dead for a year.

Key technicians: Terence Feely (writer), Pat Jackson (director), Geoff Foot (editor)

THE GENERAL

on the sanctity of education

MAIN ACTORS

Colin Gordon (Number Two), John Castle (Number 12), Peter Howell (the professor), Betty McDowall (professor's wife)

The Village tannoy summons people to attend the professor's lecture. Asking for a second coffee, Number Six is told that the café is closing. Everyone is off to their history class.

Number Six is engaged in conversation with a Number 12, who refers to the helicopters flying overhead. They must be after the professor.

Chasing across the beach, Villagers capture the fleeing professor. Following them, Number Six finds a tape recorder. He plays it. It is a warning by the professor. Guards approach and Number Six hides the recorder.

Returning to his cottage, Number Six finds his television on. The professor introduces the Speedlearn learning programme. This is followed by a fifteen-second course, displayed on the screen. After the hypnotic induction, Number Six is equipped with a vast array of factual details about a specific historical period. This amount of knowledge would normally take years of study to acquire.

Going back to the beach late at night, Number Six again meets Number 12, who has found the hidden tape recorder. Number 12 claims to be also against the system and, to prove it, he gives Number Six the recorder. He plays the message in which the professor urges revolt against Speedlearn because it is an abomination and enslaves the mind. The professor also calls for the destruction of the General, the giant computer system which has aided the implementation of Speedlearn.

Number Six locates the professor's home and meets his wife, a sculptress. One of her sculptures is a bust of Number Six. She asserts that she and her husband are in the Village quite willingly but she is obviously under duress.

Number 12 conspires with Number Six to broadcast the professor's subversive message. He provides Number Six with the means whereby he can substitute the message for a lecture and have it transmitted.

Number Six successfully infiltrates the broadcasting centre. After a tussle, Number Six takes control but, watching the surveillance cameras, Number Two detects the deception.

Guards stop Number Six in the nick of time. The official message goes out as intended.

Number Two is aware that Number Six could not have got as far as he did without help. Number Six is interrogated but reveals nothing. In frustration Number Two decides to consult the General, which has an absolutely infallible record of solving any problem.

Number 12 is about to be exposed by the computer when Number Six interrupts the proceedings, challenging the computer to answer the unanswerable. Supremely confident Number Two permits Number Six to try.

On receiving Number Six's insoluble question, the computer self-destructs. The professor is electrocuted and Number 12, in trying to rescue him, is also killed.

Key technicians: Lewis Griefer (writer) using the name 'Joshua Adam', Peter Graham Scott (director), John S Smith (editor)

MANY HAPPY RETURNS

n the impossibility of resuming the past

MAIN ACTORS

Donald Sinden (Colonel),

Patrick Cargill (Thorpe)

Number Six awakes and finds that no utilities are functioning. There is no water, no telephone, no loudspeaker music, and he has to open his front door manually. The Village is completely deserted. He commandeers a vehicle but the road goes nowhere and is surrounded by precipitously steep mountains.

Number Six builds a raft and loads it with provisions. He compiles a photographic record of the empty Village. A black cat is the only other living creature that remains.

He sets off. The sea journey is endless and, finally, he collapses from exposure and exhaustion. At night a boat approaches. Two men board the raft, steal the provisions and dump Number Six overboard.

Unseen by the two men, Number Six clambers onto their boat. He manages to overcome and lock them in a cabin. Then he sets a course towards a distant light. The two men break out of the cabin in which they'd been locked and attack Number Six. In the mêlée, Number Six jumps overboard and swims towards the shore light.

Number Six awakens on a deserted beach and scales the surrounding cliffs. He encounters a small band of gypsies who speak no English. Making his way inland, Number Six discovers he is in England. Unobserved, he boards a slow-moving lorry and passes out.

A siren startles him. He jumps off and finds himself in the middle of

London. He goes to his old home and is invited in by the current occupant. The woman is won over. She feeds and clothes Number Six, and lends him his own car. Cleaned up, he goes to reveal the existence of the village to his former superiors, Thorpe and the Colonel. He discusses his escape and hands over the pictures and his journal. His old colleagues verify the facts and are convinced that Number Six's far-fetched story is true. They calculate roughly the whereabouts of the Village. Number Six insists that he participate in the search.

A milkman slips into the pilot's quarters on an airfield. A moment later, his face concealed by a helmet, a pilot emerges. He flies Number Six off towards North Africa.

Number Six spots the Village. The pilot shows his face to be that of the milkman, and Number Six is ejected.

He parachutes onto the beach. Resignedly Number Six walks through the still, deserted Village, watched by the black cat.

As he enters his cottage, everything comes to life: shower, percolating coffee and the television. His door opens automatically and the black cat pads in, followed by the occupant of his London flat who had helped him. She is wearing a Number Two badge and is carrying a birthday cake for Number Six.

Glancing out of his window Number Six sees the Village returned to its full complement of life. Once again, he has been effectively manipulated.

Key technicians: Anthony Skene (writer), Patrick McGoohan (director) as 'Joseph Serf', Geoff Foot (editor)

DANCE OF THE DEAD

on a victim in the world of surrealism

MAIN ACTORS

Mary Morris (Number Two),

Duncan MacRae (doctor),

Norma West (number 240)

Number Six is subjected to an electrical mind-controlling treatment. Simultaneously Dutton, another Village internee not to bear a number and former colleague of Number Six, is coerced by a doctor to question Number Six. Even in his controlled condition, Number Six resists.

The experiment is curtailed by Number Two, stating that Number Six is too valuable for such risk. She invites Number Six to attend the Village carnival, and to bring a companion. Number Six notices a female apart from the others and ill at ease. He approaches her. She is Number 240. She hurries away. He tries to follow her but is prevented by an invisible force field.

That night, after eluding a patrolling Rover, Number Six collapses with exhaustion on the beach. On waking, he finds a washed-up corpse. He hides the body in a cave. He searches the body and finds a radio.

Later, as he listens to the radio, Number Six is approached by Number Two, who confiscates what he has found.

Number Six returns to the cave with a lifebelt and rope. He launches the body back into the sea with a picture of himself and a message.

A sad and weary Dutton has observed everything. Dutton tells his old friend that he could be terminated shortly, if he does not comply with what is being asked. The authorities want information that he just does not have, but they don't believe him.

At the carnival party, Number Six slips away and descends into a forbidden area. A technician hands Number Six a written message to pass on to Number Two. The message is a termination order for Dutton.

Number Six ventures into the morgue and finds the corpse he'd sent off. Number Two appears and informs Number Six that they intercepted his message.

Returning to the party, the revelry is over and the place has been converted into a courtroom. Number Six is on trial for possessing an illegal radio. Number Two is his defender and Number 240 is the prosecutor, dressed like Little Bo Peep. Number Six summons Dutton as a witness for the defence. Dressed as a clown, Dutton is in a mindless, vegetative state and cannot testify.

Number Six is found guilty and sentenced to death. He makes a run for it, pursued by a frenzied carnival horde. In a room within the labyrinthine Village underground, Number Six finds a teleprinter which he dismantles. Number Two enters accompanied by Number 240, who is despatched to placate the mob. A two-way mirror shows the hysterical mob being mollified.

In a test of wills with Number Two, Number Six insists that 'they' will never win. As if to prove this is not so, the silent, dismantled teleprinter springs back to life, a symbolic affirmation that the system can and will win through.

Key technicians: Anthony Skene (writer), Don Chaffey (director), John S Smith (editor)

CHECKMATE

on authority and conditioned responses

MAIN ACTORS

Peter Wyngarde (Number Two), Rosalie

Crutchley (The Queen),

Ronald Radd (Rook)

Everyone stops and stands deadly still. Rover is on the prowl. Number Six observes an elderly man moving, oblivious to Rover but not apprehended. Number Six joins the elderly man, an ex-count, in a game of chess. The Village inhabitants play the pieces on a board laid out on the grass.

Losing self-control, a Rook moves into Check. He is whisked away in an ambulance.

The old count informs Number Six how to distinguish between actual Villagers and planted guards. Their attitude exposes them. It is a way of seeing who can be trusted.

Number Six is pursued by the Queen, who offers to help him escape. He declines.

In hospital, the dissident Rook is reconditioned and rehabilitated. On his release, the Rook is befriended by Number Six. They plot to escape.

The Queen is hypnotically induced to believe she is in love with Number Six, in order to spy on him. Her locket contains a transmitting device.

Number Six gathers an escape team, selecting members in the way that the count instructed.

The plotters build a transmitter but they need a transistor.

Number Six acquires the transistor secreted in the Queen's locket.

The plotters send a signal. A boat responds.

At night, the Rook sets off on a raft

with the signalling device.

Number Six leads the conspirators on a mission to capture Number Two, so that he can't stop their escape. As they bind Number Two, they hear their monitoring signal cease. Number Six goes to investigate.

Seeing the boat coming in response to their signal, Number Six paddles out to reach it.

On board is a monitor screen showing Number Two in alliance with the Rook, who has betrayed Number Six. The Rook has also applied the count's methods and has determined Number Six to be more like a guard than a Villager.

Number Six overpowers the crew and sets off. The controls stop responding and Rover approaches over the water.

Key technicians: Gerald Kelsey (writer), Don Chaffey (director), Lee Doig (editor)

10
HAMMER INTO ANVIL

on the power of suggestion
and other psychologies

MAIN ACTORS

Patrick Cargill (Number Two)

A failed suicide, a woman, is sadistically interrogated by Number Two. Passing by the hospital, Number Six hears her screaming. He forces his way into the woman's room, distracting Number Two. This provides the woman with the chance to leap out of the window to her death.

Later, Number Six is forcibly taken before Number Two, and threatened with punishment for interfering in official business. A telephone call,

interrupting this meeting, indicates Number Two's extreme insecurity.

Number Six launches a series of escapades design to taunt and undermine Number Two. These cleverly contrived, red herrings start to rattle Number Two. He suspects that his superiors are onto him for he knows not what reason. He surmises that Number Six has been planted to test his loyalty. Number Six escalates his campaign against Number Two.

In a state of mounting paranoia, Number Two takes action by firing those closest to him. He is reduced to a shattered state, isolated and obsessed by Number Six.

Number Six has rendered Number Two utterly helpless. He urges Number Six to get it over with and turn him in. Number Six orders Number Two to report himself to his superiors. He does so. Number Six has redressed the balance of power.

Key technicians: Roger Woddis (writer), Pat Jackson (director), Lee Doig (editor)

11
IT'S YOUR FUNERAL

on the fabricating of political excuses

MAIN ACTORS

Derren Nesbitt (acting Number Two),
Annette Andre (watchmaker's daughter),
Andre Van Gyseghem
(retiring Number Two)

A sleeping Number Six is disturbed by Number 50. She pleads for his help to thwart a sinister plot to incriminate her gullible father, the watchmaker. She faints.

Monitoring this incident, an overconfident, young, blond, acting Number Two is delighted. All is going according to plan.

Reviving, Number 50 reveals a conspiracy of jammers, an underground group. When Number Six doesn't believe her, she rushes away.

Gloating, the acting Number Two notifies his superior that progress is being made.

Making enquiries Number Six learns about the jammers. They are a group dedicated to wasting time and misleading the authorities.

Number Six is practising a martial art on trampolines, named 'Kosho' here. In the locker room, his watch is secretly replaced.

Finding his watch has stopped, Number Six visits the watchmaker's rooms. Here, he recognizes a detonating device. Number Six's watch is repaired. On leaving he is approached by Number 50, the watchmaker's daughter. She tells Number Six about a conspiracy to blow up the old Number Two. Now Number Six believes her. The authorities could use such trouble to unleash reprisals against the community. Number Six and Number 50 plead with the elderly watchmaker but to no avail. He is committed, no matter what the consequences. This is all watched on monitors by the acting Number Two.

Number Six warns the acting Number Two about the assassination plot. Number Two is dismissive. He considers that the jammers are harmless and the likelihood of an assassination attempt ludicrous.

Number Six learns further details about the plot. On the Appreciation Day ceremony, held to honour the outgoing Number Two, the medallion round this Number Two's neck will be packed with explosives and detonated.

Intending to repeat his warning, Number Six goes to the control centre and is received by the old Number Two, who has been informed of Number Six's absurd allegations by the acting Number Two. Number Six convinces the old Number Two that it must be his own superiors who want to get rid of him. The retiring Number Two accepts the likelihood of his annihilation as inevitable and inescapable.

The Village turns out in full force for the Appreciation Day ceremony.

The mute Butler appears with the large medallion and chain on a cushion.

Number Six and the daughter search for the watchmaker and they glimpse a reflection at the top of the bell tower. They run towards it as the medallion is placed around the retiring Number Two's neck.

At the top of the tower, Number Six gains possession of the remote control detonator.

As they leave the tower, a man tries to apprehend them. This is Number 100, who had switched the watches and assisted the acting Number Two. Number Six knocks the man out.

Upon reaching the end of his speech, the retiring Number Two is astonished that he is still alive. Hurriedly he transfers the medallion to the horrified, but helpless, new Number Two. Number Six gives the detonator to the retired Number Two who rushes away to the waiting helicopter.

Number Six congratulates the new Number Two, crowding him and preventing him from taking off the medallion. The plot of the authorities has failed completely.

Key technicians: Michael Cramoy (writer), Robert Asher (director), John S Smith (editor)

12

A Change Of Mind

no political leader is inviolable

Main Actors

John Sharp (Number Two), Angela Browne (Number 86)

Number Six has created his own gymnasium in a secluded wood. Two Villagers, resenting Number Six's desire for privacy, attack him, but he drives them off.

For this act of defiance, Number Six is summoned before a committee who accuse him of antisocial tendencies. He is defined as 'un-mutual'. Number Six is shunned, and an article denouncing his nonconformist tendencies appears in the daily newspaper.

Number Two warns Number Six of the seriousness of his situation.

A woman, Number 86, is assigned to tutor Number Six in sociability. His attitude persists and he disrupts a social group.

Number Six is hospitalized for a check-up. He witnesses brutal aversion therapy. He meets a patient, once un-mutual like Number Six, who is now placidly indifferent. Number Six is a candidate for the same therapy.

Still unwilling to conform, Number Six is ostracized and spied upon. Nevertheless he will not alter his behaviour. An intolerant Village committee physically subdues Number Six and forces him to attend hospital for remedial therapy. Number Six is tranquillized and, apparently, given a lobotomy. He wakes with a plaster on his forehead. Groggily he leaves the hospital. He is cheered now as a less aggressive, more social citizen.

In his cottage, Number Six is served a drugged tea by Number 86. Unseen, Number Six disposes the tea without drinking it.

On waking later, Number Six is interrogated by Number Two. Number Six displays unreformed, aggressive tendencies and still refuses to cooperate.

Again Number 86 serves drugged tea. But this time Number Six switches cups and it is Number 86 who swallows the drug. Number Six hypnotizes her and implants a suggestion of his own.

Number Six goes to Number Two and offers to tell him what he wants, but in a public place at four o'clock.

The Villagers duly assemble and Number Six delays his address until the town clock strikes the hour of four. This triggers his posthypnotic suggestion and Number 86 publicly accuses Number Two of being un-mutual. The people turn on him in pandemonium and he flees for his life. He is violently hounded to his lair.

Key technicians: Roger Parkes (writer), Patrick McGoohan (director) as 'Joseph Serf', Lee Doig (editor)

13

Do Not Forsake Me Oh My Darling

on mental manipulations

in pursuit of power

Main Actors

Clifford Evans (Number Two), Nigel Stock (the Colonel), Zena Walker (Janet)

A coterie of secret service personnel examines slides but fails to decipher the code that will reveal where Doctor

Seltzman is hiding.

A Colonel flies to the Village and is told by Number Two that Seltzman devised a means of transferring one person's mind in another's body. The Village has a Seltzman machine but needs to locate the Doctor and to ascertain whether he has perfected the reverse-transfer process. The Colonel is to have his mind switched with Number Six's in order to discover the whereabouts of the Doctor, his friend.

The transfer proceeds. Number Six is set free but in the body of the Colonel. His own body remains in the Village, with the Colonel's mind.

In the Colonel's body, Number Six wakes up back in his old London home. Looking in the mirror, he sees that he is inside another man's body. He is visited by Janet, who was his fiancee. She saw the car outside and thought he had returned, after an absence of a year. Number Six assures her that by the evening of her birthday, later the same day, he will bring her a message from her fiancée.

Number Six goes to Janet's father, Sir Charles, for whom he worked. Number Six cannot convince Sir Charles of the incredible thing that has happened. He leaves, followed by an agent sent by Sir Charles.

At the birthday party, Number Six asks Janet for a vital piece of paper he left with her, a year ago. Her doubts vanish with an impassioned kiss. She is convinced only her fiancée could kiss like that, even if in another's body.

The slip is a receipt for photographs. By projecting the superimposed transparencies Number Six can decode the address contained within a correct combination of pictures.

As Number Six sets off to find Seltzman, he is followed by Sir Charles' agent.

In Austria, Number Six successfully convinces Seltzman that he is his old friend, but in a different body. To bring matters back to normal, the Doctor

agrees to help his friend. Sir Charles's agent bursts in on them but, while they tussle, an agent from the Village appears and releases a gas.

In the Village, the Doctor agrees to perform the reverse process operation. In a laboratory, he links himself to Number Six and the Colonel.

After the mind-transfer, the Colonel is congratulated and thanked as he leaves the Village. The doctor regains consciousness but is dying. It is not the mind of the Doctor that speaks but that of the Colonel. The Doctor has escaped, in a younger and better body, and Number Six has his own mind returned to his own body.

Key technicians: Vincent Tilsley (writer), Pat Jackson (director), Eric Boyd-Perkins (editor)

14

LIVING IN HARMONY

on experimenting with the frontier

of the mind

MAIN ACTORS

Valerie French (Cathy), Alexis Kanner (The Kid), David Bauer (the Judge)

A Sheriff, Number Six, hands in his badge and his gun. He is finished with law enforcement.

Crossing the desolate countryside, horseless but with his saddle slung across his shoulder, the ex-Sheriff is attacked by a gang, beaten up and dumped unconscious onto the ground in the town of Harmony. The ex-lawman has never heard of the town before. It is not on any map. In the saloon he is offered the job of Sheriff by a corrupt Judge who knows all about him. He refuses.

Cathy, the attractive bar hostess, takes a shine to the ex-lawman. A mute gunslinger keen on Cathy picks on the stranger and draws his gun, but is punched out. This increases Cathy's admiration for the new man in town.

Attempting to leave Harmony, the stranger finds it is near impossible. The townspeople resent his wanting to leave. They're proud and satisfied with their town and they think that he should be, too. Feeling against the stranger mounts and the townspeople let loose. The stranger is beaten into submission and, for his own protection, the Judge locks him in the jail. To placate the angry mob, the Judge releases the only other prisoner. The crowd lynch him. The innocent victim is Cathy's brother.

Cathy visits the jail where she finds The Kid on guard. She gets him drunk and releases the stranger.

The stranger is soon caught and taken to the saloon. A trial is underway. Cathy is found guilty of helping a prisoner escape. That the stranger was not guilty of anything is irrelevant. The stranger cannot permit Cathy to be left alone in the jail with The Kid, and says that he will wear the badge but not carry the gun.

The Kid is edgy. He taunts someone into a fight and shoots him dead.

On the Judge's orders, the town spokesman is murdered and his body dumped in the jail. The Sheriff makes a determined effort to escape Harmony and take Cathy with him. They arrange to meet at the town border. Cathy does not appear to meet him and he returns to town.

Meanwhile, Cathy has been attacked by The Kid and strangled. The Sheriff buries her, takes off his badge and straps on his gun. He outshoots The Kid and kills him.

The Judge's men ambush the Sheriff. He outguns them but is shot finally by the Judge's derringer. He wakes up in the saloon as Number Six, wearing the piped Village uniform and a radio headset.

Number Six runs through the western town, discovering it to be all life-sized, cut-outs and façades. He goes to the control centre, and meets the main characters from Harmony. The Judge is Number Two; The Kid is Number Eight; and Cathy is Number 22. Number Six leaves in disgust.

Number Two and Eight argue over their failure. Number 22 cannot withhold her tears and flees to the saloon, followed by Number Eight. His western character kicks back in and, he strangles Number 22 when she resists him.

Number Six finds her and she dies in his arms. The unhinged Number Eight throws himself from the balcony to his death.

Key technicians: David Tomblin (writer and director) from a story by David Tomblin and Ian Rakoff, Noreen Ackland (editor)

THE GIRL WHO WAS DEATH

on a fantasy beyond the Village confines

MAIN ACTORS

Justine Lord (Sonia) and Kenneth Griffith (Schnipps, the mad scientist)

Out of a children's story book comes a game of cricket with the assassination of a batsman by an exploding ball.

Number Six, investigating a mad scientist's bid to blow up London, appears on the same cricket pitch. He thwarts another assassination and chases after a mysterious blonde, Sonia. This results in a series of dangerous traps, snares, bombs and idiosyncrasies of mayhem. Doggedly, Number Six

keeps on the trail of Sonia. The battles between them lead to a lighthouse occupied by her father, Schnipps, a mad scientist. The scientist is dressed as Napoleon and commands a band of uniformed troops. His lighthouse has been converted to function as a rocket.

Number Six sabotages the rocket and outwits the troops. He escapes, leaving Schnipps and his daughter marooned. They are destroyed in the ensuing explosion.

The story book is closed and Number Six takes his leave of children everywhere.

Watching a monitor are Number Two, seen in the story as Schnipps, and Number Two's assistant, Sonia in the story; they admit to failure in their attempt to induce Number Six to let drop his guard.

Key technicians: Terence Feely (writer), David Tomblin (director), Eric Boyd-Perkins (editor)

ONCE UPON A TIME

on role reversal and the psychology of disintegration

MAIN ACTORS

Leo McKern (Number Two)

A familiar Number Two contacts Number Six while watching him on the surveillance screen. He asks Number Six why he cares.

Reviewing the highlights of Number Six's history of rebellion, Number Two telephones his superior for permission to implement the radical 'degree absolute'. This is a desperate undertaking. Based on psychoanalytical principles, it is a test of wills. Either Number Two or Number Six will

survive, not both.

Number Six is put into a hypnotically induced trance and regressed to infancy. The two of them, along with the Butler, are locked in a large underground room, the embryo room. The doors are inescapably sealed for the seven-day duration of the ultimate test.

Number Two leads Number Six through the seven ages of man, intermittently bombarding him with the question of why he resigned. Number Two assumes different roles as Number Six goes through the different ages. Number Two becomes in turn, father, teacher, athletic coach, employer, judge, officer and prison guard. The grilling progressively intensifies. It becomes confrontational, even violent.

Gradually, Number Six matures and learns the nature of what is going on. He realizes the extraordinary, potentially fatal risk that Number Two is taking. They drink, laugh, and argue together, attended by the silent Butler. In the last stage, Number Six manoeuvres Number Two into a cage and locks him in. The power has switched, and the Butler becomes more responsive to Number Six, who interrogates the imprisoned Number Two, ruthlessly.

Number Two loses confidence and dignity, has a mental breakdown, panics, grovels, and in the final countdown Number Six urges Number Two to die. The reversal of roles has been completed and it is Number Two who drops to his death.

The Supervisor enters and takes the victorious Number Six to meet Number One.

Key technicians: Patrick McGoohan (writer and director), Lee Doig (editor)

17

Fall Out

on the exultation of individualism

Main Actors

Main actors: Leo McKern (Number Two),

Alexis Kanner (Number 48),

Kenneth Griffith (The President)

This is a continuation of the previous episode. In a subterranean room, Number Six is given his own clothes from a life-sized mannequin of himself. He proceeds along a corridor hewn out of the rocks and lined with juke boxes, accompanied by the Butler and the Supervisor. The music of the Beatles' 'All You Need Is Love' is heard.

They enter a large, underground cavern. Rows of masked and robed figures occupy seats like a waiting jury.

The President acknowledges the significance of Number Six's achievement as an individual. Consequently he is to assume the throne as the new ultimate leader.

While the dead Number Two is resuscitated, the President summons rebellious youth personified by The Kid, a.k.a. Number 48. He causes havoc and has to be restrained.

Number Two, brought back to life, is irreverent and troublesome. He, too, is restrained.

The President declares that Number Six is honoured and saluted for being a revolutionary of the right calibre. He is free to lead or leave the Village.

Number Six's speech is applauded to a point of inaudibility. He is invited to meet Number One.

Ascending a spiral staircase into a circular room Number Six unmasks a hooded figure. The face is that of a chimpanzee and then of himself. Number Six chases Number One who escapes, shutting a trapdoor behind him.

Number Six tackles the control panel and starts the countdown of a rocket, of which the circular room is the control centre. Simultaneously, he sets about the destruction of the Village.

Number Six then releases The Kid and Number Two. Along with the Butler, they overpower the armed guards, shoot up the place and escape in the cage, mounted on a pantechnicon. The Butler drives.

The pantechnicon crashes out of a tunnel and the rocket takes off.

En route to London, The Kid leaves them. In London Number Two also goes his own way. Finally the Butler and Number Six abandon the vehicle and make for Number Six's old home. His door opens electronically.

Number Six drives off in his Lotus.

The conclusion questions whether the prisoner has actually escaped.

Key technicians: Patrick McGoohan (writer and director), Noreen Ackland and Eric Boyd-Perkins (editors)

Acknowledgements

One way or another, a number of people helped me in stitching together the disparate slices of those celluloid days. So it's quite a bunch of thanks that are due. Richard Reynolds commissioned me in the first place, so that's that one. Steven Edgell made sense and ensured the joins between my words didn't stick out too much. Dave Barrie, the founding father of the very concept of appreciating *The Prisoner*, backed my play, collaborated and corroborated, and convinced me that my stance was valid. Steve-Ricks knew *The Prisoner* and had the photographs. Huge thanks to John S Smith for his openness and faith in my ability. To Nic Roeg for mulling over the bones of our mutual past; and much the same with Stephen Frears. To the many colleagues and friends from my film history; Sue Michie, Alan Sapper, David Woodward, Roy Benson, Chris Sutton, Mark Davies, Tony Sloman, Michael Ellis, David Gladwell and Alan Patillo. And to those good companions from my Memorial days, the well-meaning Albert Finney and Michael Medwin who returned those excellent days to my recall; also Daphne Hunter, Phil Davis and David Barber, who had time for conversation. And, for supplementary support during the slog of writing, to Helen James, Paul Gravett, Nina Scott-Stoddart, my sister Lorna and, not to forget he who often kept my computer paranoia at bay, Colin Howard.

As the late Lindsay would have asked, isn't that enough of this nonsense...?

Publisher's Note

Executive Editor Richard Reynolds (Number Two) and Author Ian Rakoff (Number Six) give especial thanks to Steve Edgell (Number 12), Steven Ricks (Number 48), David Barrie (Number 51), Lucinda Williams (Number 58) and Frank Ratcliffe (Number 130) for their help above and beyond the call of duty. Without their support, it would not have been possible to publish this book in its present form - and without incurring the displeasure of the ever-vigilant Number One. This book may contain occasional disguised code words to guard against unauthorized use of the information it contains.

Thanks are also due to Polygram Licensing International for kind permission to reproduce their copyright illustrations. Other illustrations courtesy of the author with the exception of British Film Institute pages 133, 150; Dell comics, pages 42, 70, 73; Gold Key comics, page 22; Polygram Licensing Ltd pages 24, 27, 29, 31, 44, 46, 56, 58, 68, 76, 80, 86, 95a, 95b, 96, 99, 100, 159 and cover photographs.

Six of One is the official Prisoner appreciation society. For further information, send s.a.e. to: Six of One, Box 66, Ipswich IP2 9TZ.

SELECT BIBLIOGRAPHY

(The following are some of the books and videos I referred to. This is by no means a definitive list of any kind)

The Official Prisoner Companion , Matthew White & Jaffer Ali, Sidgwick & Jackson, London, 1988.

The Prisoner, A televisionary masterpiece, Alain Carraze & Helene Oswald, W. H. Allen & Co, London, 1990.

The Gillis Guide to The Prisoner, S. J. Gillis, SJG Communication Service Ltd, UK, 1997.

Alert, Number Six, In The Village, magazines. Published by Six of One, The Prisoner Appreciation Society, Ipswich, IP2 9TZ, UK. 1977 - 1998.

Sixties British Cinema , Robert Murphy, British Film Institute, London, 1992.

Once Upon A Time magazine, Carolina,1997.

Learning and Self-counselling Through Television Entertainment, Snow, Robert P., and Cuthbertson, Beverley Ann, Arizona, 1979.

The Prisoner Puzzle, Ontario Education Communications Authority, Ontario 1978.

Going Mad In Hollywood and Life with Lindsay Anderson , David Sherwin, Penguin, London, 1997.

The World Encyclopaedia of Comics, Edited by Maurice Horn, Chelsea House, New York, 1976.

VIDEO TAPES

The Prisoner Investigated Steven Ricks 1990

The Prisoner in Conclusion Steven Ricks 1994

GENERAL INDEX

Figures in **bold** refer to illustrations